CANNAE

By

General Fieldmarshal Count Alfred von Schlieffen

MAPS VOLUME

The Naval & Military Press Ltd

Published by

The Naval & Military Press Ltd
Unit 5 Riverside, Brambleside
Bellbrook Industrial Estate
Uckfield, East Sussex
TN22 1QQ England

Tel: +44 (0)1825 749494

www.naval-military-press.com
www.nmarchive.com

In reprinting in facsimile from the original, any imperfections are inevitably reproduced and the quality may fall short of modern type and cartographic standards.

CONTENTS

Map 1: BATTLE OF CANNAE, 2 AUGUST, 216 B.C., GENERAL MAP.

Map 2: BATTLE OF CANNAE, 2 AUGUST, 216 B.C., POSITION BEFORE THE BATTLE, AND CAVALRY ENGAGEMENT

Map 3: BATTLE OF CANNAE, 2 AUGUST, 216 B.C., COLLISION OF THE TWO ARMIES.

Map 4: BATTLE OF LEUTHEN, 5 DECEMBER, 1757

Map 5: BATTLE OF ZORNDORF, MOVEMENTS FROM 23 TO 25 AUGUST, 1758

Map 6: BATTLE OF ZORNDORF, 25 AUGUST, 1758

Map 7: BATTLE OF ZORNDORF, 25 AUGUST, 1758

Map 8: BATTLE OF ZORNDORF, 25 AUGUST, 1758

Map 9: BATTLE OF KUNERSDORF, 12 AUGUST, 1759

Map 10: BATTLE OF KUNERSDORF, 12 AUGUST, 1759

Map 11: CAMPAIGN IN ITALY, 1800

Map 12: CAMPAIGN IN GERMANY, 1805

Map 13: ADVANCE ON JENA, 7 TO 13 OCTOBER, 1806

Map 14: BATTLE OF AUSTERLITZ, 2 DECEMBER, 1805

Map 15: BATTLE OF AUSTERLITZ, 2 DECEMBER, 1805

Map 16: CAMPAIGN OF PRUSSIAN-EYLAU, JANUARY, 1807

Map 17:   CAMPAIGN OF PRUSSTAN-EYLAU, 4 TO 8 FEBRUARY, 1807

Map 18:   CAMPAIGN OF REGENSBURG, APRIL, 1908, SITUATION ON 17 APRIL, 1809

Map 19:   CAMPAIGN OF REGENSBURG, SITUATION ON 18 APRIL, AND FIRST MOVEMENTS ON 19 APRIL.

Map 20:   CAMPAIGN OF REGENSBURG, SITUATION IN THE EVENING OF 19 APRIL

Map 21:   CAMPAIGN OF REGENSBURG, MOVEMENTS ON 20 APRIL

Map 22:   CAMPAIGN OF REGENSBURG, MOVEMENTS ON 21 APRIL, AND SITUATION THAT EVENING

Map 23:   CAMPAIGN OF REGENSBURG, SITUATION AT NOON, 22 APRIL

Map 24:   CAMPAIGN OF REGENSBURG, SITUATION ON THE EVENING OF 22 APRIL

Map 25:   BATTLE OF TORGAU, 3 NOVEMBER, 1760

Map 26:   CAMPAIGN OF FRIEDLAND-TILSIT, JUNE, 1807

Map 27:   MOVEMENTS FROM THE MIDDLE OF AUGUST TO THE END OF SEPTEMBER, 1813

Map 28:   MOVEMENTS FROM THE END OF SEPTEMBER, 1813, UNTIL THE BATTLE OF LEIPZIG.

Map 29:   BATTLE OF LIEGNITZ, 15 AUGUST, 1760

Map 30:   CAMPAIGN IN THE NETHERLANDS, 1815.

Map 31:   BATTLE OF LIGNY, 16 JUNE, 1815

Map 32:   BATTLE OF LIGNY, 16 JUNE, 1815

Map 33:   BATTLE OF BELLE ALLIANCE (WATERLOO), 18 JUNE, 1815

Map 34:   GENERAL MAP OF THE AUSTRO-PRUSSIAN WAR, 1866

Map 35:   SITUATION ON 20 JUNE, 1866, AND MOLTKE'S PLAN

Map 36:   SITUATION ON 21 JUNE, 1866

Map 37:   SITUATION ON 22 JUNE, 1866

Map 38:   SITUATION ON 23 JUNE, 1866

Map 39:   SITUATION ON 25 JUNE, 1866

Map 40:   SITUATION ON 26 JUNE, 1866

Map 41:   ENGAGEMENT AT LANGENSALZA, 27 JUNE, 1866

Map 42:   SITUATION ON THE EVENING OF 27 JUNE, 1866

Map 43:   OPERATIONS TO INCLUDE 27 JUNE, 1866

Map 44:   SCHEME FOR THE PRUSSIAN ADVANCE BASED ON MOLTKE'S PLAN OF CAMPAIGN

Map 45:   ENGAGEMENT AT NACHOD, 27 JUNE

Map 46:   ENGAGEMENT AT TRAUTENAU, 27 JUNE

Map 47:   ENGAGEMENT AT SKALITZ, 28 JUNE

Map 48:   ENGAGEMENT AT BURKERSDORF, 28 JUNE

Map 49:   OPERATIONS FROM 28 JUNE TO THE NIGHT OF 30 JUNE

Map 50:   ENGAGEMENT AT SCHWEINSCHADEL, 29 JUNE

Map 51:   ENGAGEMENT AT GITSCHIN, 29 JUNE

Map 52:   PROBABLE SITUATION ON THE EVENING OF 1 JULY, IF MOLTKE'S DIRECTIONS (TELEGRAM IN THE NIGHT OF 30 JUNE–1 JULY, OCCASIONED BY THE CHANGES IN THE SITUATION THAT DAY) HAD BEEN FOLLOWED

Map 53:   LOCATION OF THE PRUSSIAN ARMIES ON 1-2 JULY. PLAN OF THE PRUSSIAN MOVEMENTS ON 3 JULY, IN ACCORDANCE WITH MOLTKE'S INSTRUCTIONS.

Map 54:   GENERAL MAP OF THE BATTLE OF KONIGGRATZ, 3 JULY, 1866

Map 55:   BATTLE OF KONIGGRATZ, MOVEMENTS DURING FORENOON

Map 56:   BATTLE OF KONIGGRATZ, SITUATION IN THE AFTERNOON

Map 57:   BATTLE OF KONIGGRATZ, SITUATION IN THE EVENING

Map 58:   SITUATION IN THE EVENING OF 13 JULY, 1866

Map 59:   SITUATION AT OLMUTZ ON THE EVENING OF 14 JULY, 1866

Map 60:   ENGAGEMENT AT TUBITSCHAU, 15 JULY, 1866

Map 61:   SITUATION OF THE PRUSSIANS ON THE EVENING OF 15 JULY, 1866, AND RETREAT OF THE AUSTRIAN NORTHERN ARMY DOWN THE VALLEY OF THE WAAG

Map 62:   SITUATION ON THE EVENING OF 21 JULY, 1866

Map 63:   THE FRANCO-PRUSSIAN WAR, 1870. PROBABLE CONCENTRATION AREAS OF THE FRENCH, AND ORIGINALLY PLANNED CONCENTRATION AND ADVANCE OF THE GERMANS

Map 64:   MOLTKE'S SCHEME FOR THE ADVANCE OF THE GERMAN ARMIES FROM THEIR POINTS OF DETRAINMENT BEYOND THE RHINE

Map 65:   ACTUAL CONCENTRATIONS AND ADVANCE OF THE GERMANS PRIOR TO THE BATTLES OF WORTH AND SPICHERN. FRENCH POSITIONS ON THE EVENING OF 5 AUGUST

Map 66:   MOVEMENTS OF THE THIRD ARMY AND OF MACMAHON'S TROOPS FROM THE EVENING OF 3 AUGUST TO THE EVENLNG OF 5 AUGUST

Map 67:   SITUATION OF THE THIRD ARMY ON THE EVENING OF 5 AUGUST. MACMAHON'S POSS113LE ENVELOPING OFFENSIVE.

Map 68:   BATTLE OF WORTH, 6 AUGUST, 1870

Map 69:   MACMAHON'S SITUATION ON THE EVENING OF 5 AUGUST. POSSIBLE OFFENSIVE OF THE THIRD ARMY

Map 70:   BATTLE OF SPICHERN, 6 AUGUST, 1870

Map 71:   RETREAT OF THE FRENCH AFTER THE BATTLE OF WORTH AND SPICHERN

Map 72:   PLAN FOR THE ADVANCE OF THE FIRST AND SECOND ARMIES TO AND BEYOND THE MOSELLE

Map 73:   MOLTKE'S PLAN FOR THE ADVANCE OF THE FIRST AND SECOND ARMIES TO THE MOSELLE

Map 74:   FRENCH POSITIONS ON 10 AUGUST. HEADQUARTERS' PLAN FOR OPERATIONS BY THE SECOND ARMY

Map 75: SITUATION ON THE EVENING OF 14 AUGUST

Map 76: SITUATION ON THE EVENING OF 12 AUGUST. PLAN FOR THE FURTHER ADVANCE TO THE MOSELLE

Map 77: BATTLE OF COLOMBEY-NOUILLY 14 AUGUST, 1870

Map 78: SITUATION ON THE EVENING OF 15 AUGUST, AND MOVEMENTS ON 16 AUGUST

Map 79: SITUATION AT NOON, 15 AUGUST. PROBABLE ADVANCE OF THE FIRST AND SECOND ARMIES ON THE AFTERNOON OF 15 AUGUST AND ON 16 AUGUST IN CASE MOLTKE'S PURPOSE TO ADVANCE NORTH OF METZ WITH THE FIRST ARMY, SHOULD BE EFFECTED

Map 80: MARS LA TOUR, 16 AUGUST, 1870

Map 81: SITUATION ON THE EVENING OF 16 AUGUST, AND MOVEMENTS UNTIL THE EVENING OF 17 AUGUST

Map 82: PLAN FOR THE MOVEMENT OF THE GERMANS ON THE AFTERNOON OF 17 AUGUST AND FOR THE ADVANCE ON 18 AUGUST

Map 83: SITUATION ON THE MORNING OF 18 AUGUST AND ADVANCE OF THE GERMANS.

Map 84: BATTLE OF GRAVELOTTE–ST. PRIVAT, 18 AUGUST, 1870, MOVEMENTS AND ENGAGEMENTS FROM THE BEGINNING OF THE BATTLE TILL ABOUT 3:00 PM.

Map 85: BATTLE OF GRAVELOTTE–ST. PRIVAT, MOVEMENTS AND COMBATS FROM 3:00 PM TILL ABOUT 6:00 PM.

Map 86: BATTLE OF GRAVELOTTE–ST. PRIVAT, MOVEMENTS AND COMBATS AFTER 6:00 PM.

Map 87: BATTLE OF GRAVELOTTE–ST. PRIVAT, SITUATION AT THE END OF THE BATTLE.

Map 88: SITUATION ON THE NIGHT 18-19 AUGUST, AND RETREAT OF THE FRENCH

Map 89: SITUATION ON 22 AND 25 AUGUST. MARCHES ON 26 AUGUST

Map 90: PLAN FOR THE ADVANCE OF THE GERMANS FROM 23 TO 29 AUGUST

Map 91:   SITUATION ON AUGUST 26. MARCHES ON 27 AND 28 AUGUST

Map 92:   SITUATION ON THE EVENING OF 28 AUGUST, MOVEMENTS ON 29 AUGUST

Map 93:   SITUATION OF THE GERMANS ON THE EVENING OF 29 AUGUST. MOVEMENTS OF THE GERMANS AFTER 30 AUGUST, ACCORDING TO MOLTHE'S PLAN

Map 94:   SITUATION ON EVENING OF 29 AUGUST. MOVEMENTS ON 30 AUGUST

Map 95:   BATTLE OF BEAUMONT, 30 AUGUST, 1870, MOVEMENTS AND COMBATS UNTIL ABOUT 3:00 PM

Map 96:   BATTLE OF BEAUMONT, SITUATION ABOUT 3:00 PM. MOVEMENTS AND COMBATS UNTIL EVENING.

Map 97:   SITUATION IN THE NIGHT 30-31 AUGUST. MARCHES ON 31 AUGUST

Map 98:   POSSIBLE RETREAT OF THE ARMY OF CHALONS, ON 1 SEPTEMBER

Map 99:   BATTLE OF SEDAN, 1 SEPTEMBER, 1870, POSITIONS OF THE FRENCH ON 1 SEPTEMBER. ADVANCE OF THE THIRD ARMY BASED ON THE ORDER FROM GENERAL HEADQUARTERS. MOLTKE'S PLAN FOR THE ADVANCE OF THE MEUSE ARMY

Map 100:   BATTLE OF SEDAN, MOVEMENTS AND ENGAGEMENTS UP TO NOON

Map 101:   BATTLE OF SEDAN, ENGAGEMENTS AND MOVEMENTS IN THE AFTERNOON

Map 1.

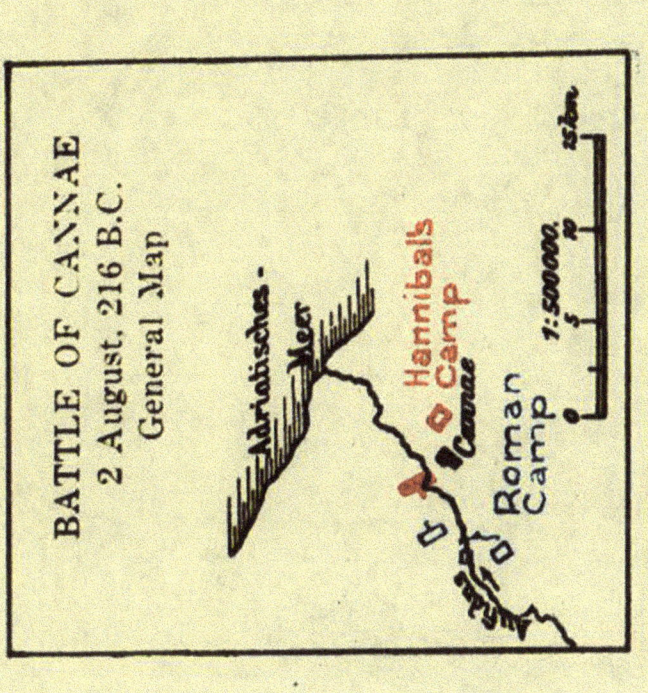

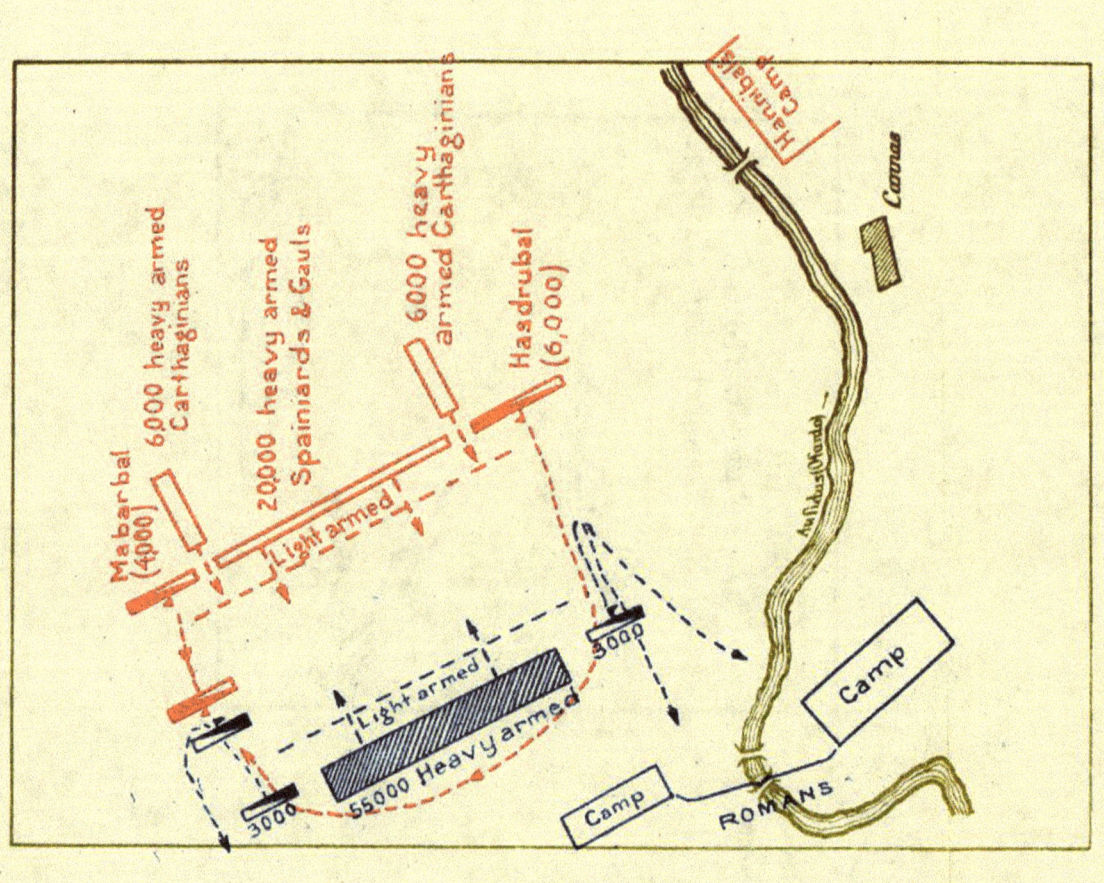

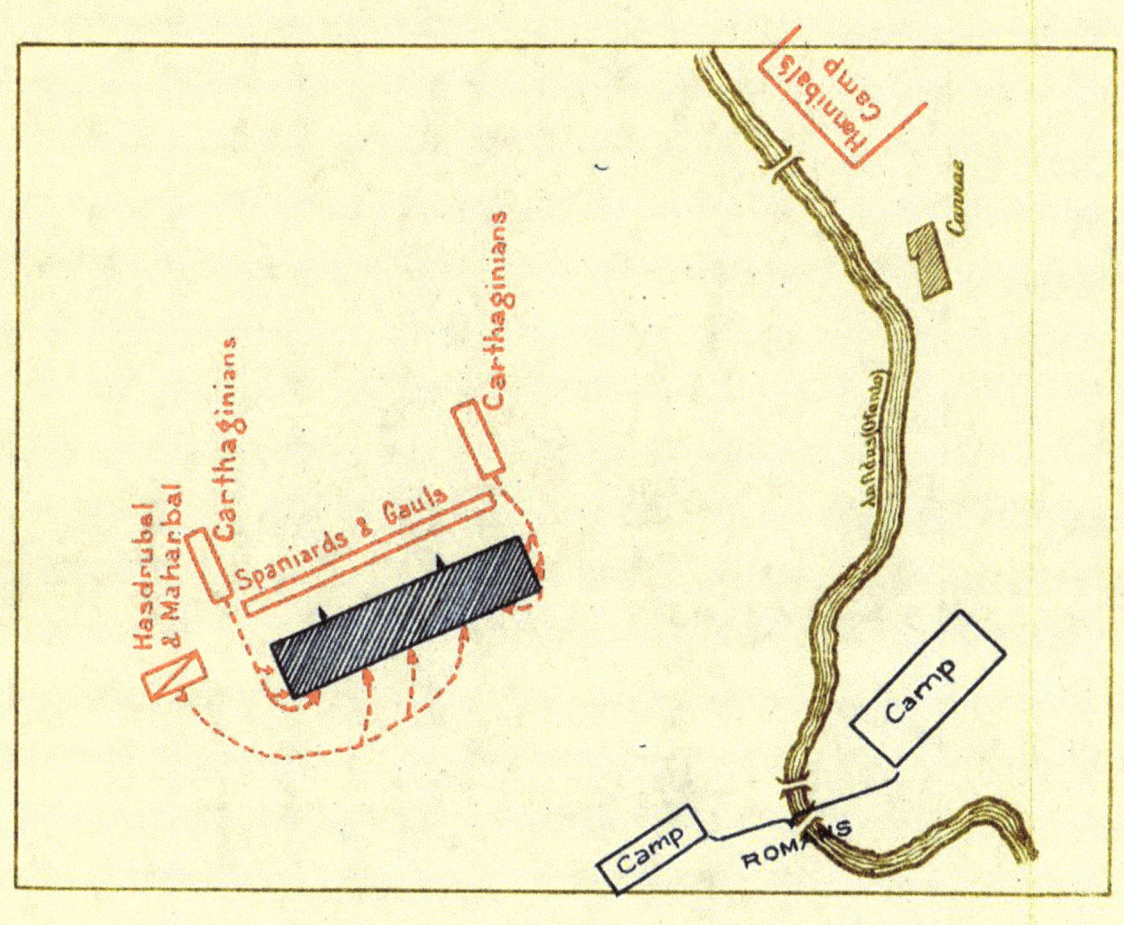

Map 4.

BATTLE OF LEUTHEN
5 December, 1757

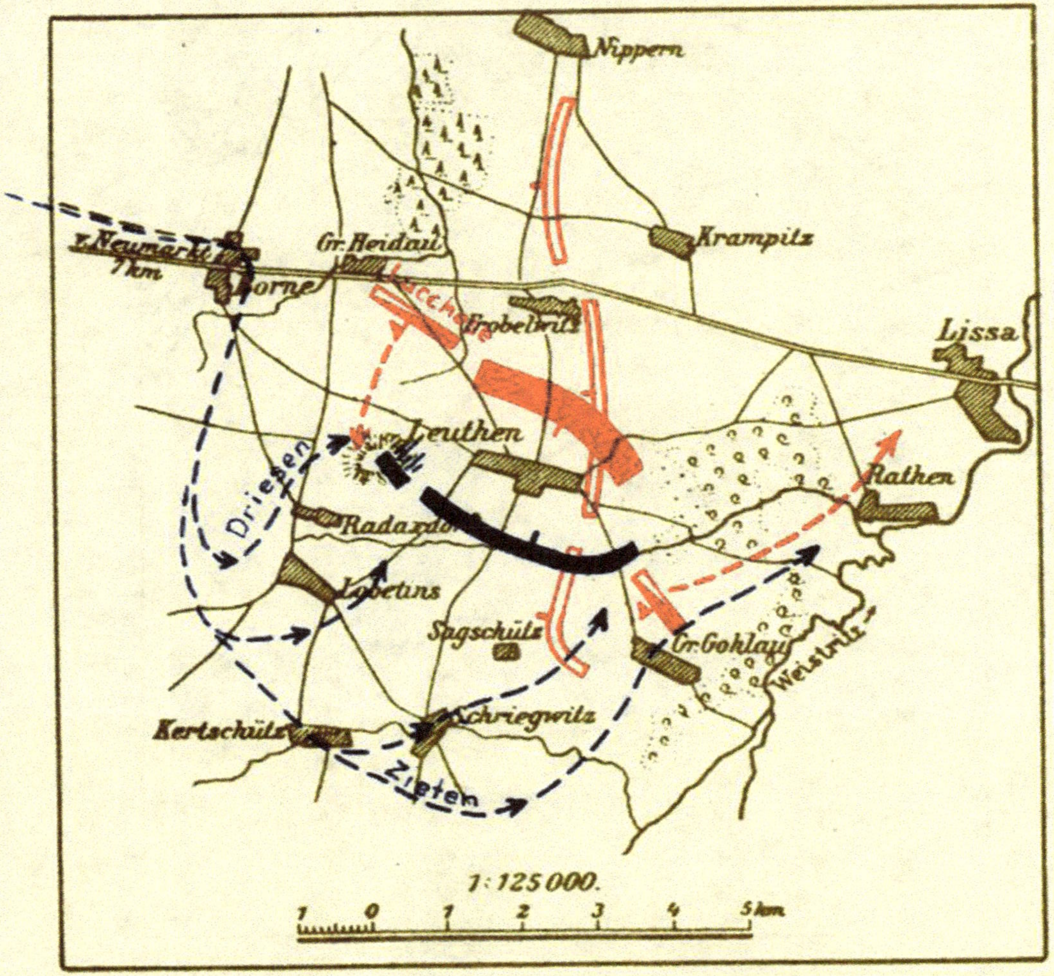

1:125 000

Map 5.

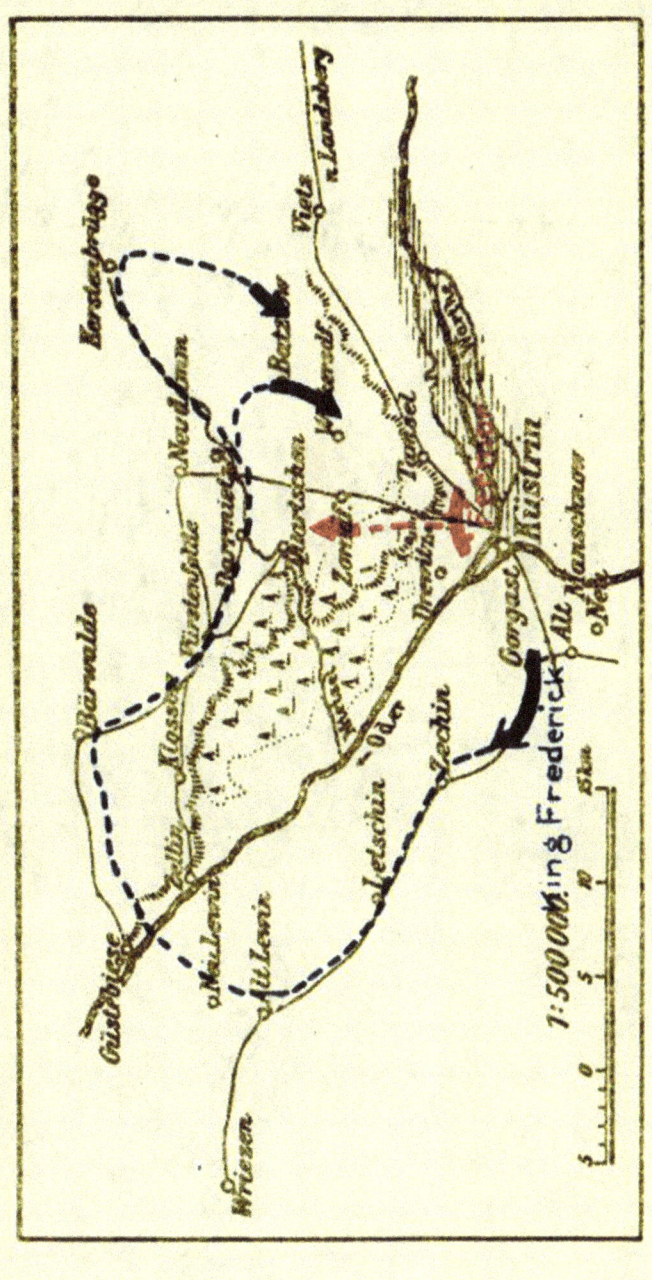

BATTLE OF ZORNDORF
Movements from 23 to 25 August, 1758

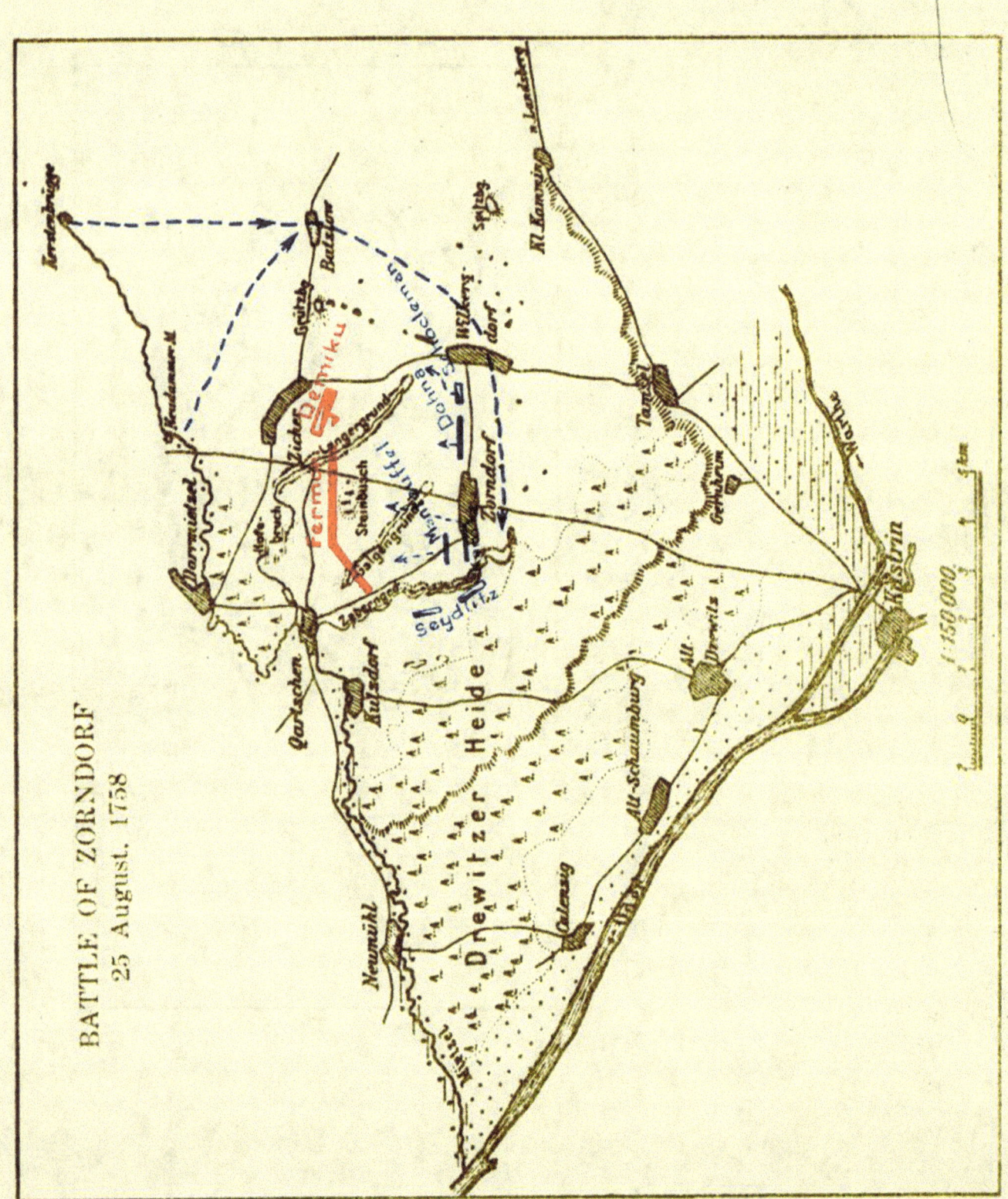

Map 7.

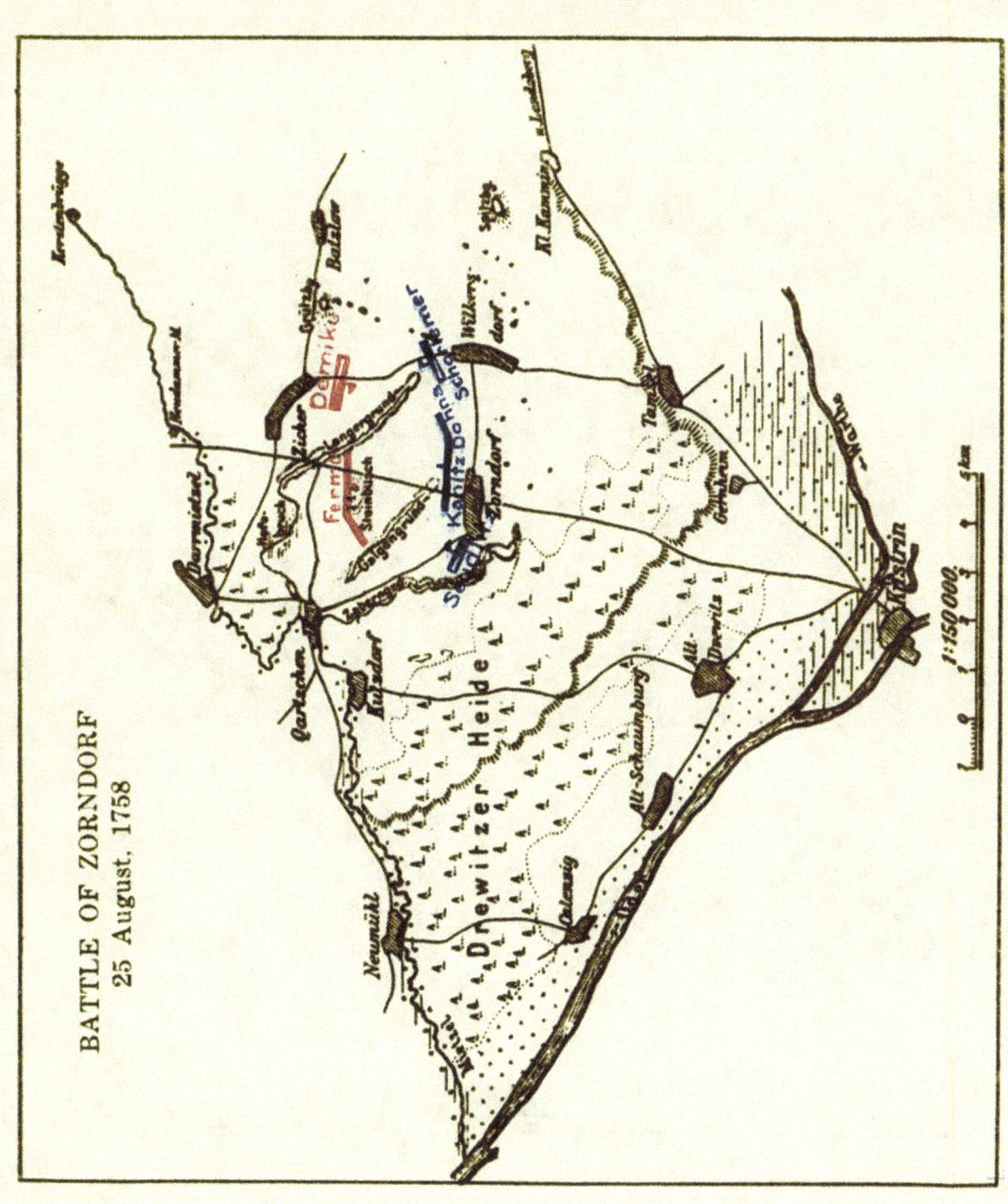

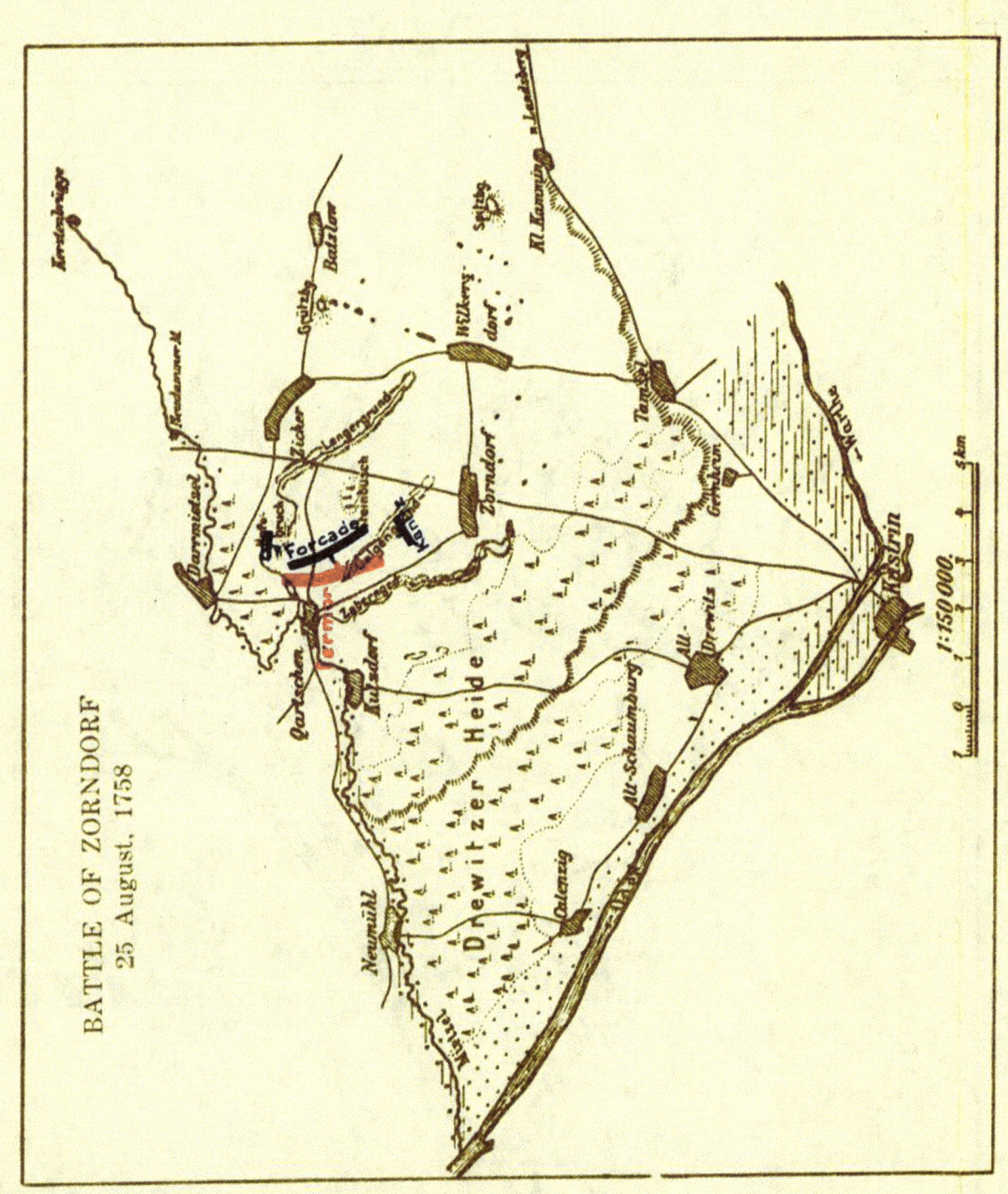

Map 9.

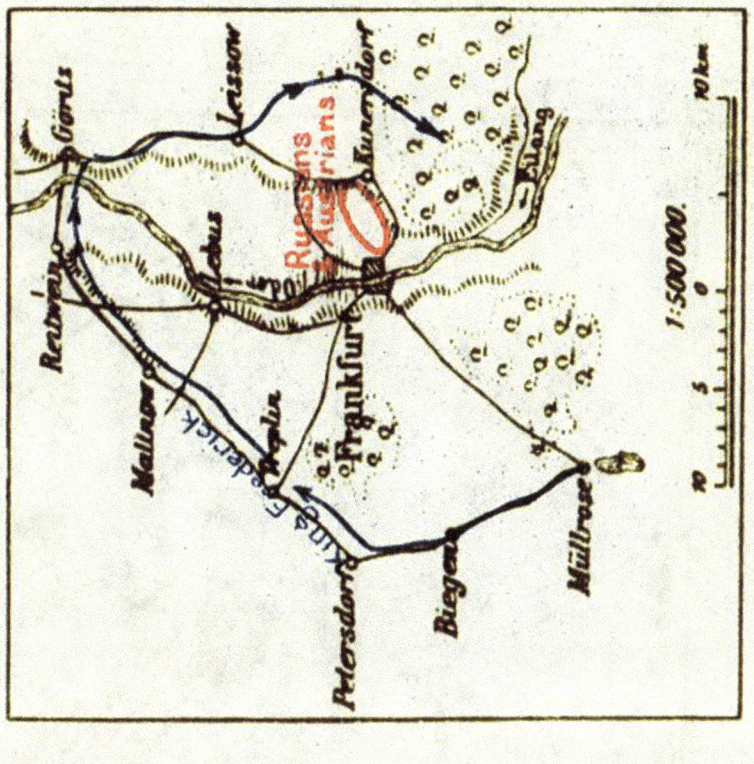

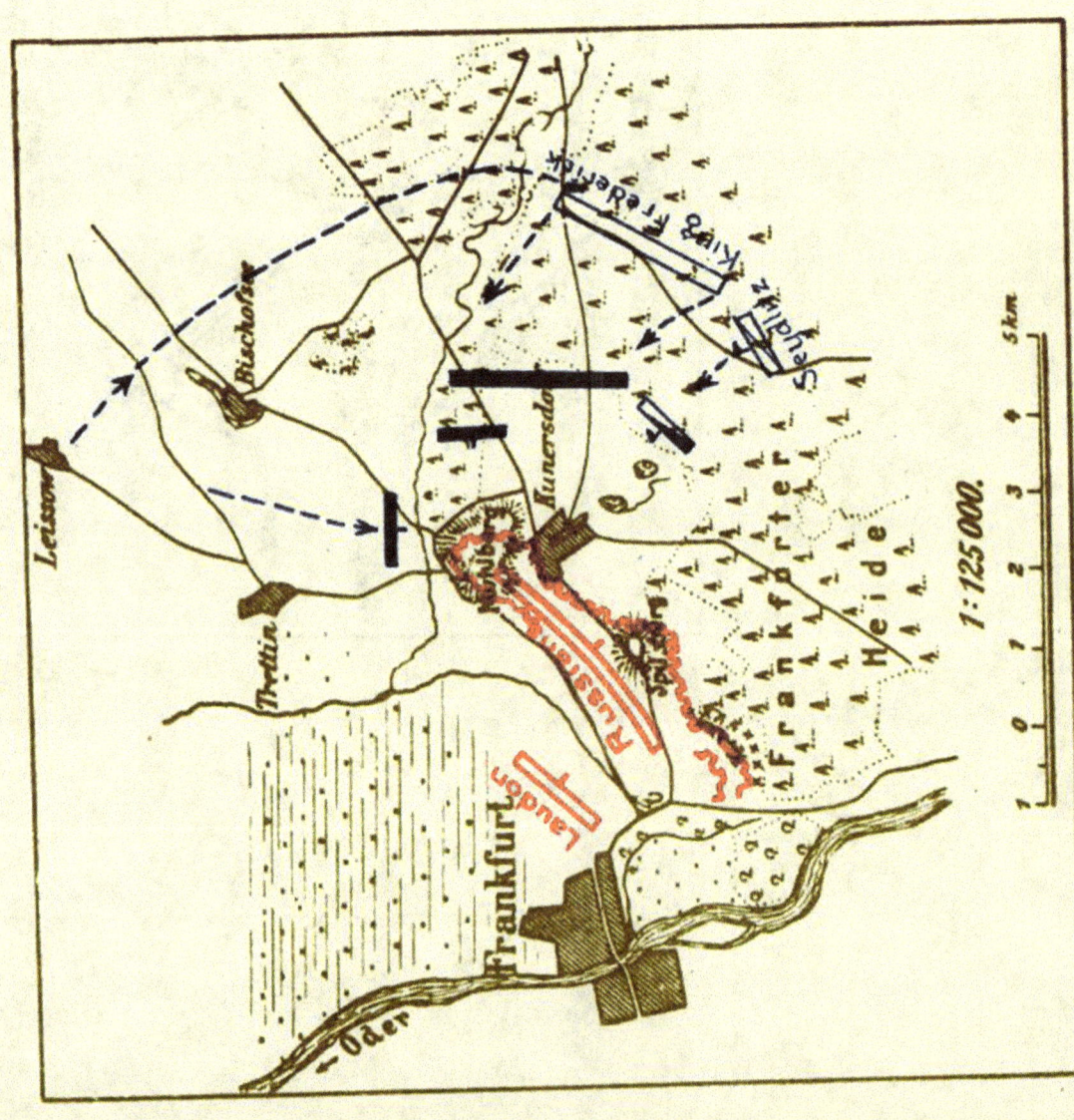

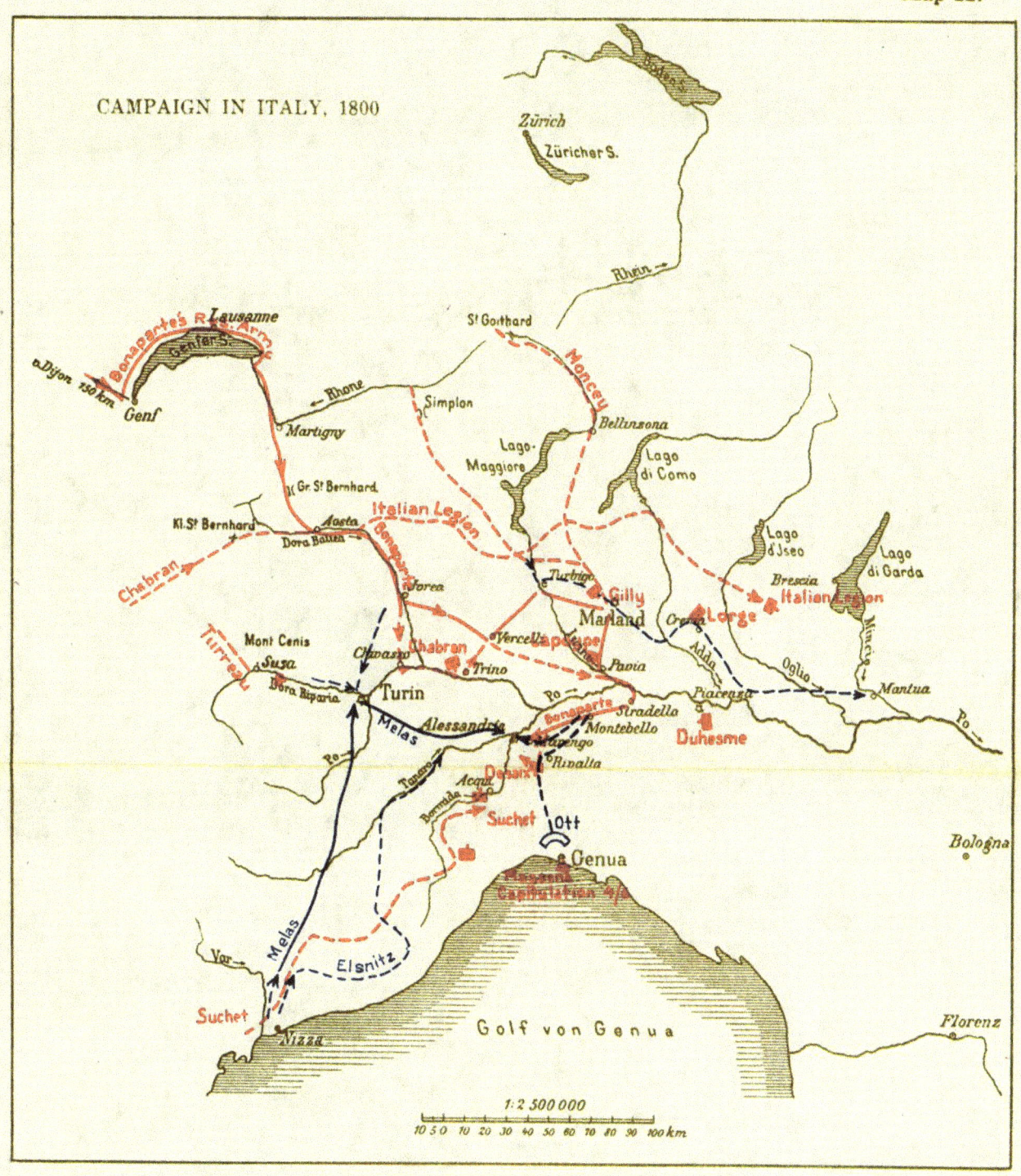

Map 12.

CAMPAIGN IN GERMANY 1805

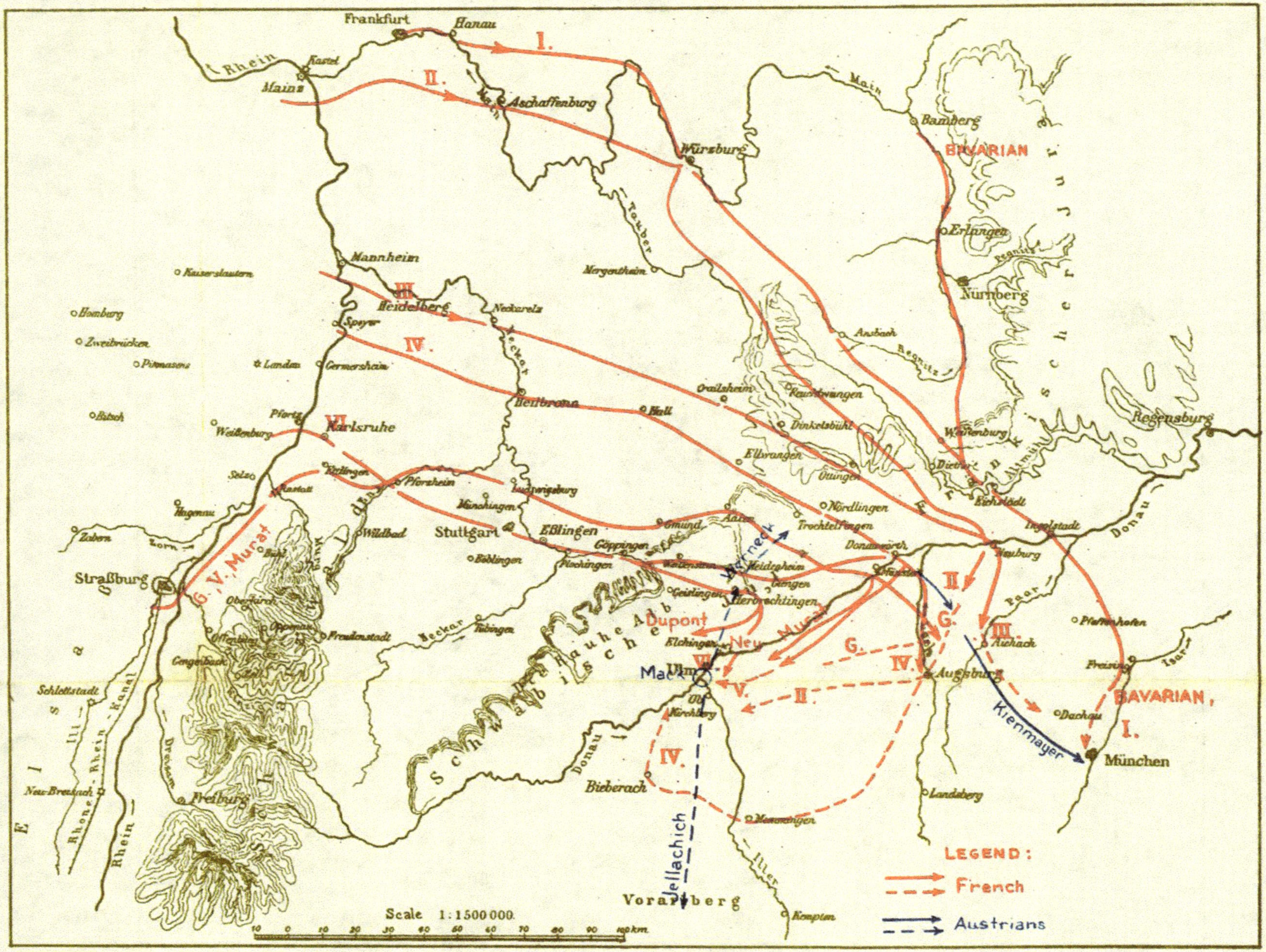

LEGEND:
French →
Austrians →

Scale 1:1.500.000.

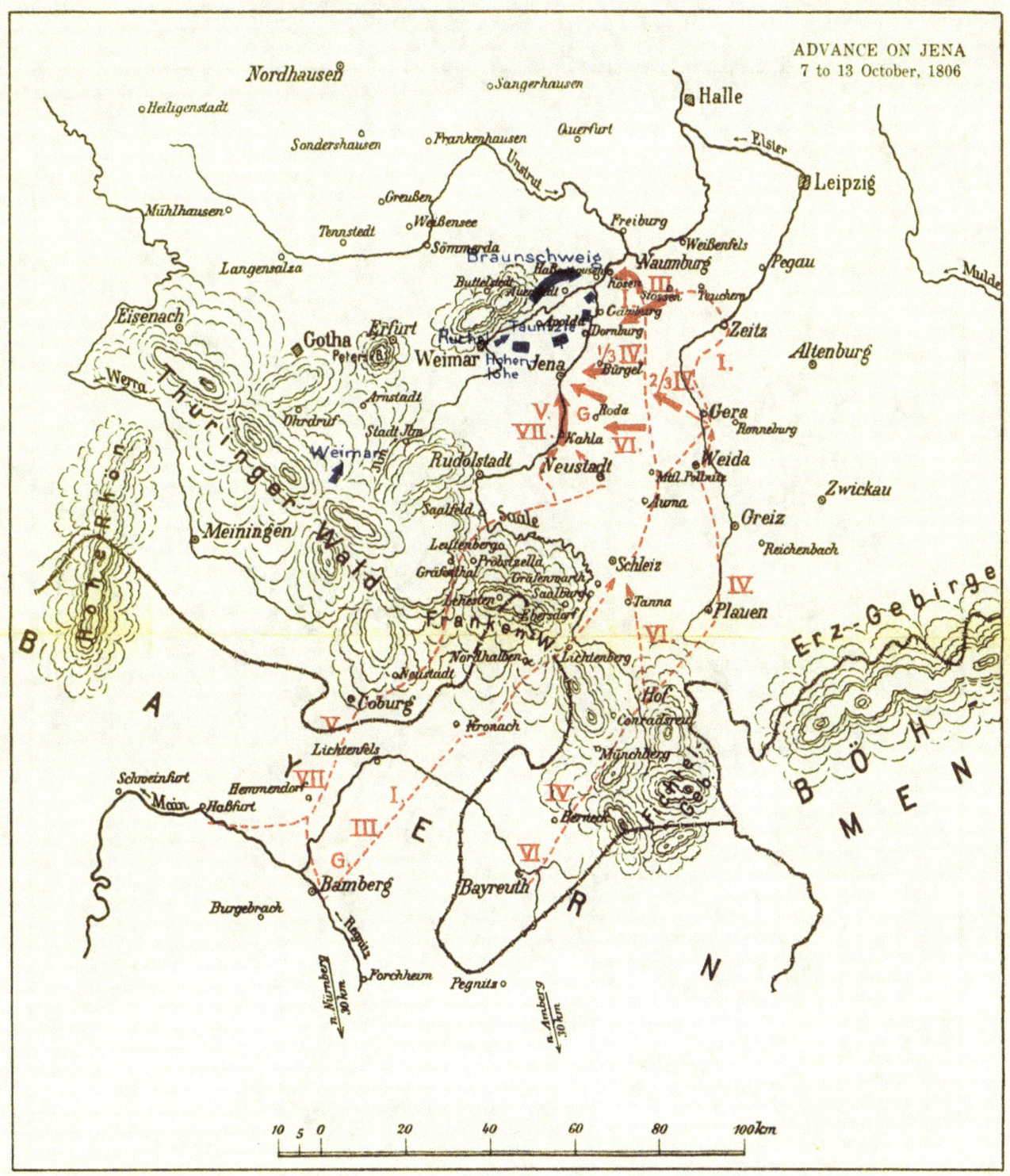

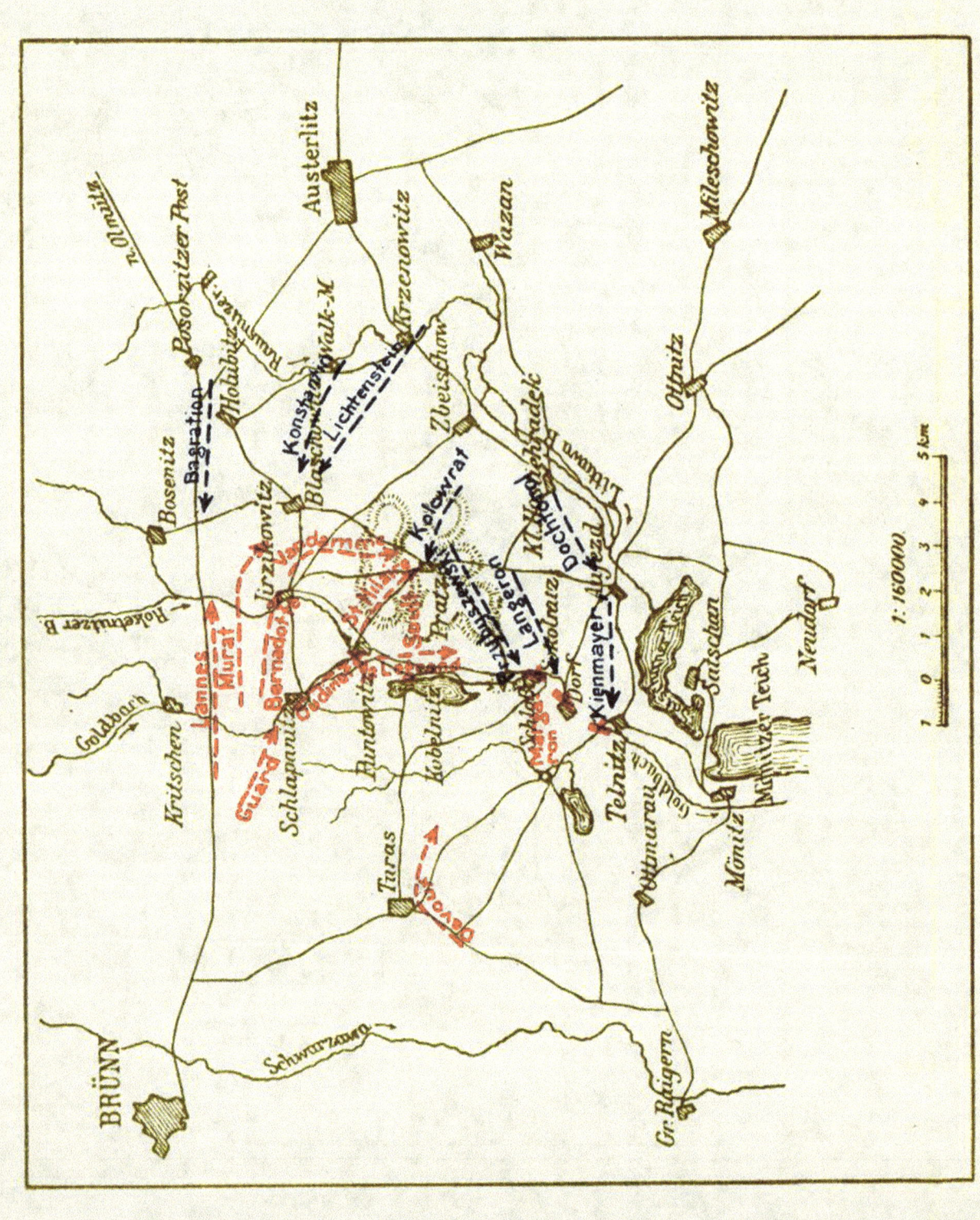

Map 14.

BATTLE OF AUSTERLITZ
2 December, 1805

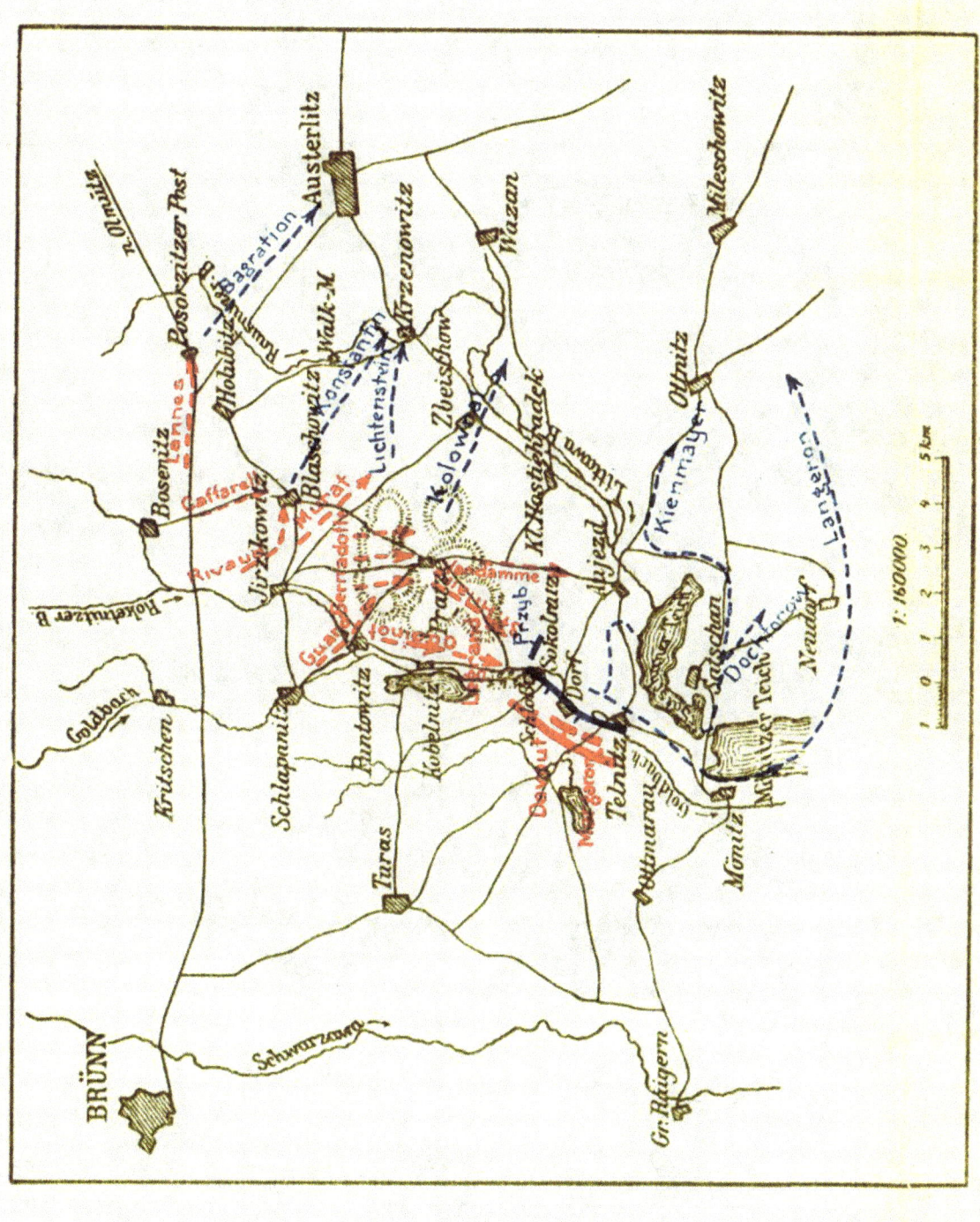

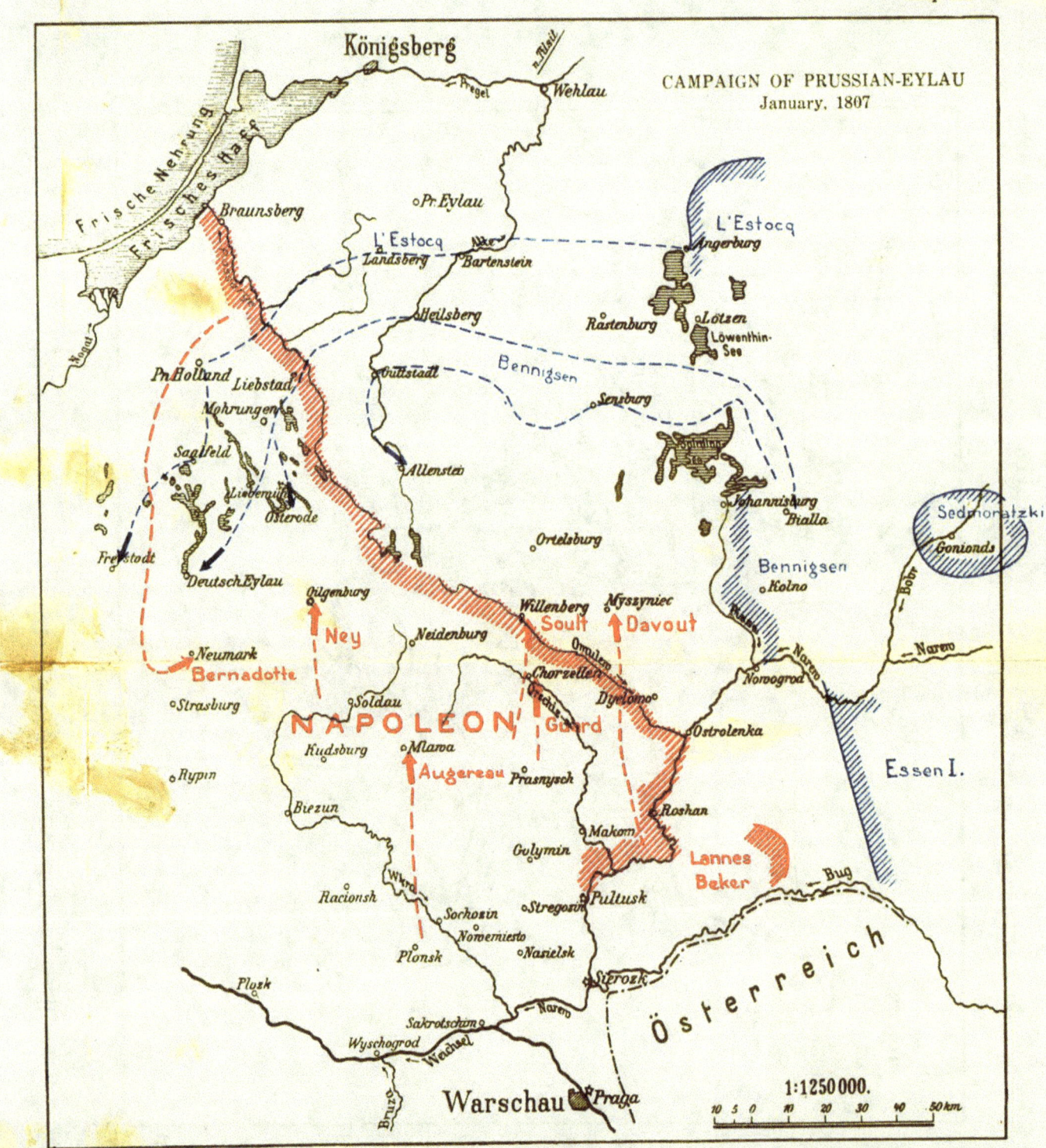

Map 17.

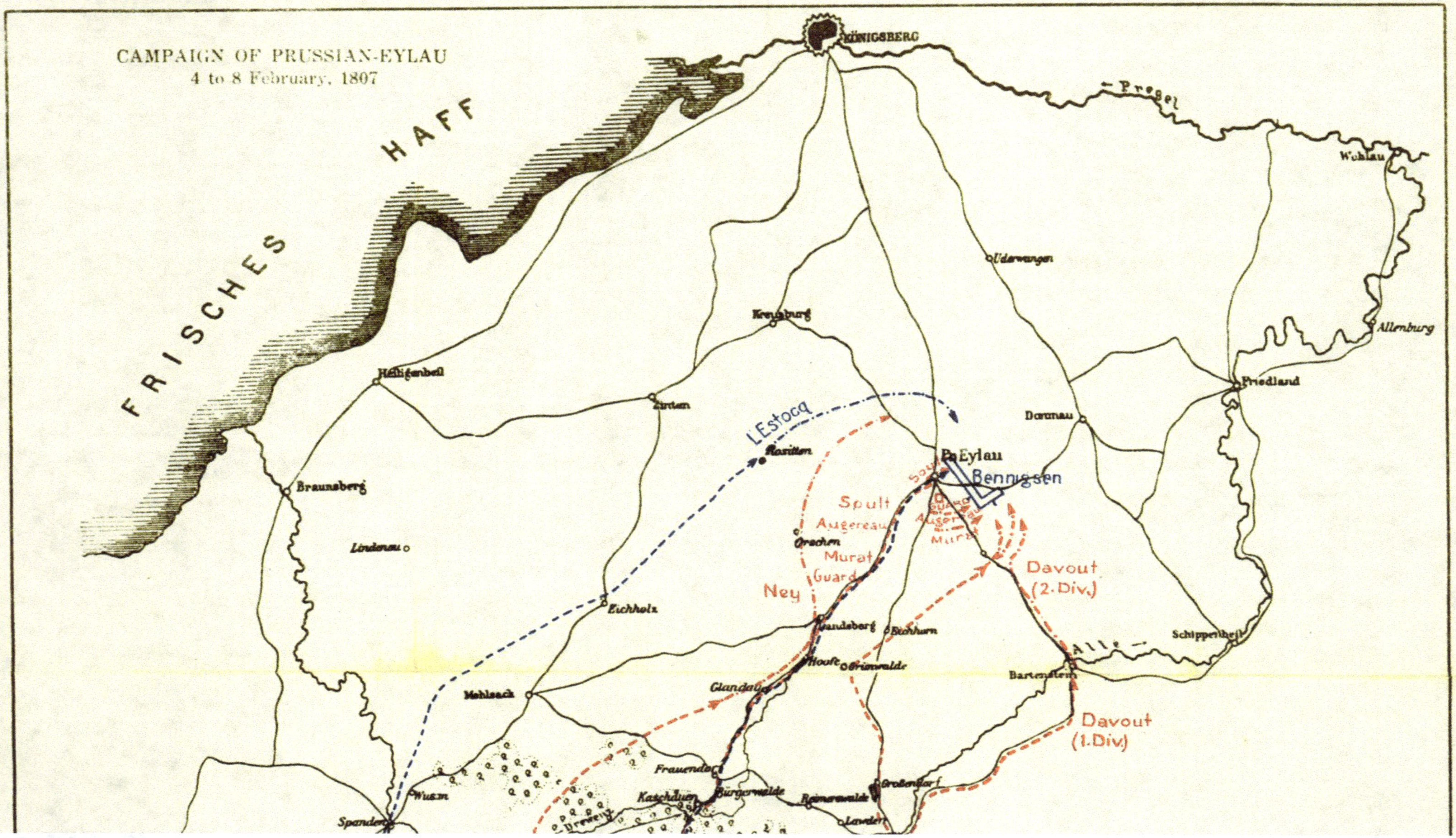
CAMPAIGN OF PRUSSIAN-EYLAU
4 to 8 February, 1807
FRISCHES HAFF
KÖNIGSBERG
Pregel
Wehlau
Allenburg
Friedland
Uderwangen
Kreuzburg
Heiligenbeil
Zinten
Braunsberg
Lindenau
Rositten
Eichholz
Mehlsack
Domnau
Pr. Eylau
Bennigsen
L'Estocq
Soult
Augereau
Murat
Guard
Ney
Davout (2. Div.)
Davout (1. Div.)
Orschen
Landsberg
Eichhorn
Hoofe
Grünwalde
Glandau
Bartenstein
Schippenbeil
Alle
Frauendorf
Kashdum
Burgerwalde
Reimerswalde
Großendorf
Lawden
Wusen
Spanden

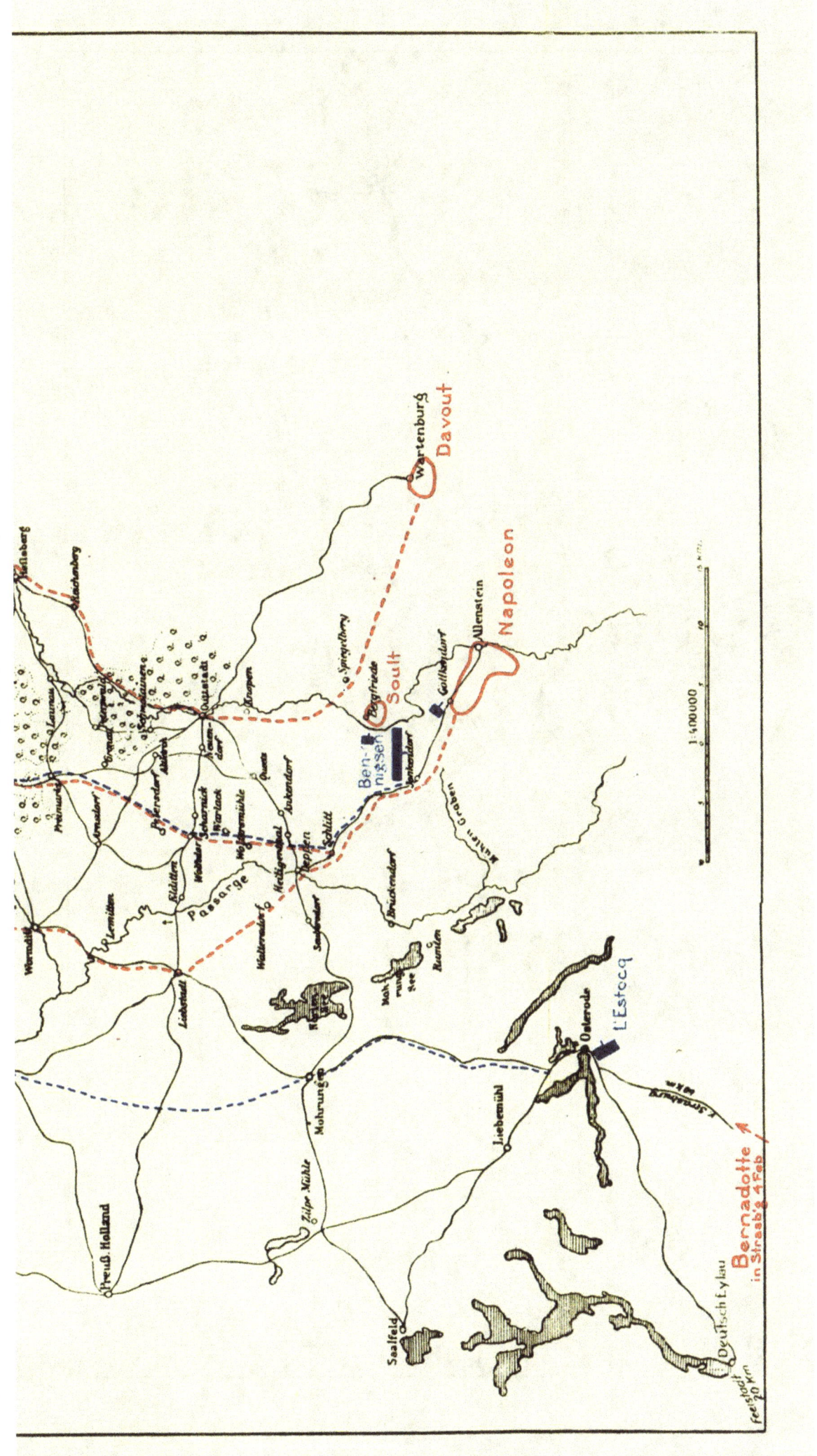

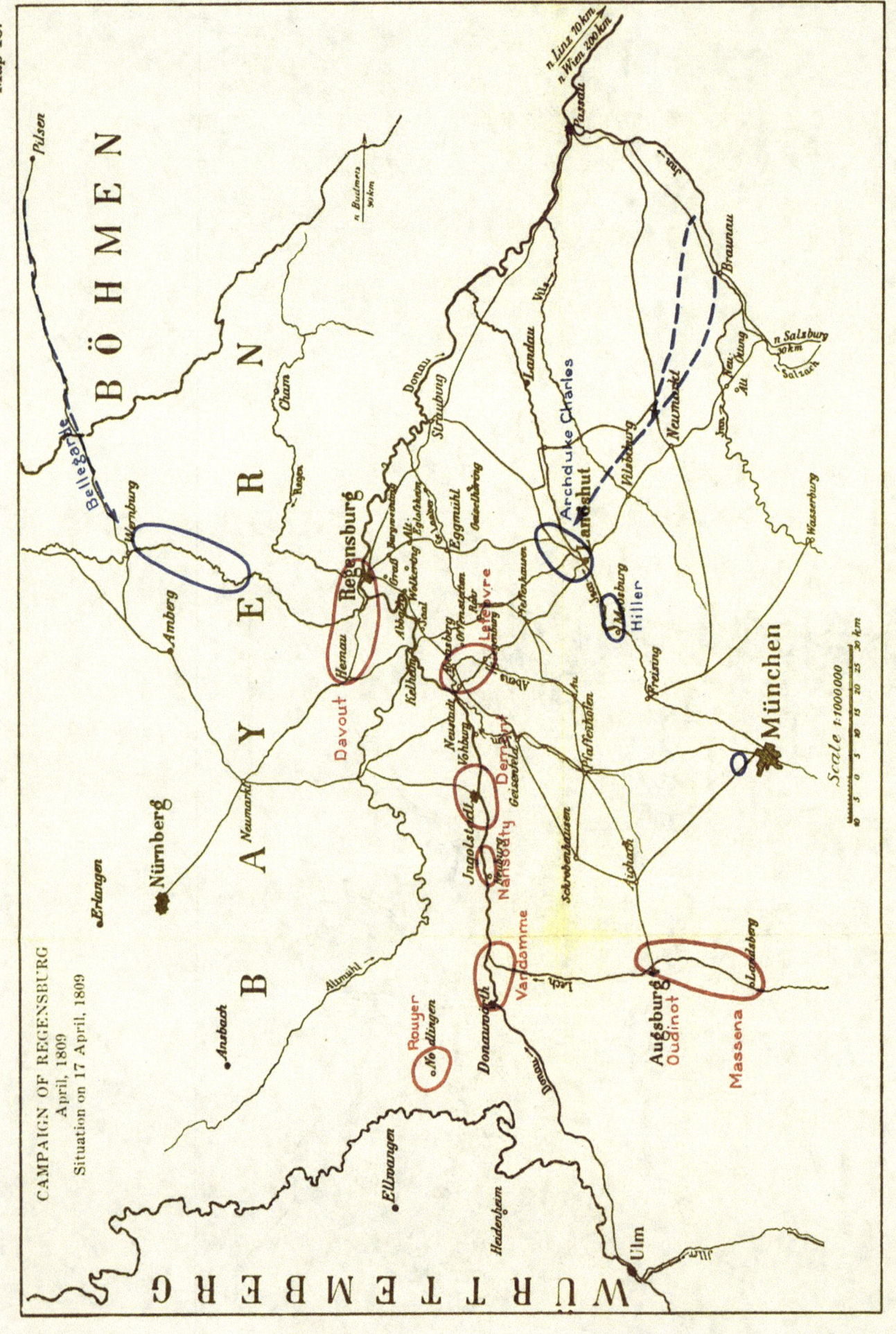

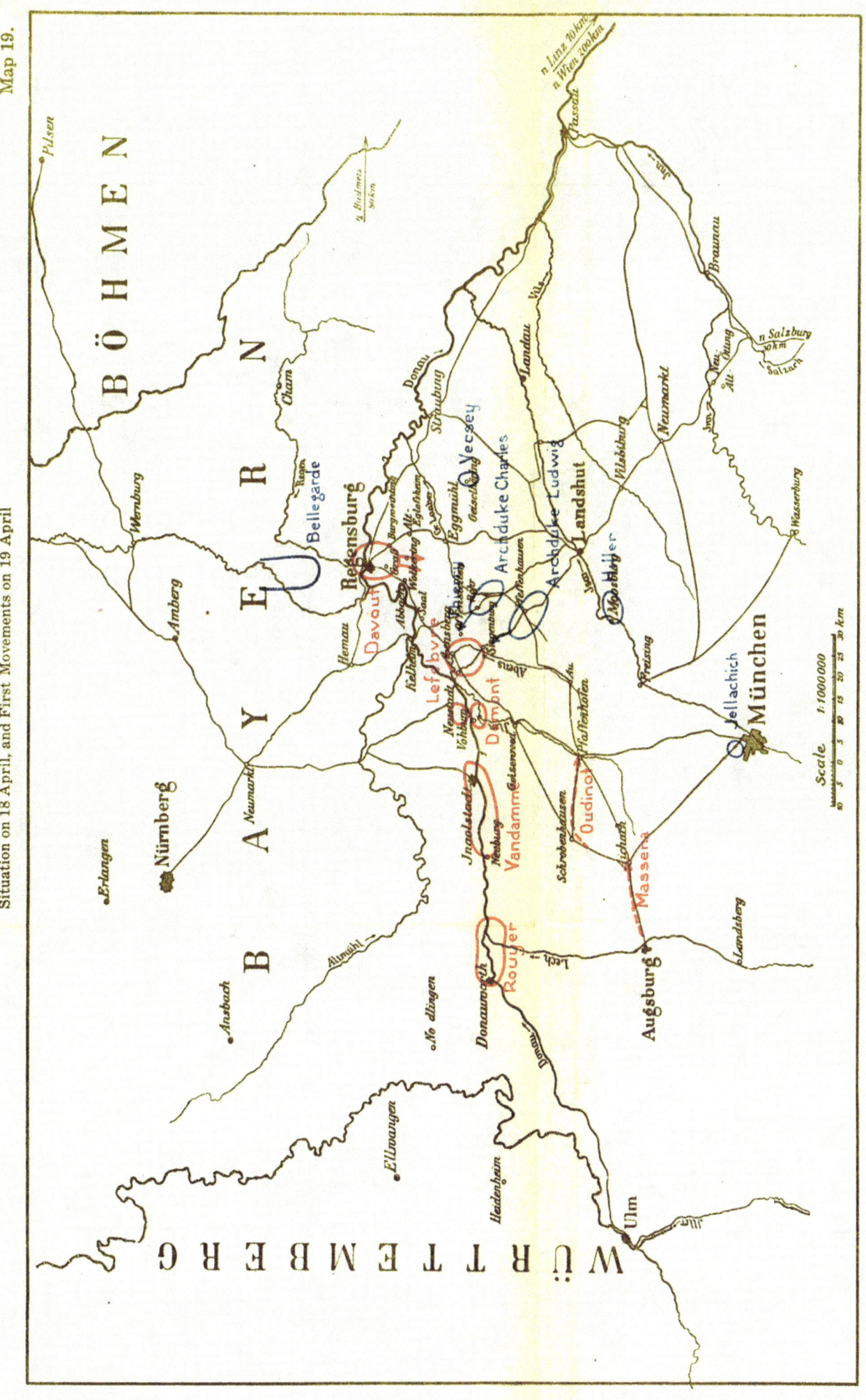

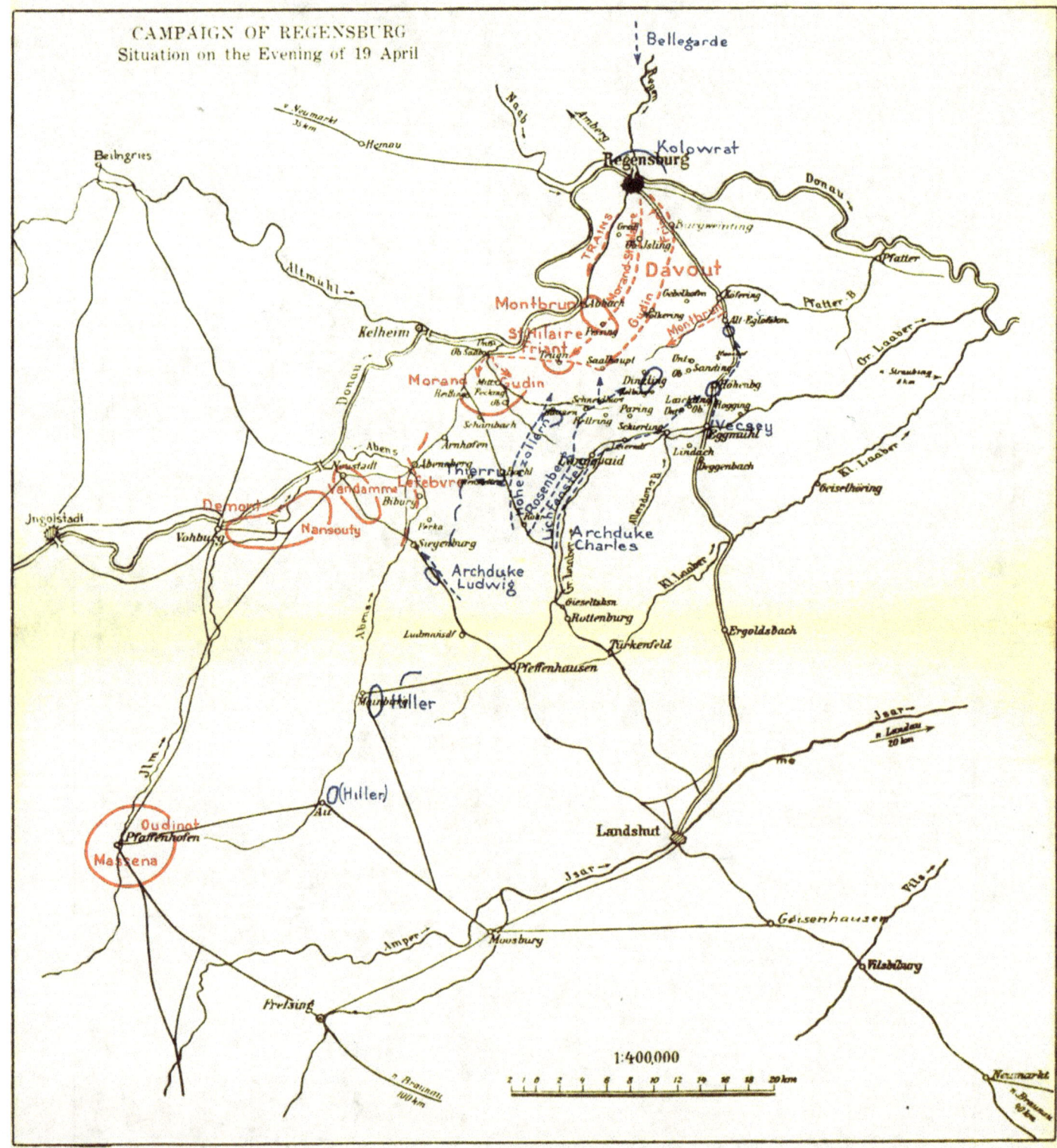

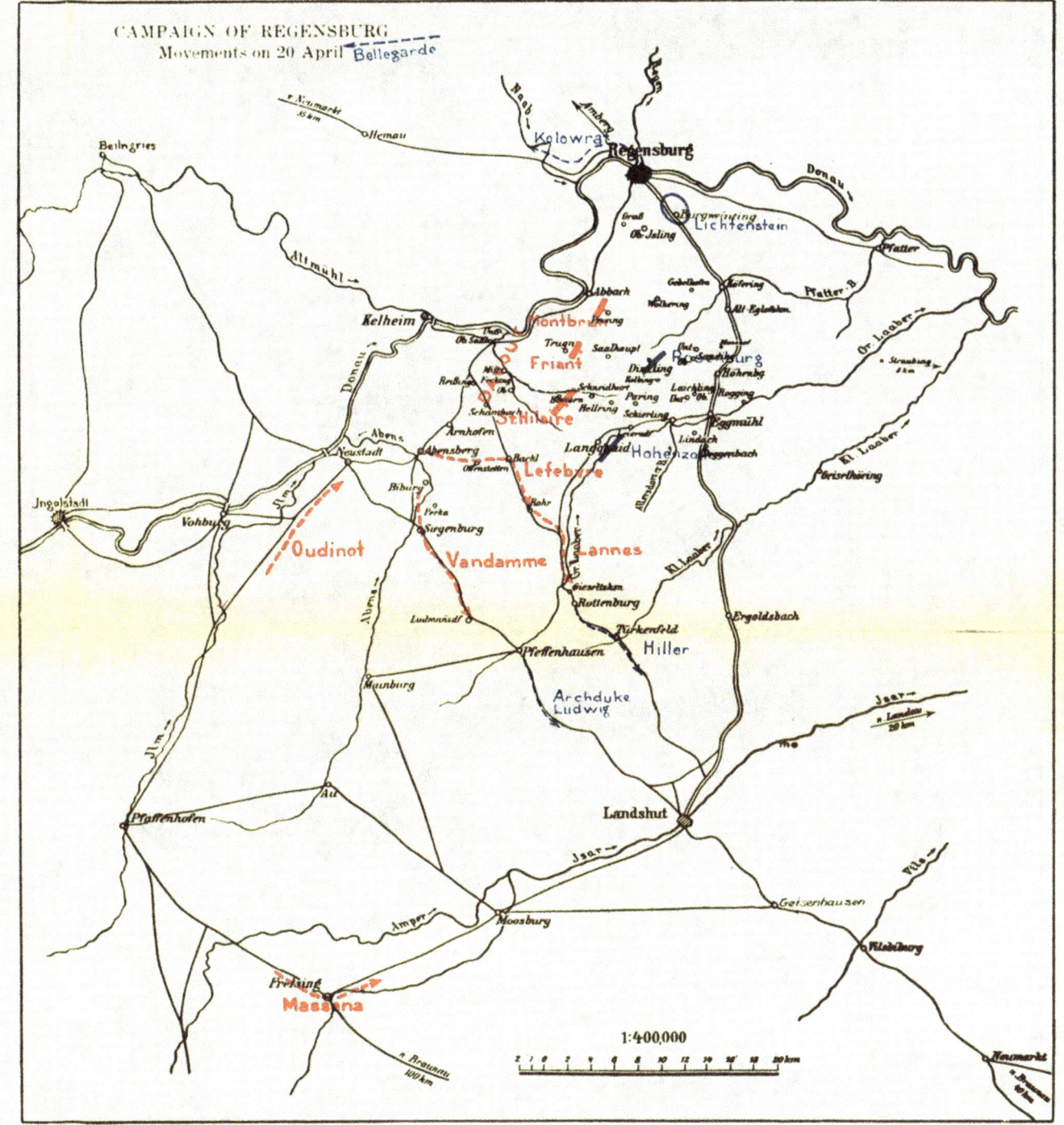

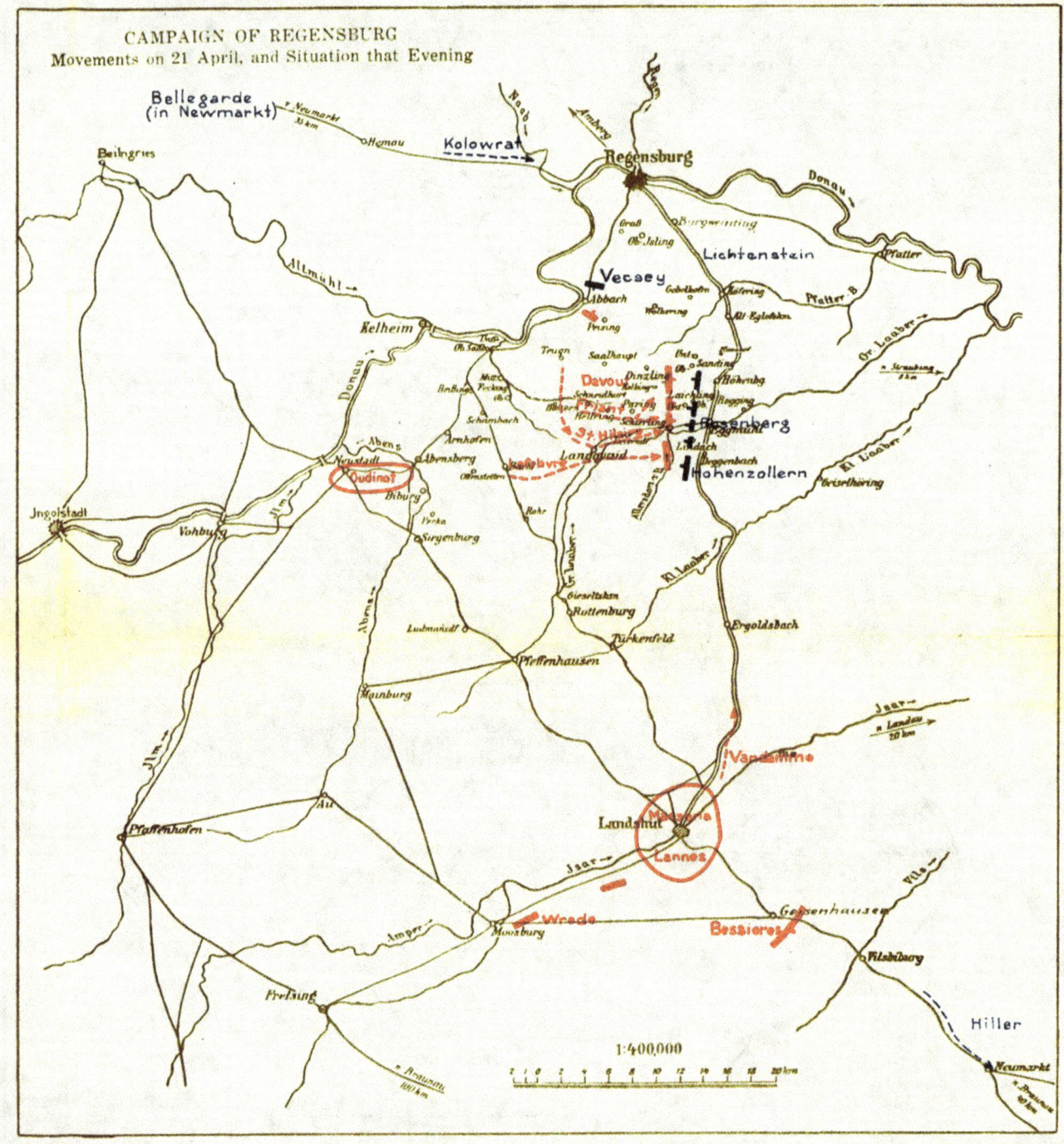

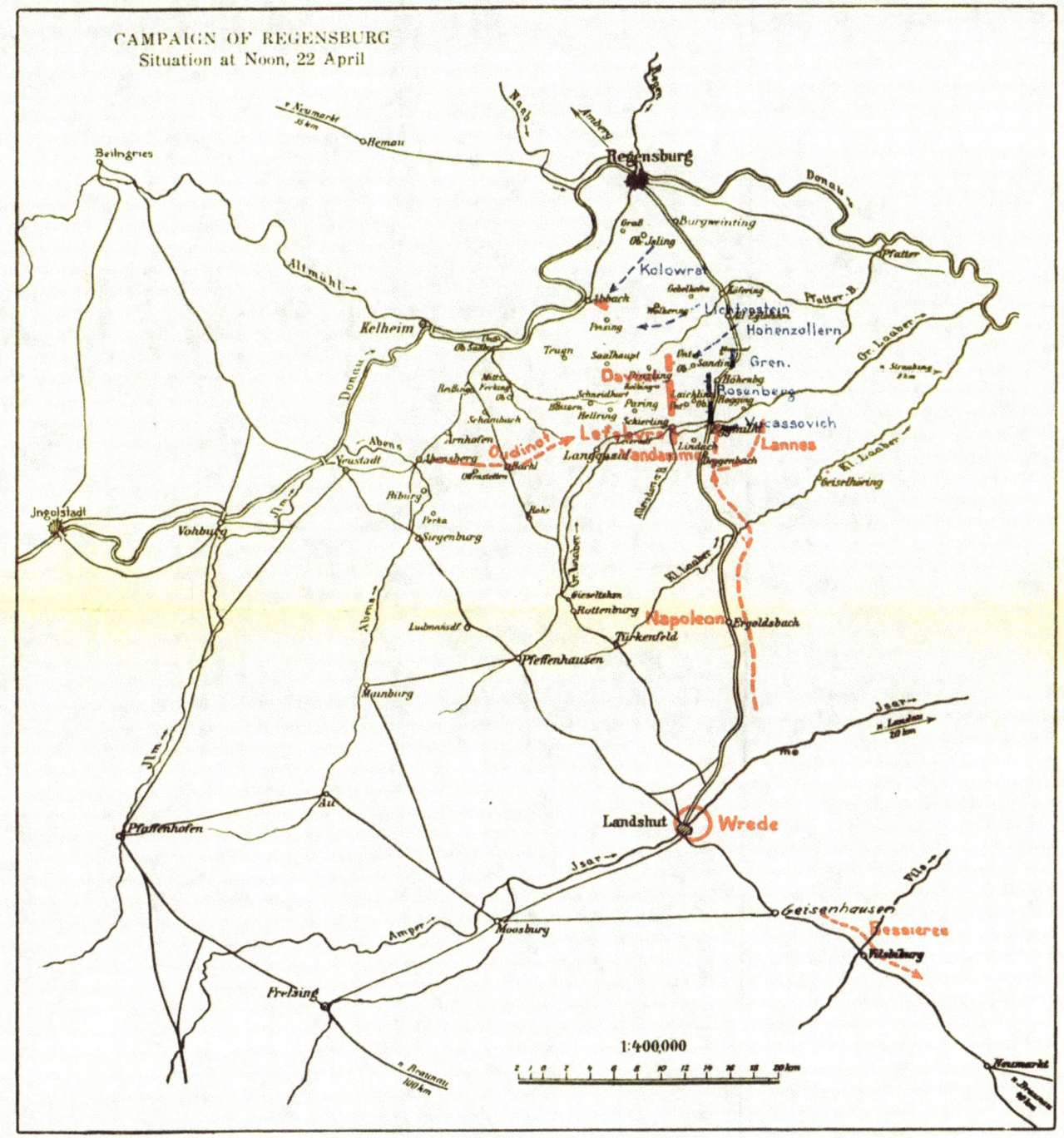

Map 24.

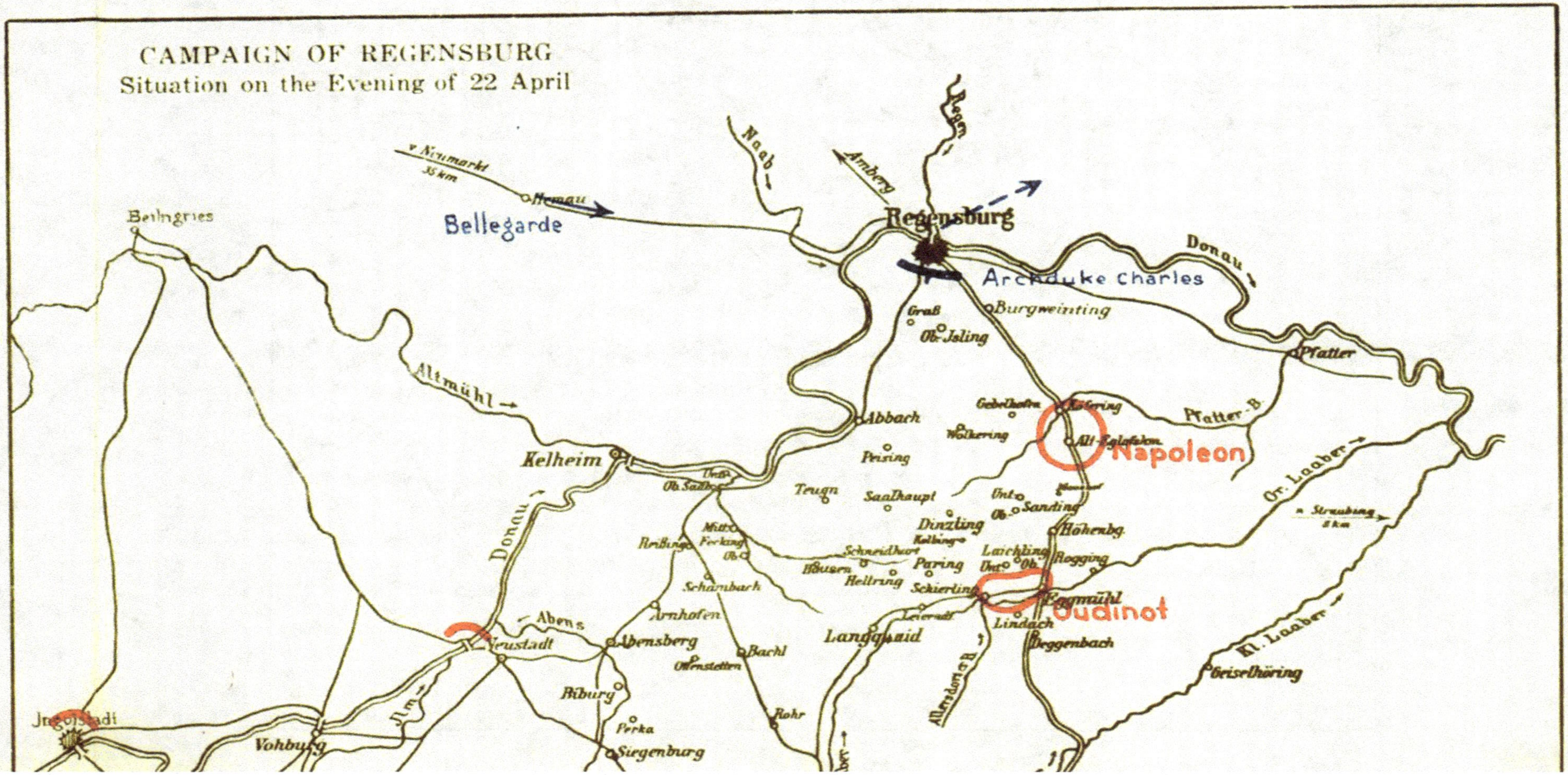
CAMPAIGN OF REGENSBURG
Situation on the Evening of 22 April
Regensburg
Bellegarde
Archduke Charles
Napoleon
Oudinot
Donau
Naab
Regen
Amberg
Altmühl
Kelheim
Abbach
Burgweinting
Pfatter
Beilngries
Neustadt
Abensberg
Langquaid
Eggmühl
Vohburg
Siegenburg

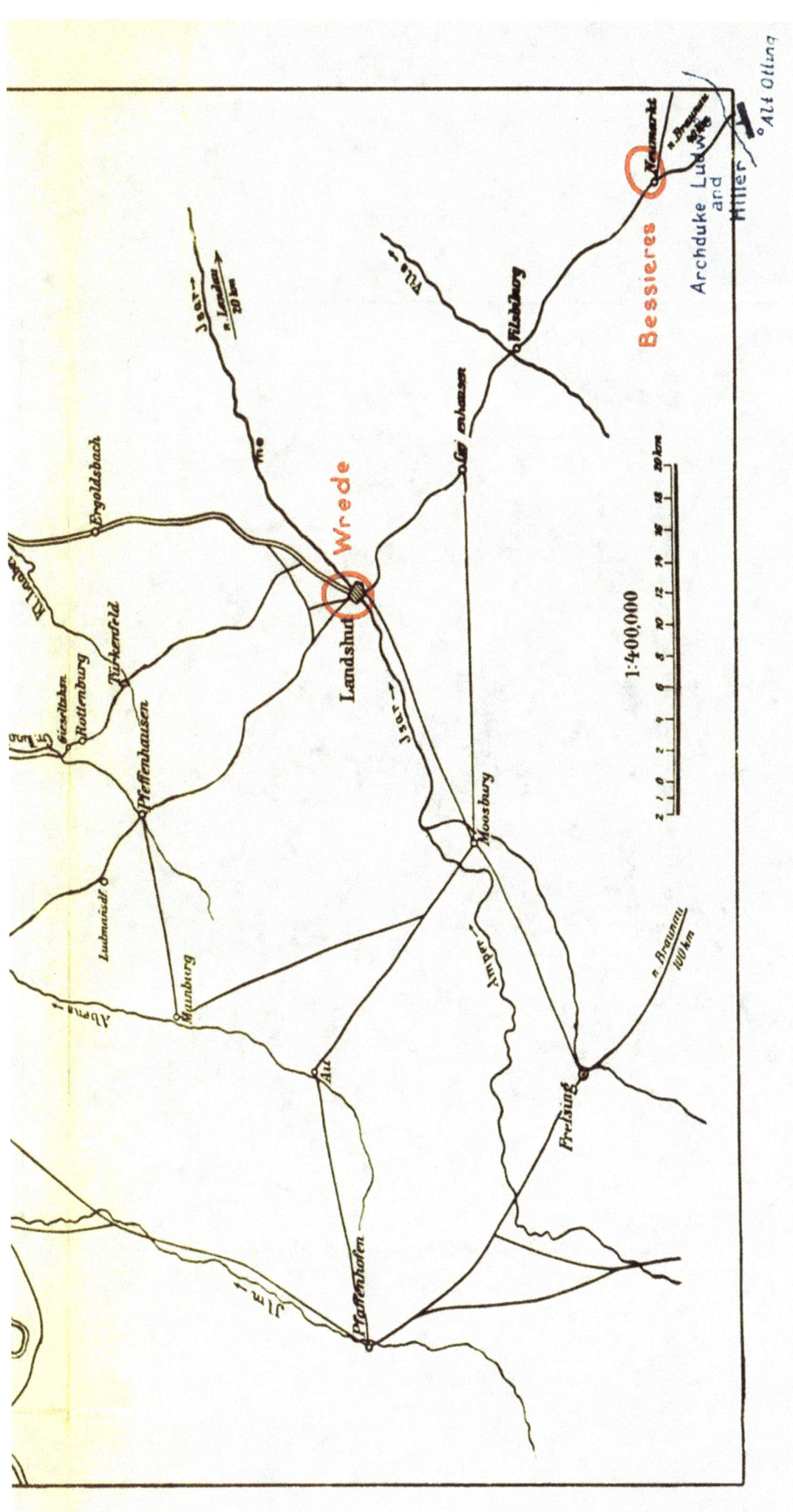

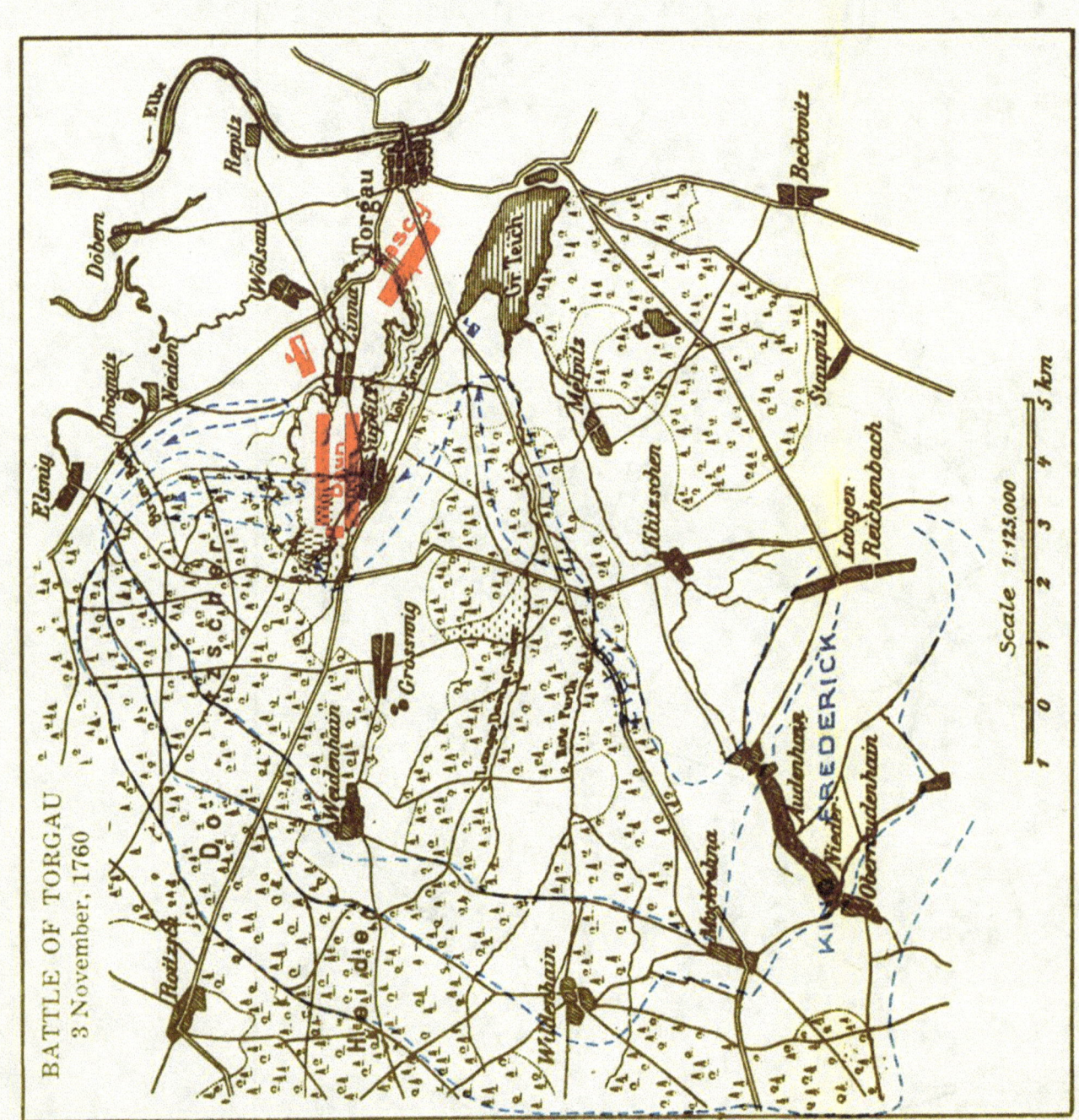

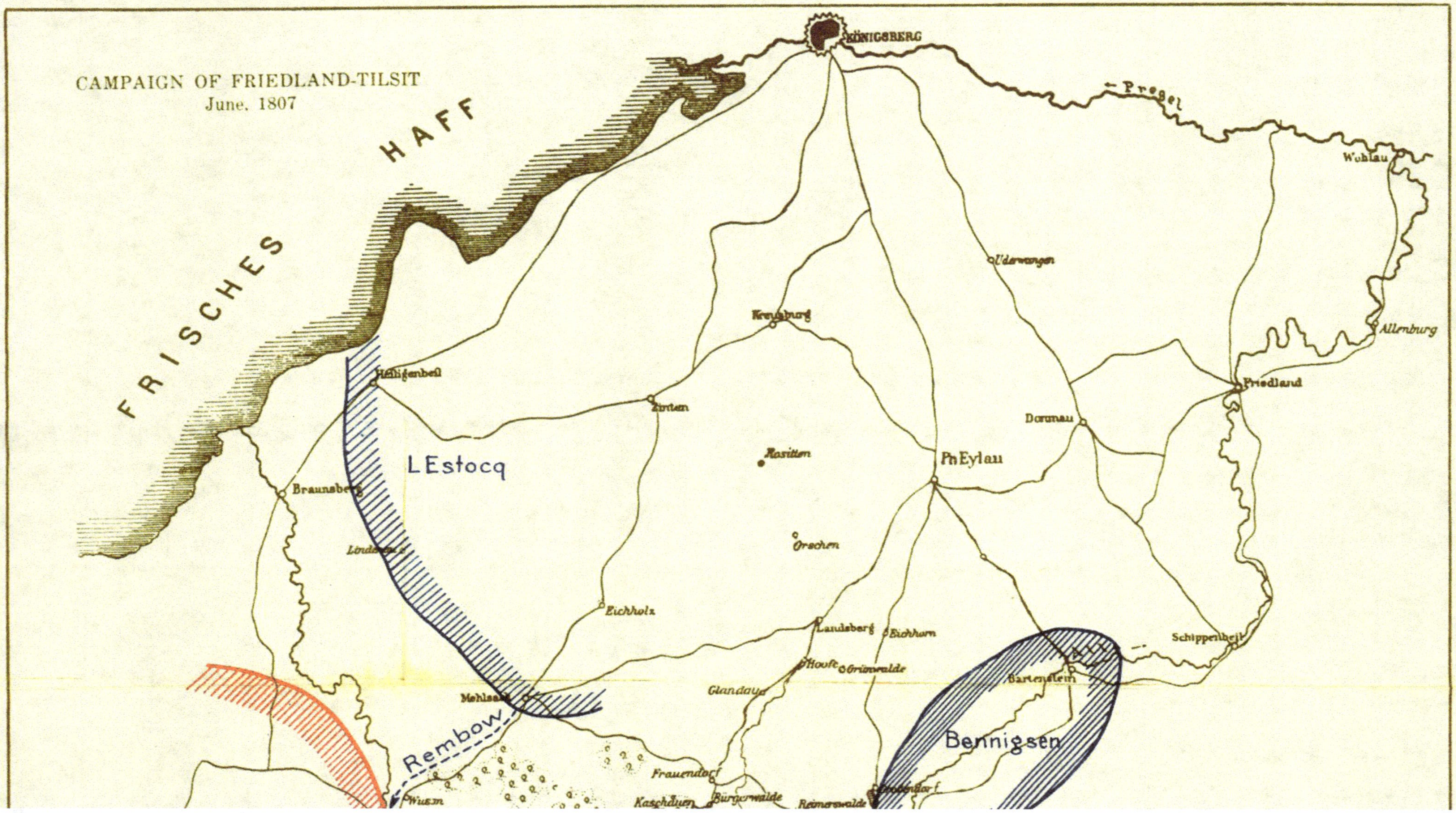

Map 26.

CAMPAIGN OF FRIEDLAND-TILSIT
June. 1807

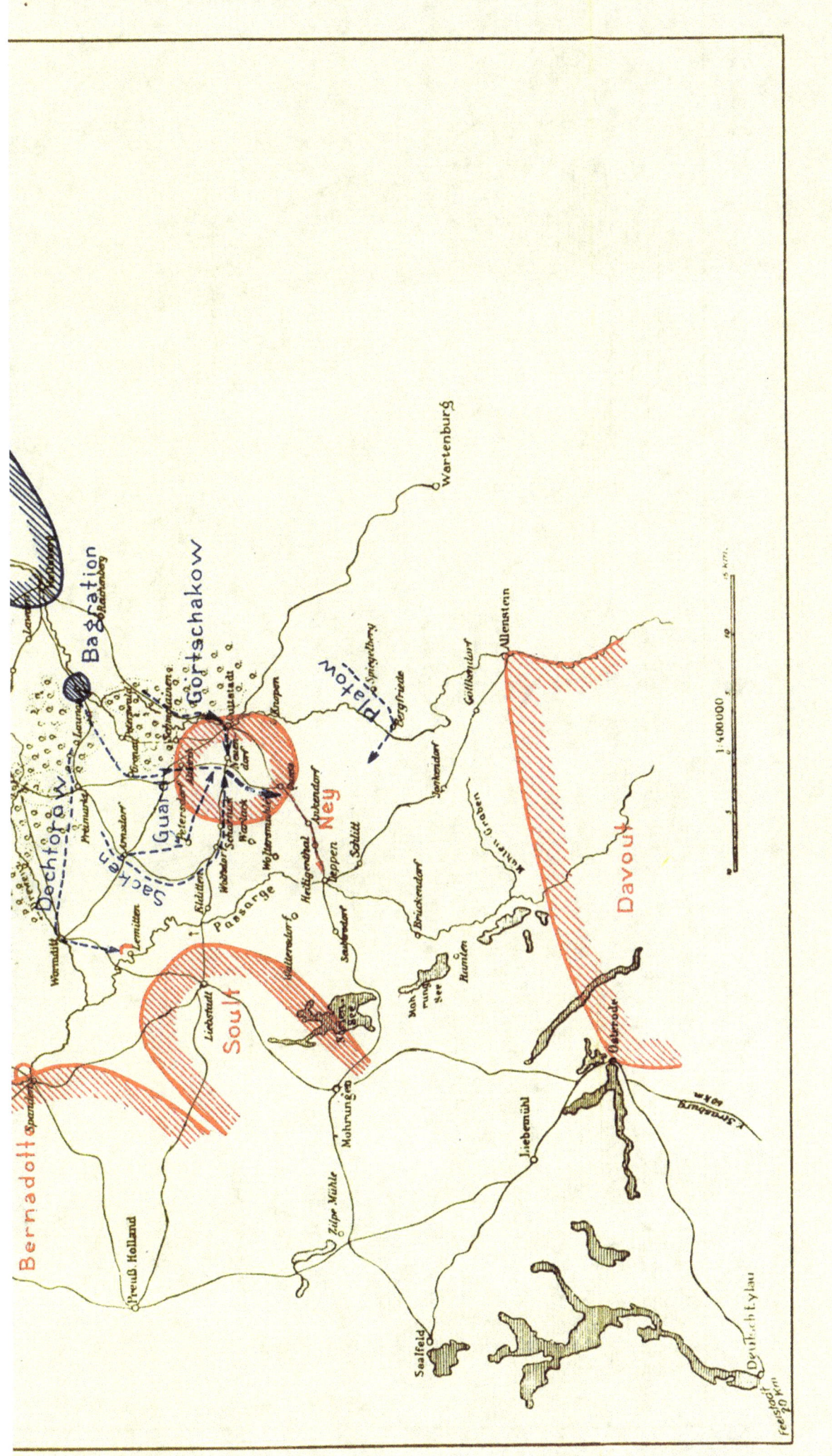

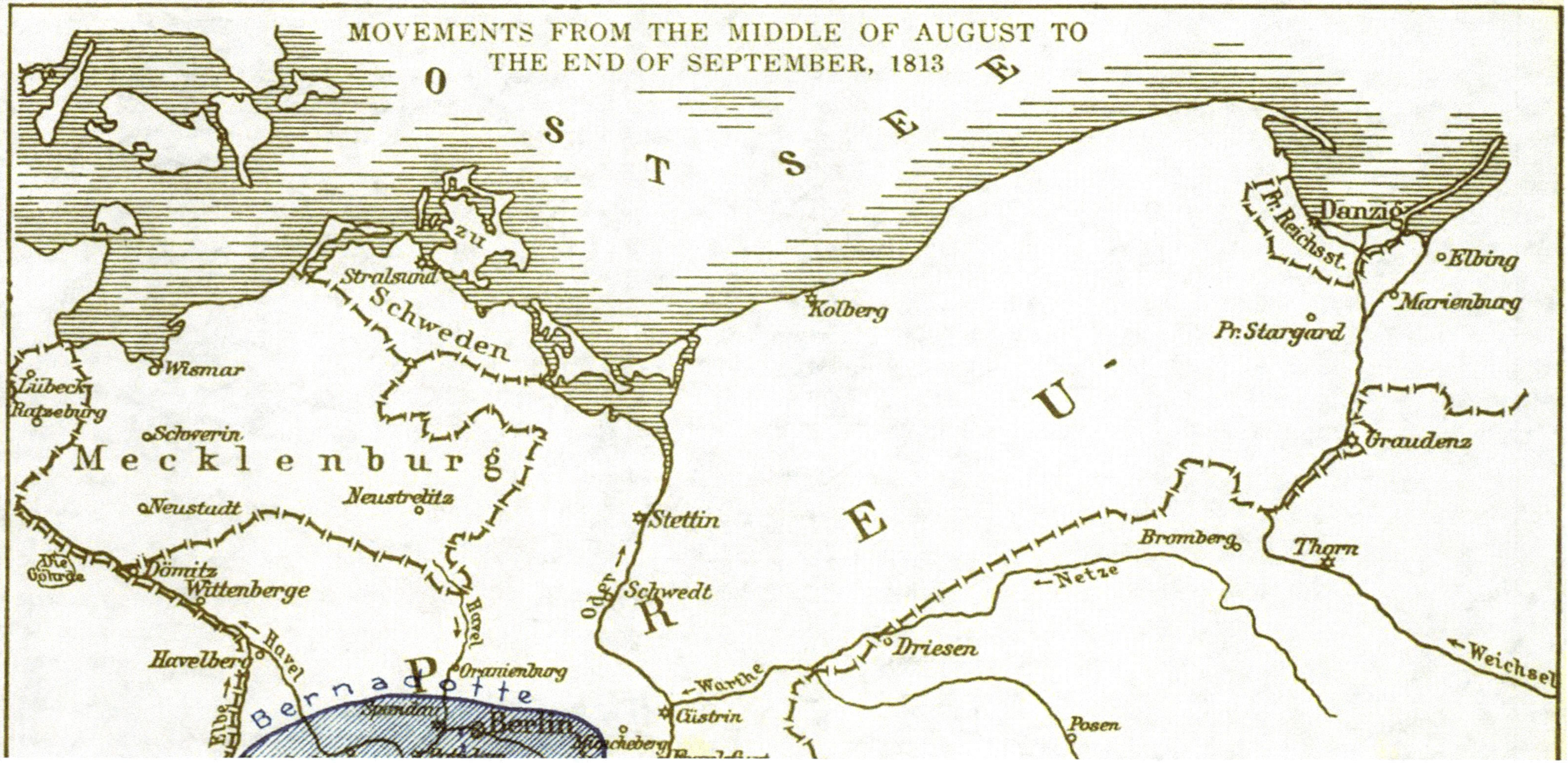

Map 27.

MOVEMENTS FROM THE MIDDLE OF AUGUST TO THE END OF SEPTEMBER, 1813

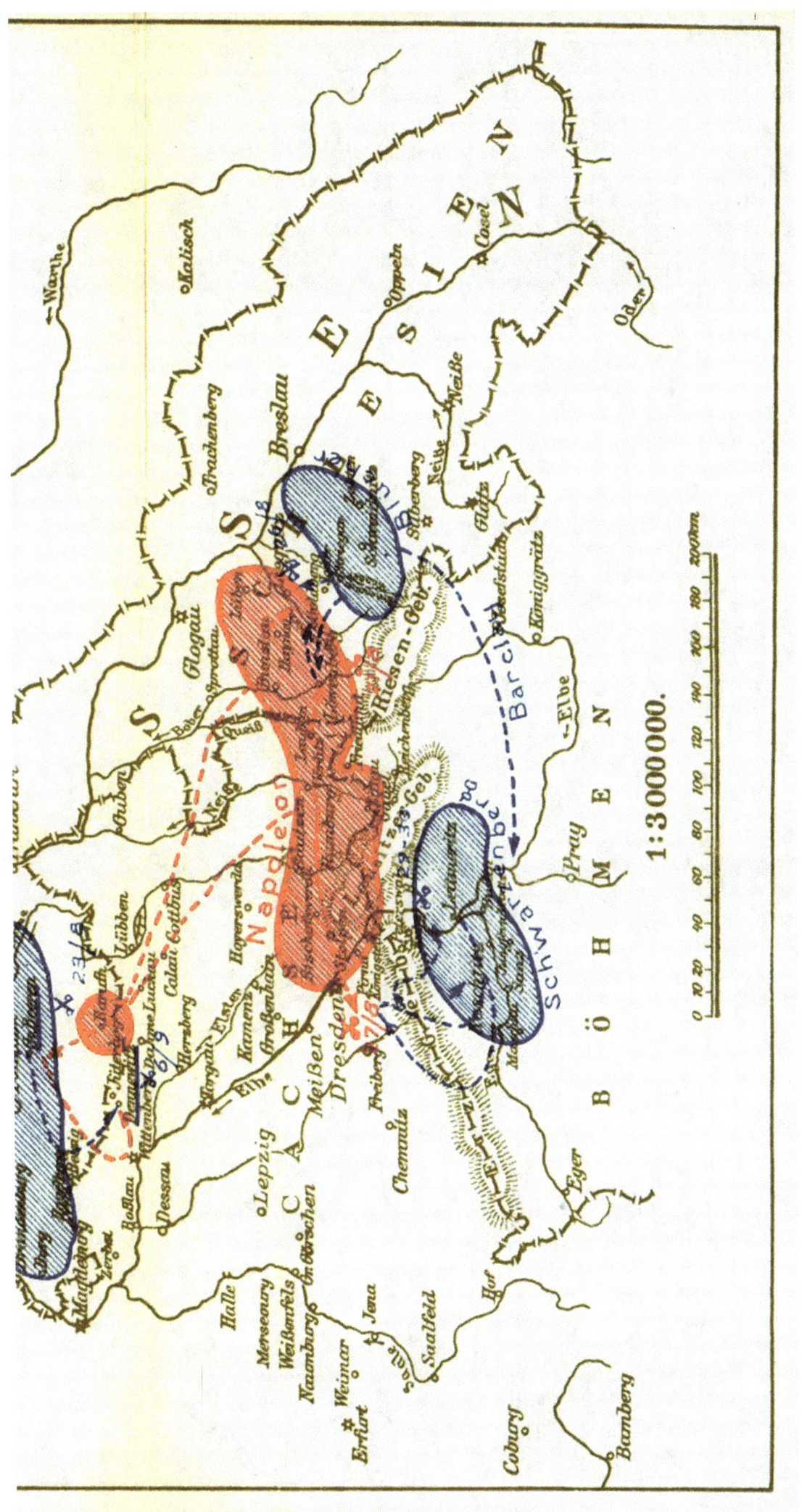

Map 28.

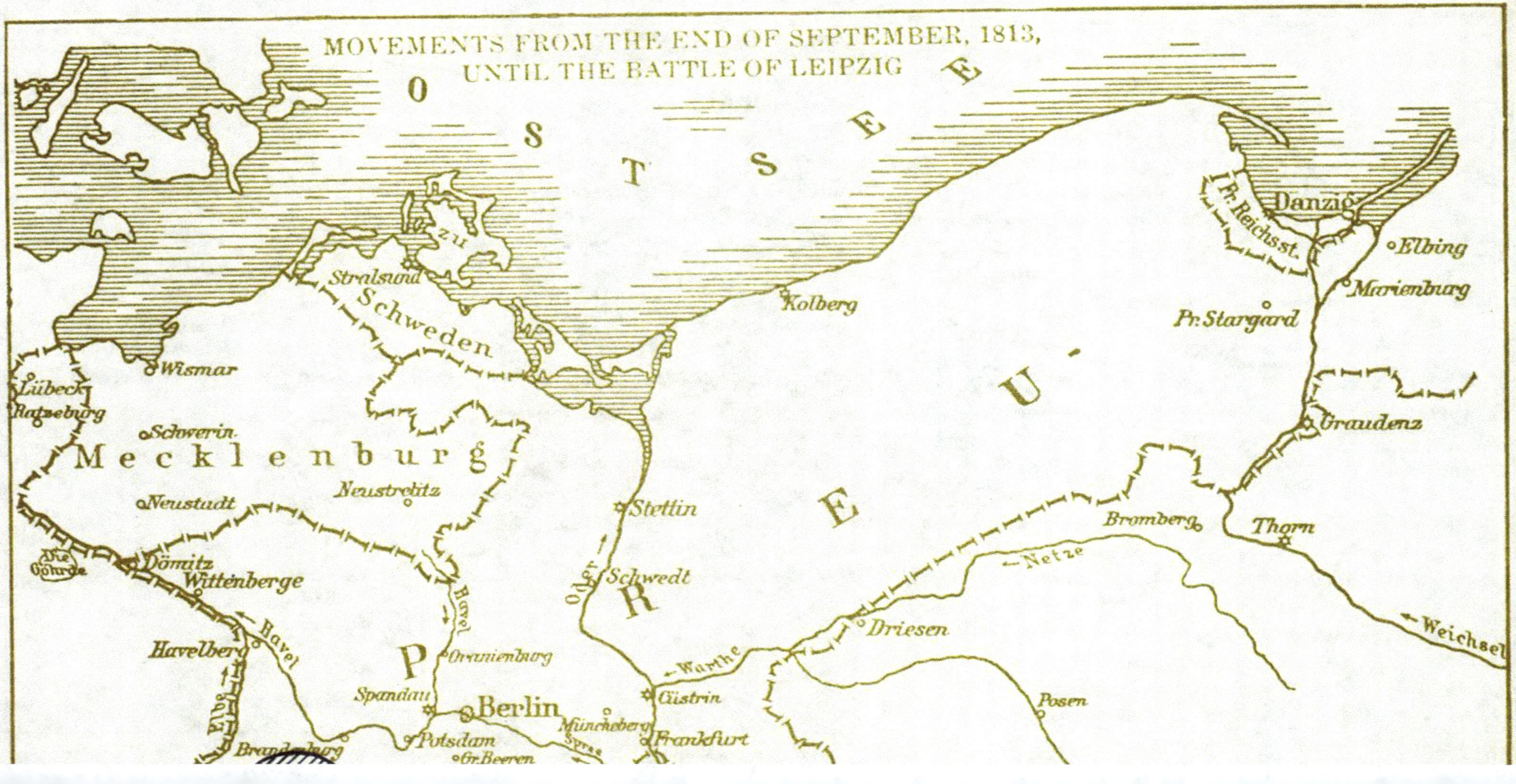
MOVEMENTS FROM THE END OF SEPTEMBER, 1813,
UNTIL THE BATTLE OF LEIPZIG
O S T S E E
Danzig
Elbing
Marienburg
Pr. Reichsst.
Pr. Stargard
Graudenz
Thorn
Bromberg
Netze
Weichsel
Posen
Driesen
Kolberg
Stralsund
Schweden
Wismar
Lübeck
Ratzeburg
Schwerin
Mecklenburg
Neustrelitz
Neustadt
Dömitz
Wittenberge
Die Göhrde
Havelberg
Havel
Elbe
Stettin
Schwedt
Oder
Warthe
Cüstrin
Frankfurt
Müncheberg
Spree
Berlin
Oranienburg
Spandau
Potsdam
Gr. Beeren
P R E U

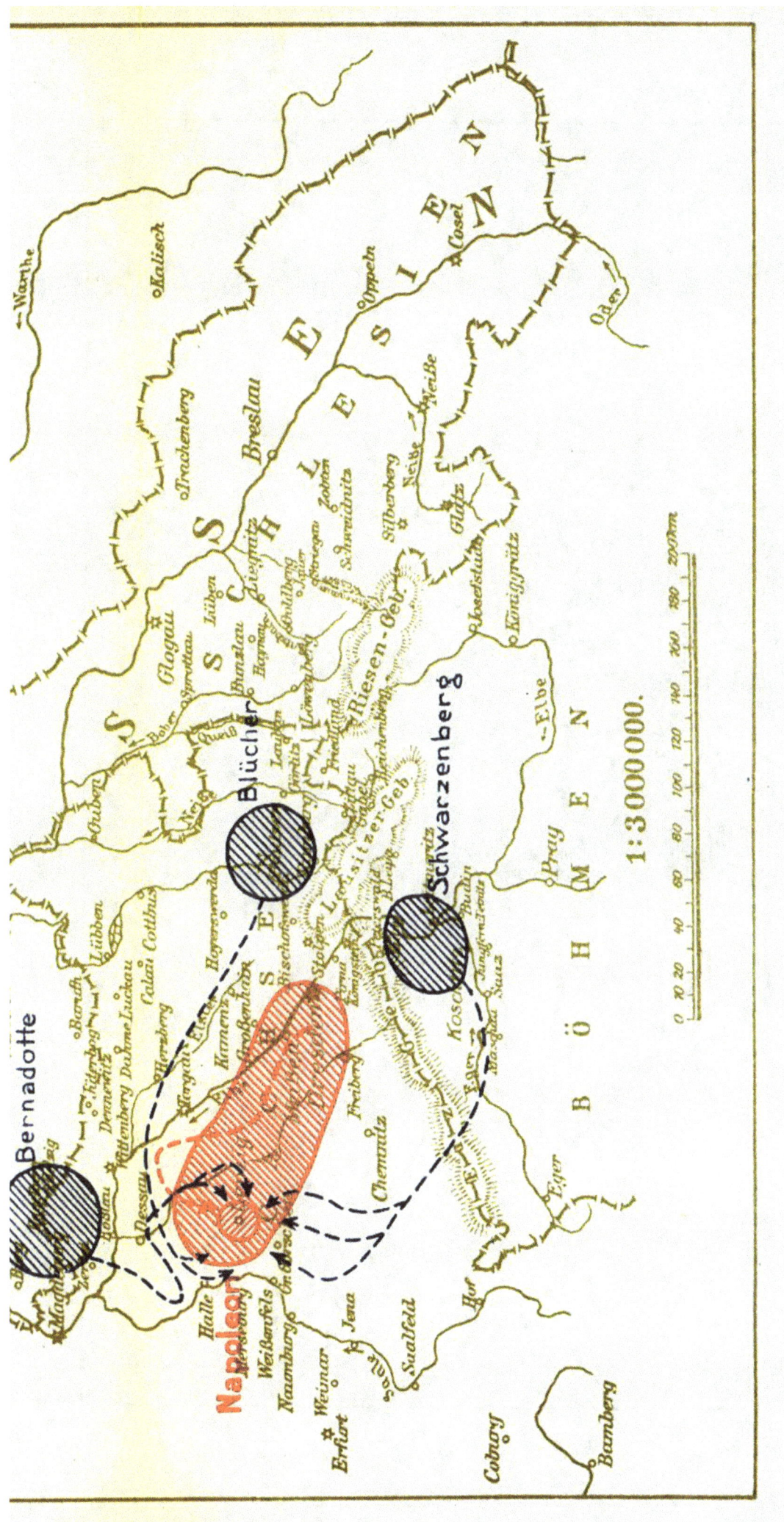

Map 29.

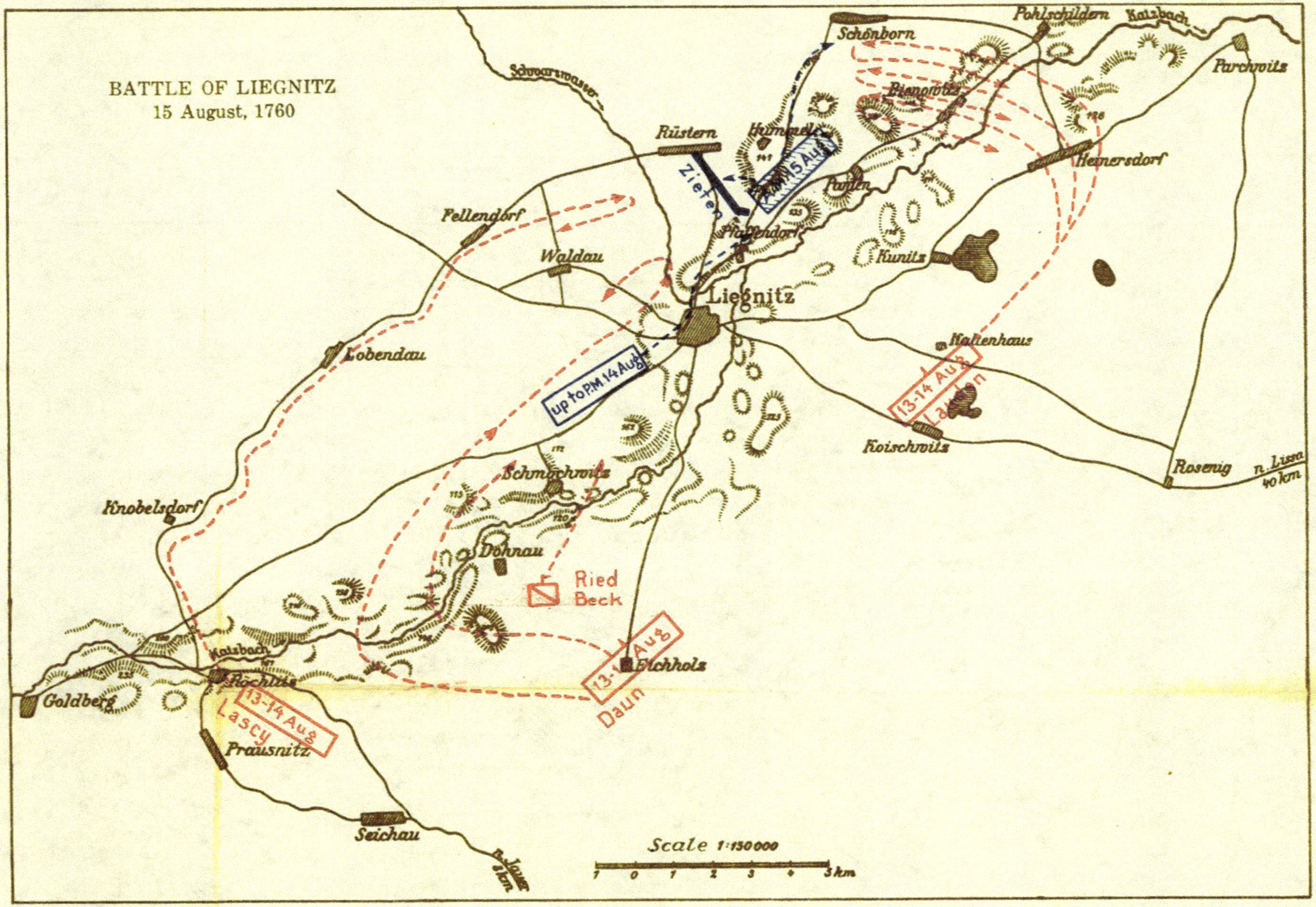

BATTLE OF LIEGNITZ
15 August, 1760

Scale 1:150000

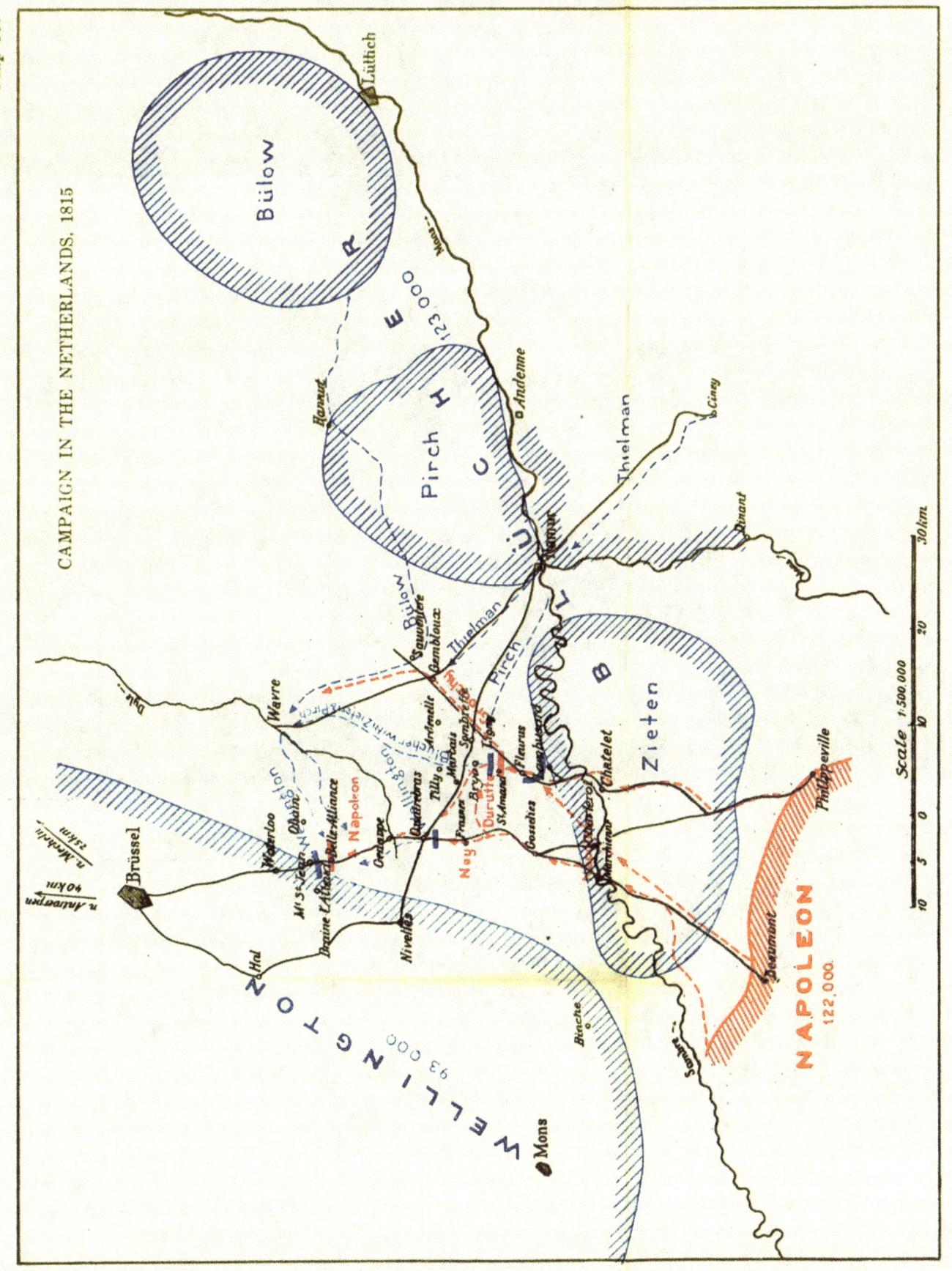

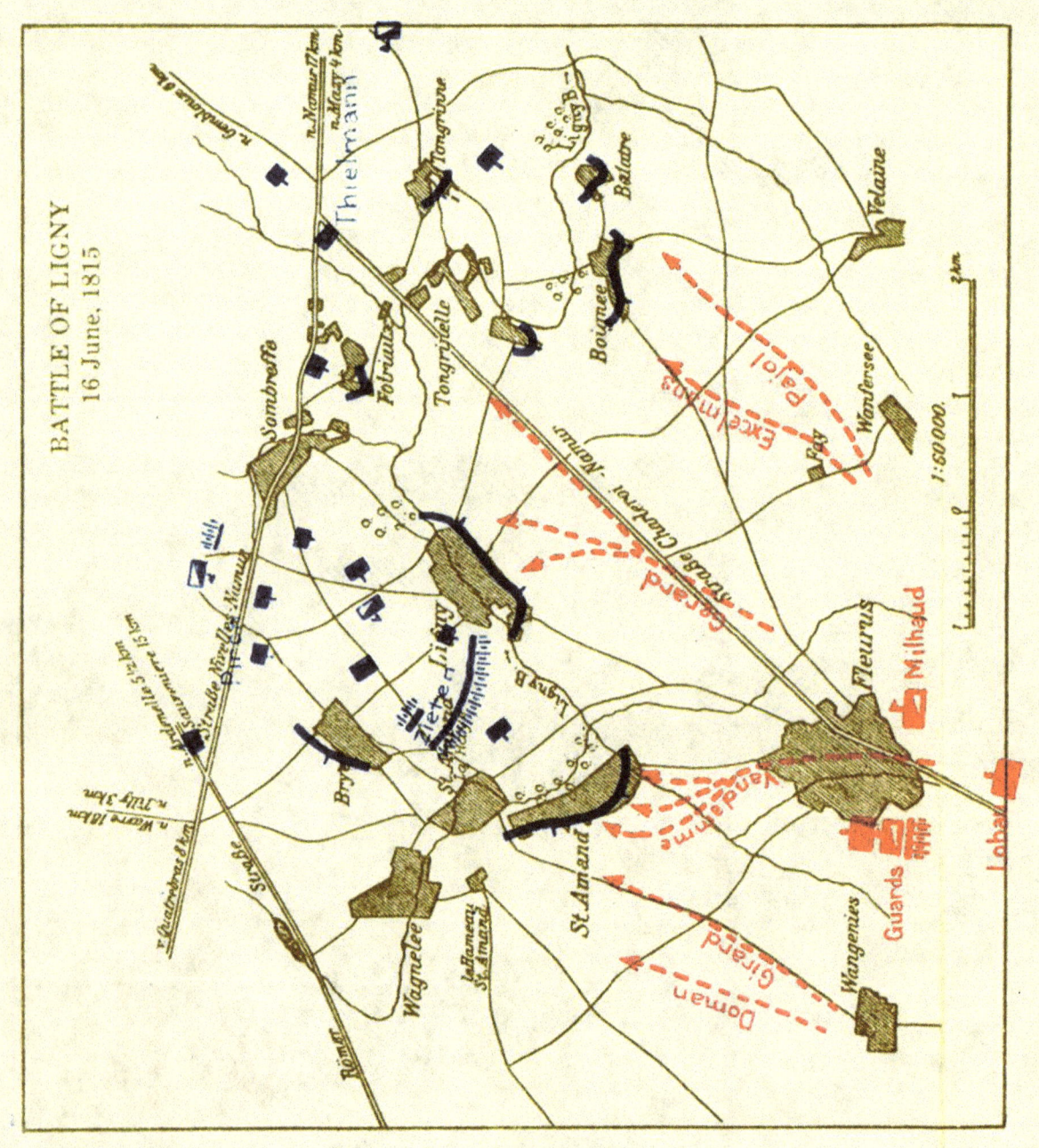

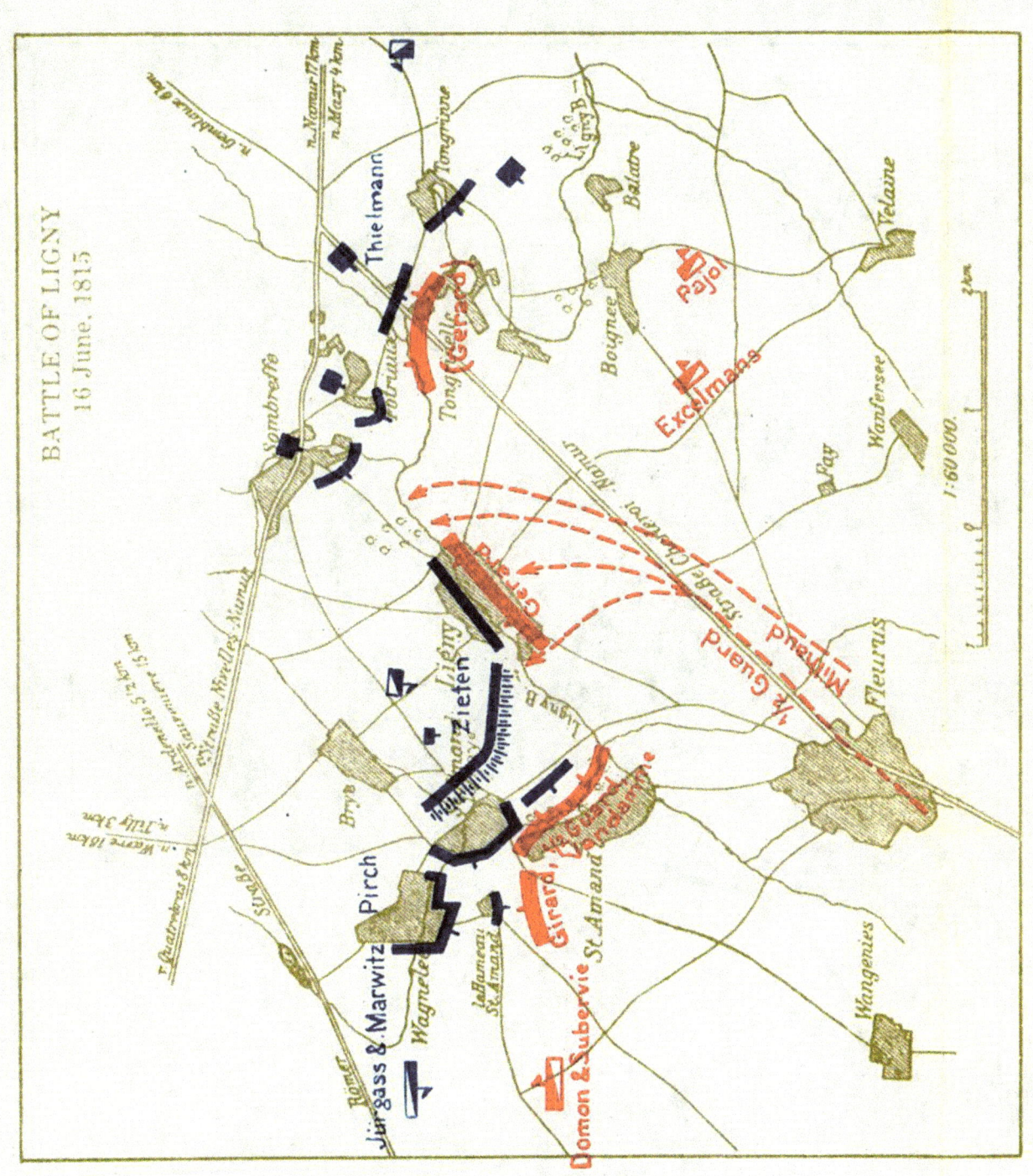

Map 32. BATTLE OF LIGNY, 16 June, 1815

Map 33.

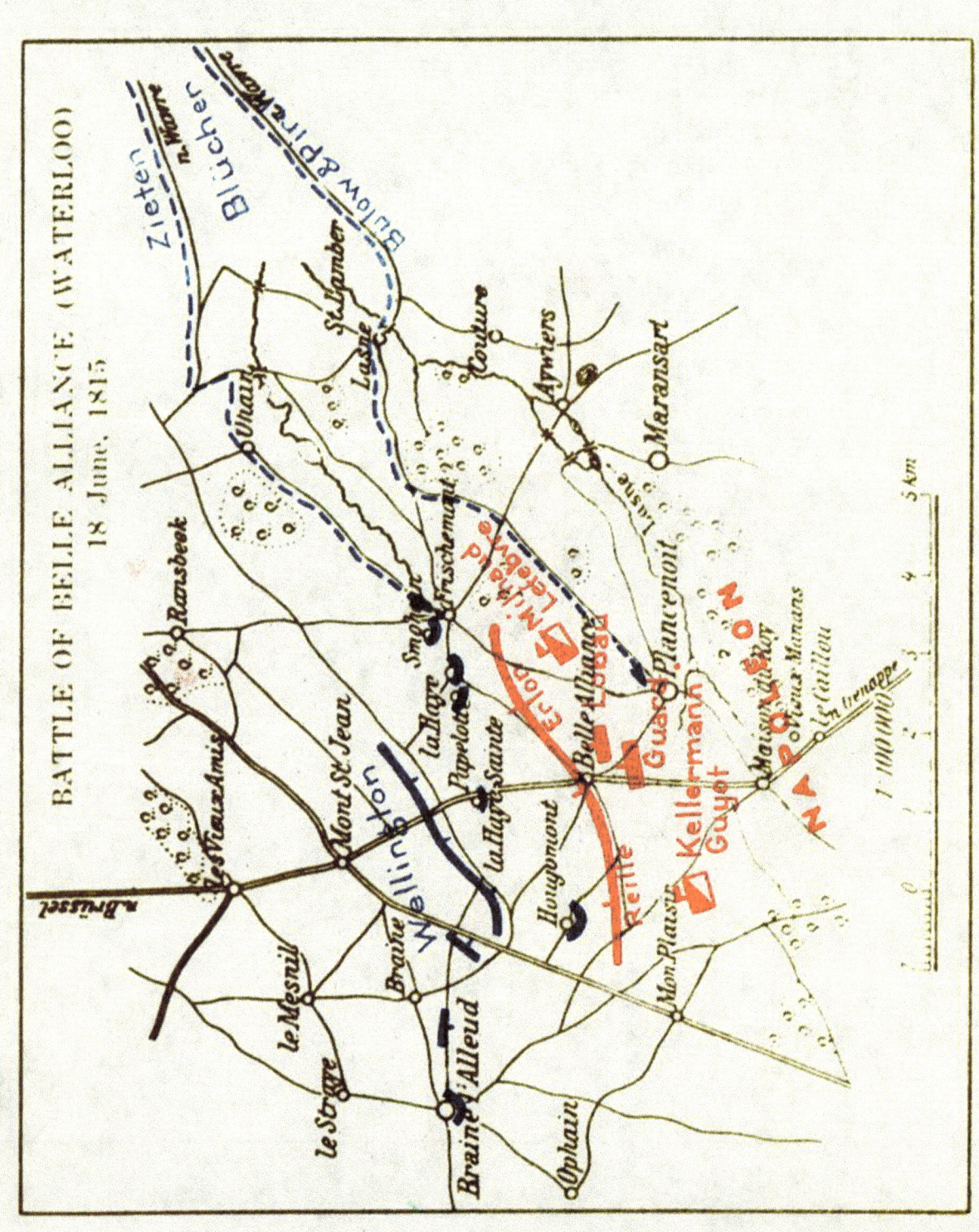

AUSTRO-PRUSSIAN WAR, 1866

Map 34.

Map 35.

SITUATION ON 20 JUNE, 1866, AND MOLTKE'S PLAN

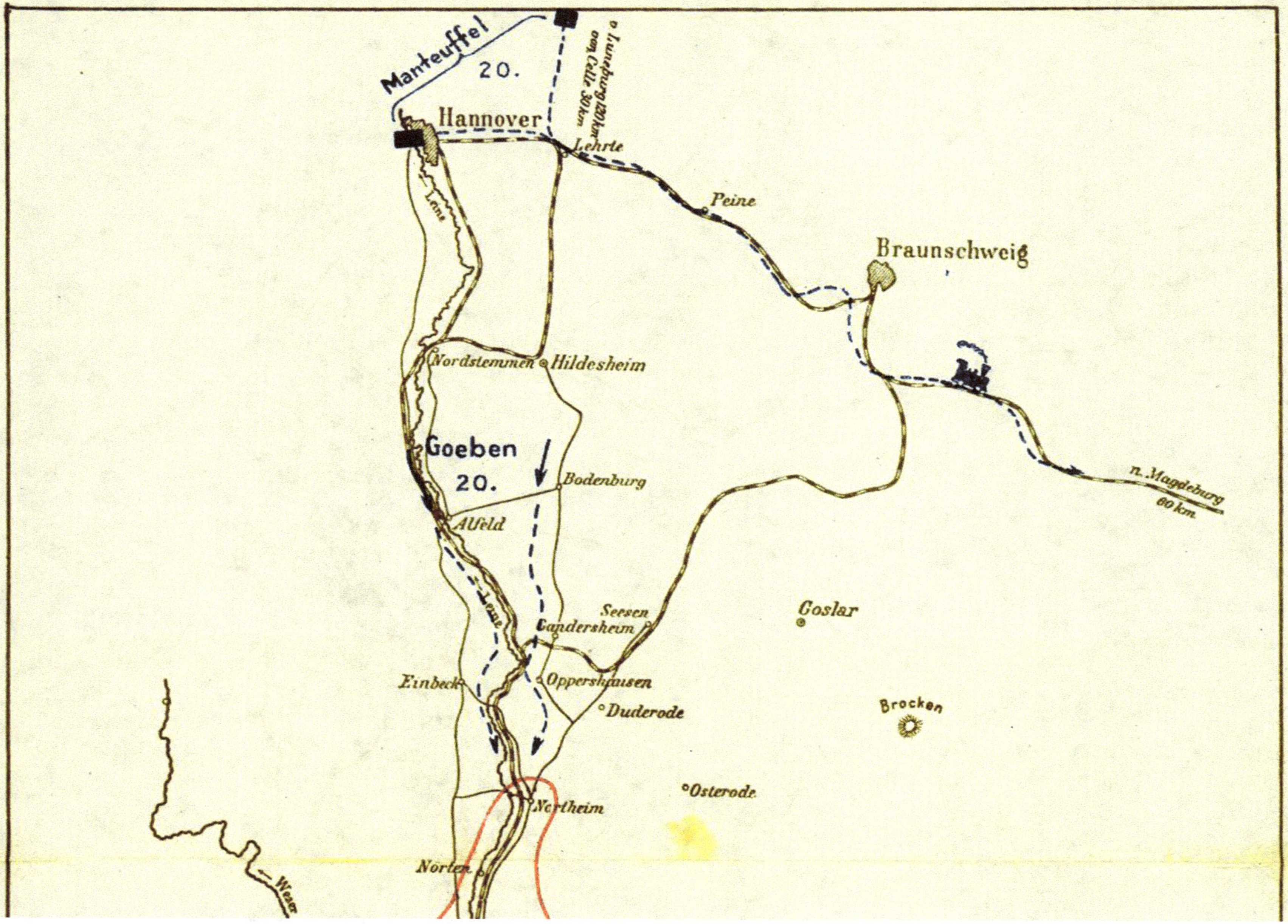

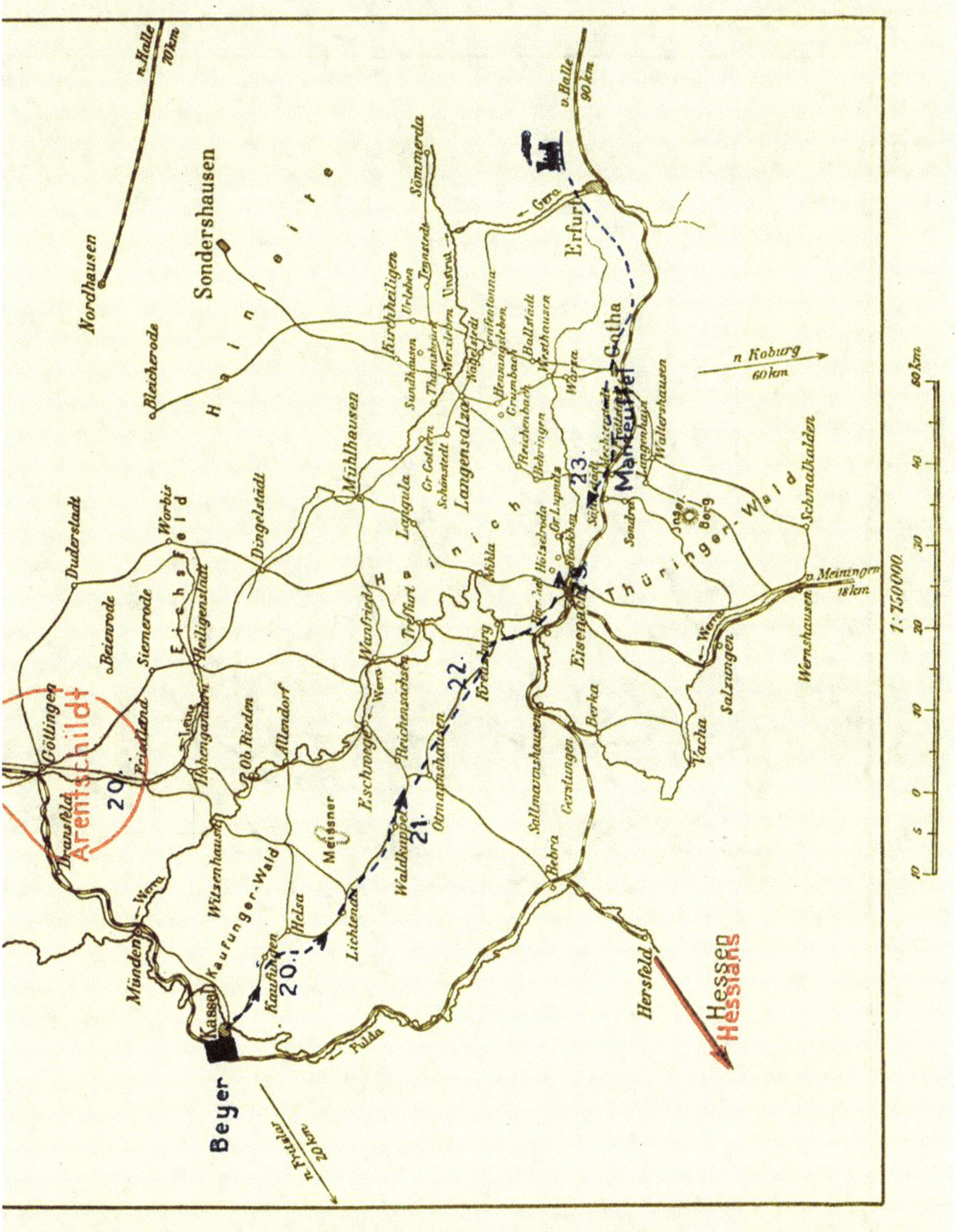

Map 36.

SITUATION ON 21 JUNE, 1866

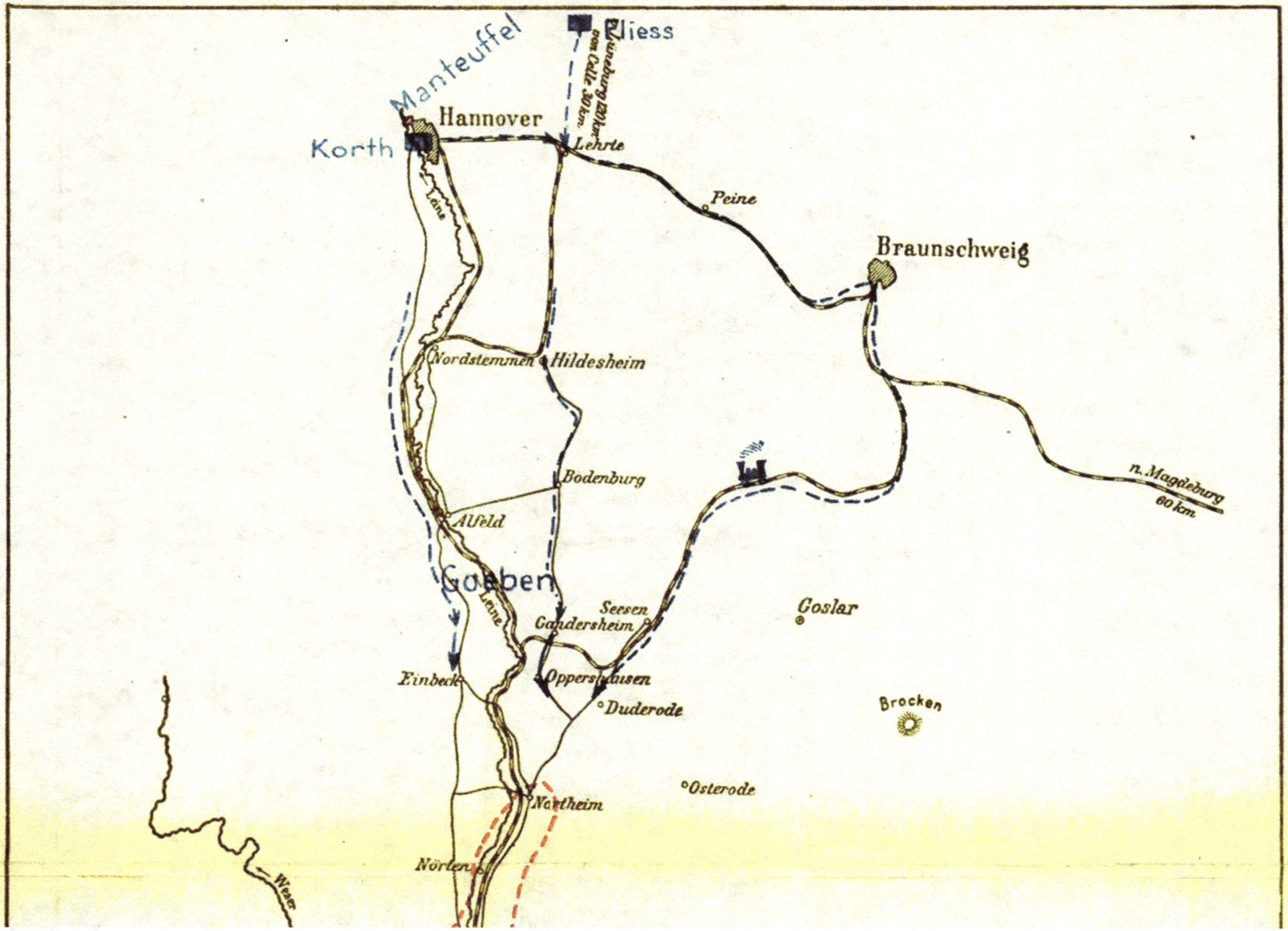

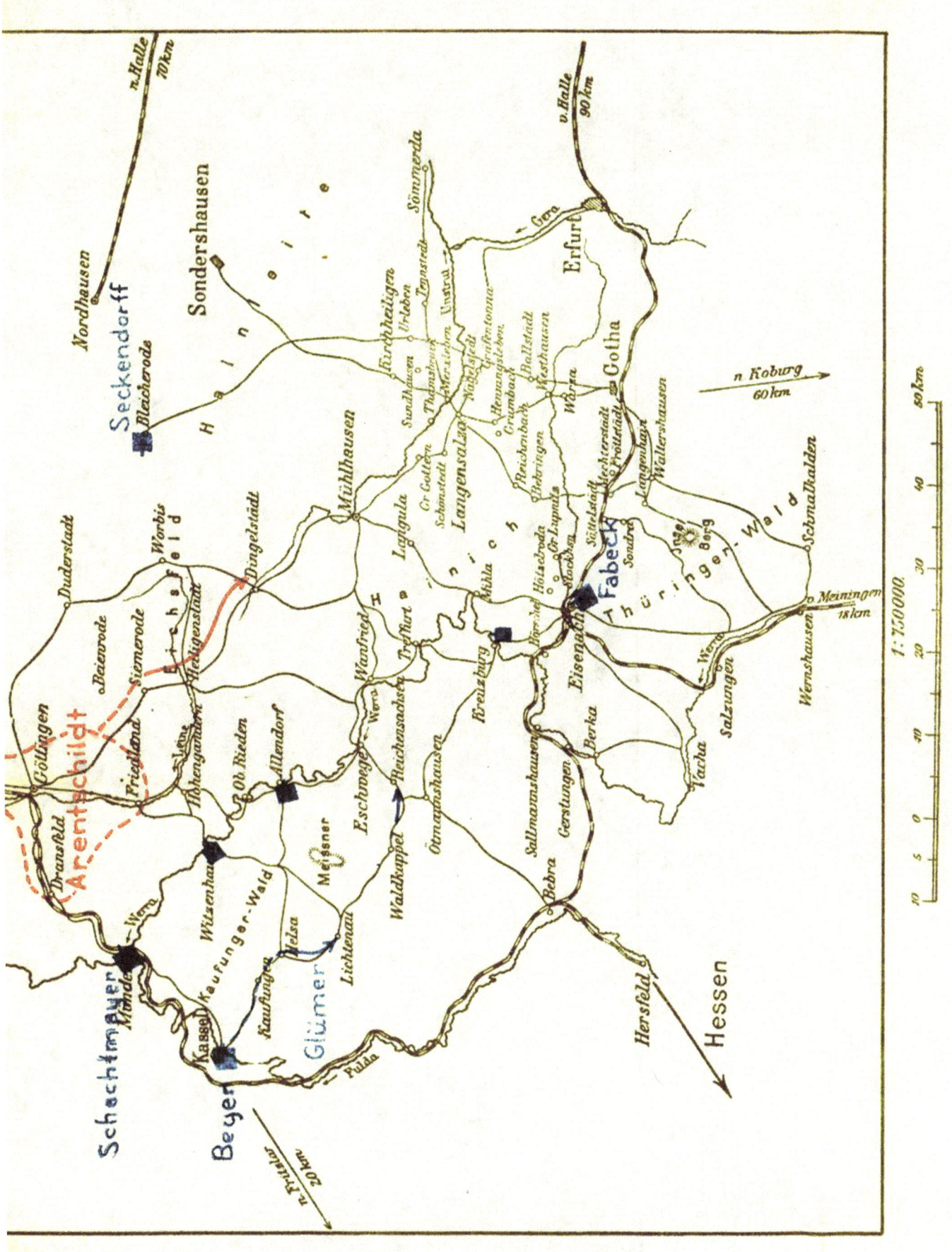

Map 37.

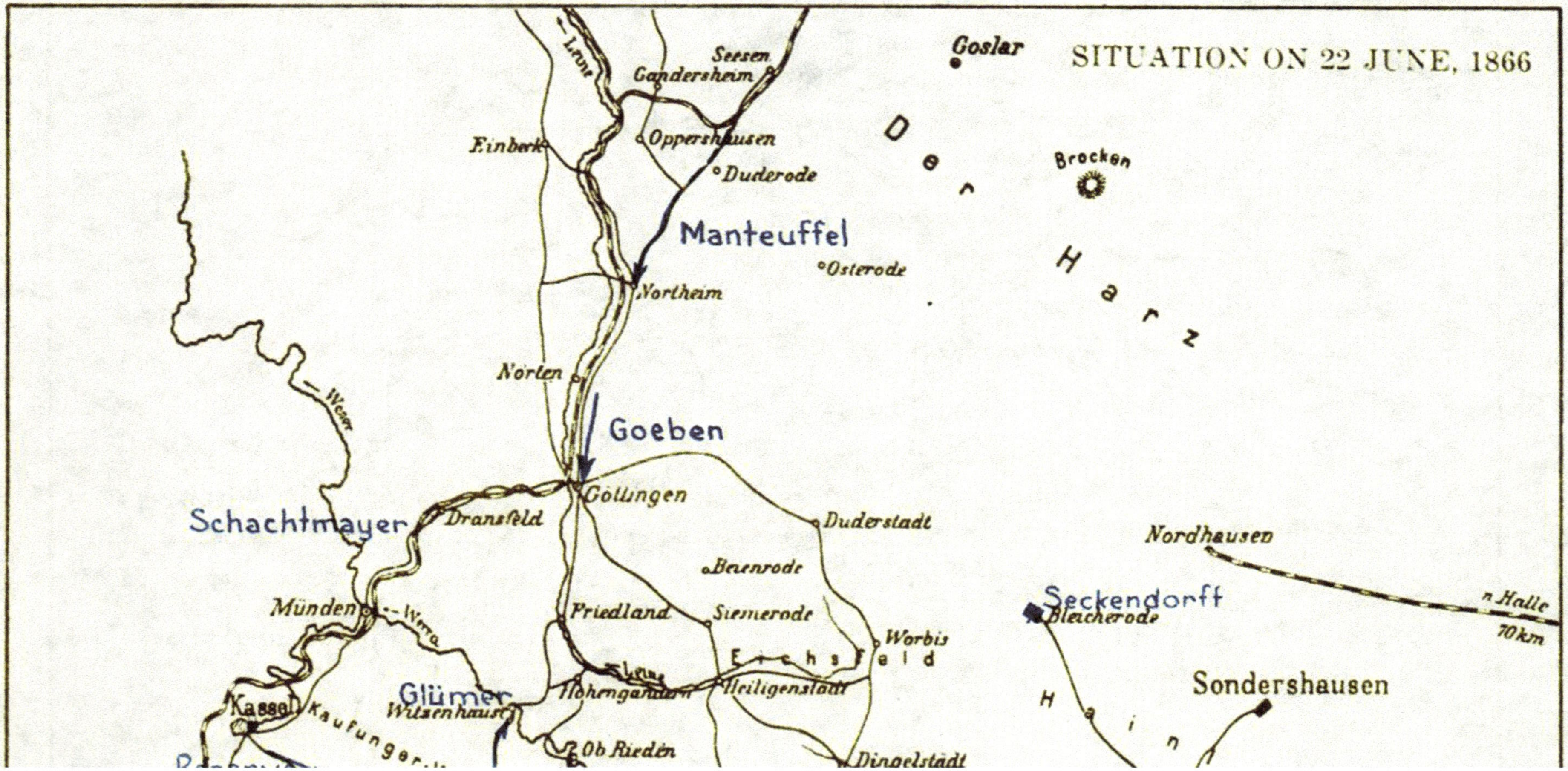
SITUATION ON 22 JUNE, 1866
Goslar
Brocken
Der Harz
Seesen
Gandersheim
Oppershausen
Einbeck
Duderode
Manteuffel
Osterode
Northeim
Leine
Nörten
Goeben
Weser
Göttingen
Schachtmayer
Dransfeld
Duderstadt
Nordhausen
Münden
Werra
Friedland
Siemerode
Worbis
Eichsfeld
Seckendorff
Bleicherode
n Halle
70 km
Glümer
Kassel
Witzenhausen
Hohengandern
Heiligenstadt
Sondershausen
Hain
Ob Rieden
Dingelstädt

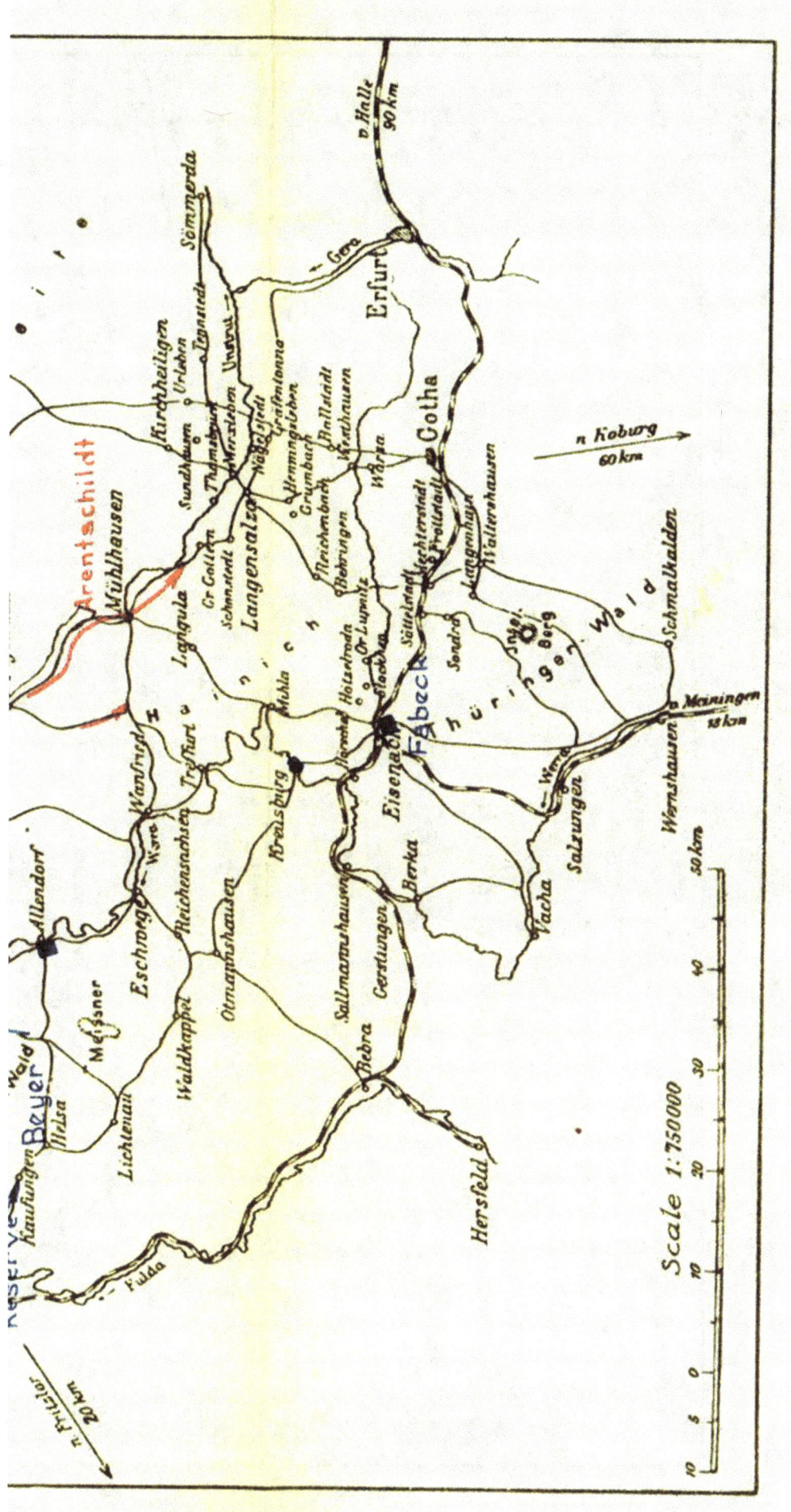

Map 38.

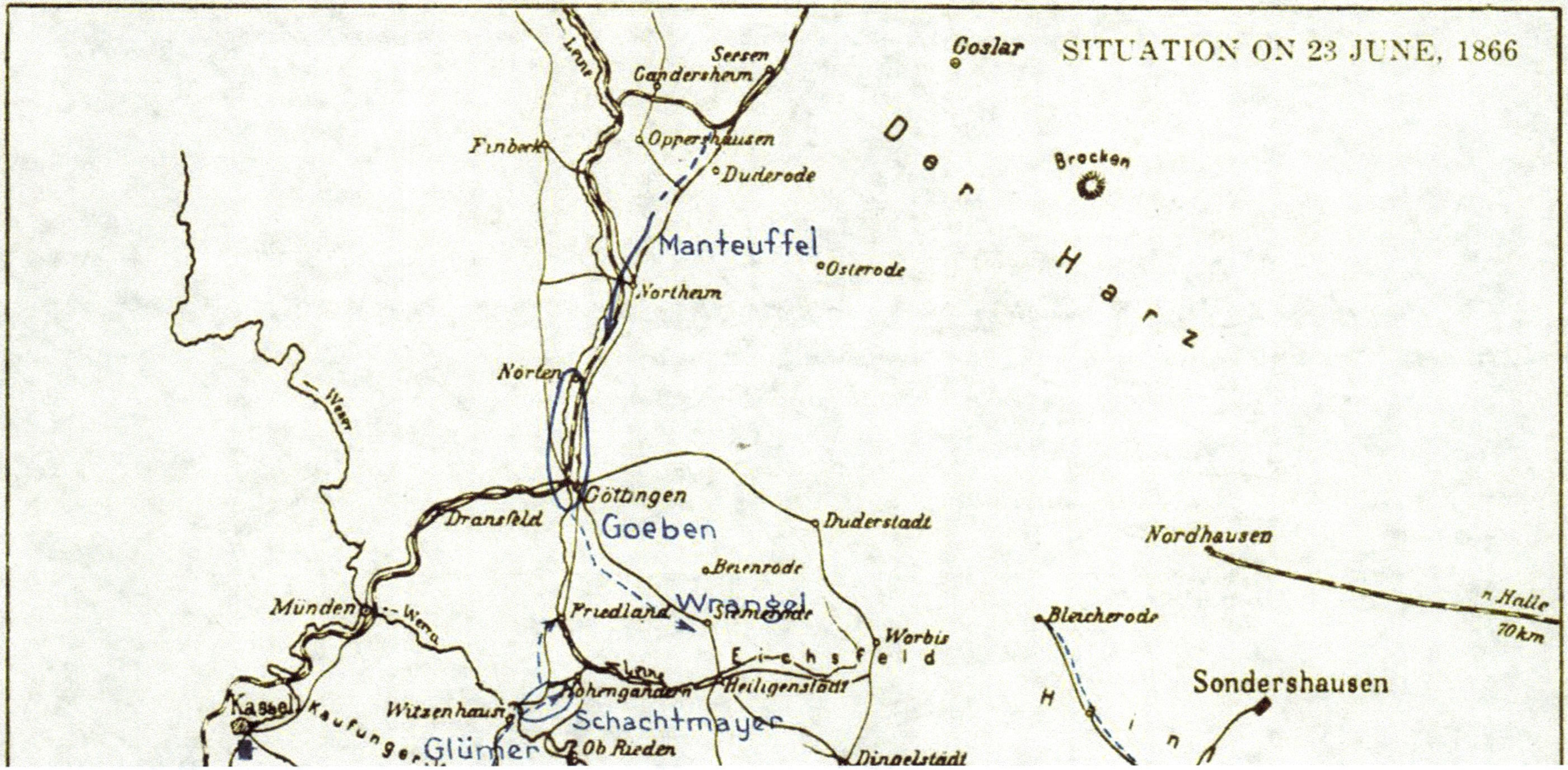
SITUATION ON 23 JUNE, 1866
Goslar
Seesen
Gandersheim
Leine
Finbeck
Oppershausen
Duderode
Der Harz
Brocken
Manteuffel
Osterode
Northeim
Nörten
Weser
Göttingen
Goeben
Dransfeld
Duderstadt
Nordhausen
n. Halle
70 km
Beienrode
Münden
Werra
Friedland
Wrangel
Siemerode
Worbis
Bleicherode
Eichsfeld
Hohengandern
Heiligenstadt
Sondershausen
Kassel
Witzenhausen
Schachtmayer
Kaufungen
Glümer
Ob Rieden
Dingelstädt

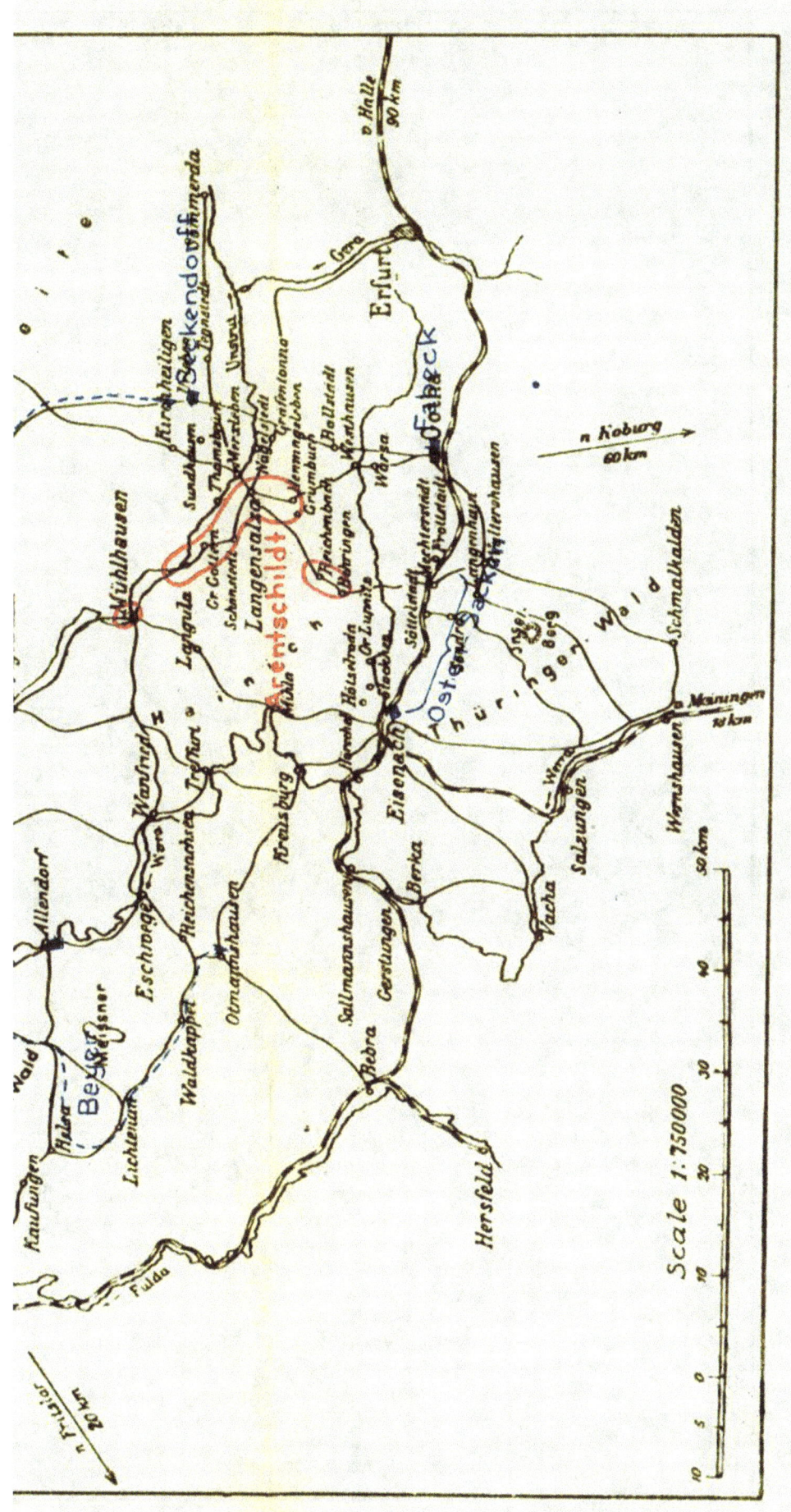

Map 39.

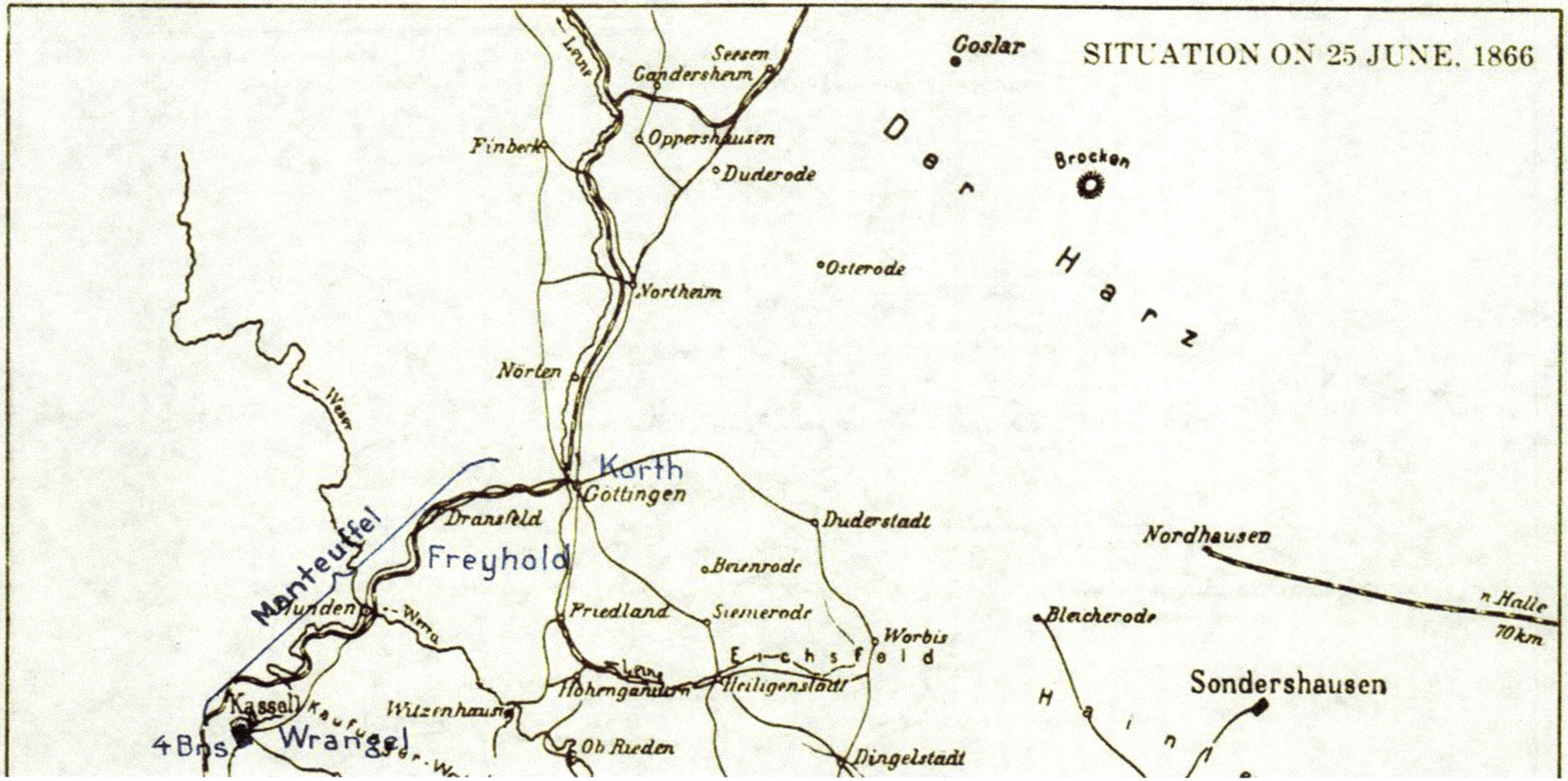
SITUATION ON 25 JUNE. 1866
Goslar
Seesen
Gandersheim
Oppershausen
Duderode
Finbeck
Der Harz
Brocken
Osterode
Northeim
Nörten
Weser
Leine
Korth
Göttingen
Dransfeld
Freyhold
Manteuffel
Münden
Werra
Duderstadt
Nordhausen
n Halle
70 km
Bleicherode
Friedland
Siemerode
Worbis
Eichsfeld
Heiligenstadt
Hohengandern
Witzenhausen
Kassel
4 Bns.
Wrangel
Kaufungen
Ob Rieden
Dingelstädt
Sondershausen

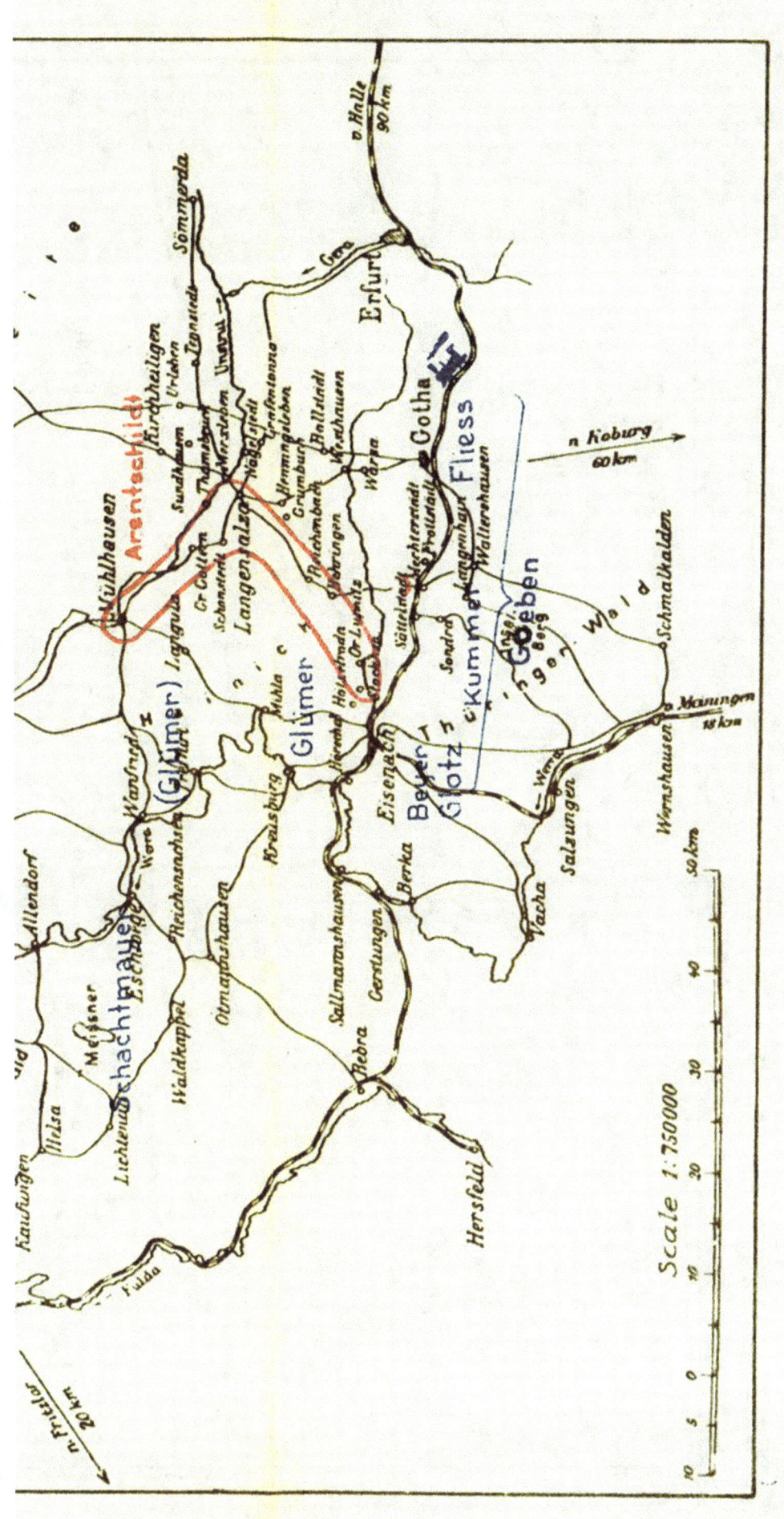

Map 40.

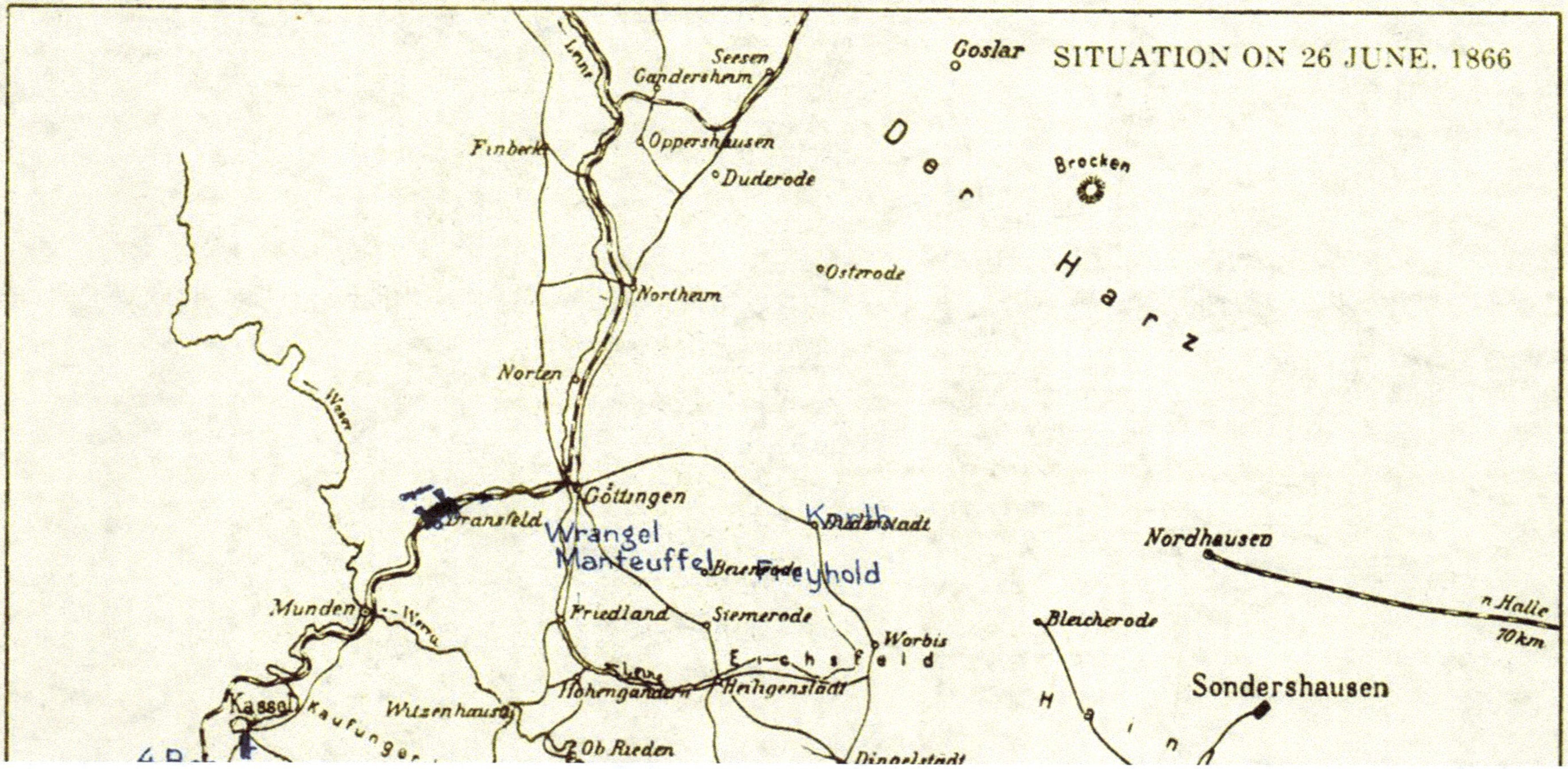

SITUATION ON 26 JUNE. 1866
Goslar
Brocken
Der Harz
Seesen
Gandersheim
Oppershausen
Duderode
Finbeck
Ostrode
Northeim
Norten
Weser
Göttingen
Dransfeld
Wrangel
Manteuffel
Freyhold
Nordhausen
n Halle
70km
Munden
Werra
Friedland
Siemerode
Worbis
Eichsfeld
Bleicherode
Kassel
Witzenhausen
Hohengandern
Heiligenstadt
Sondershausen
Ob Rieden

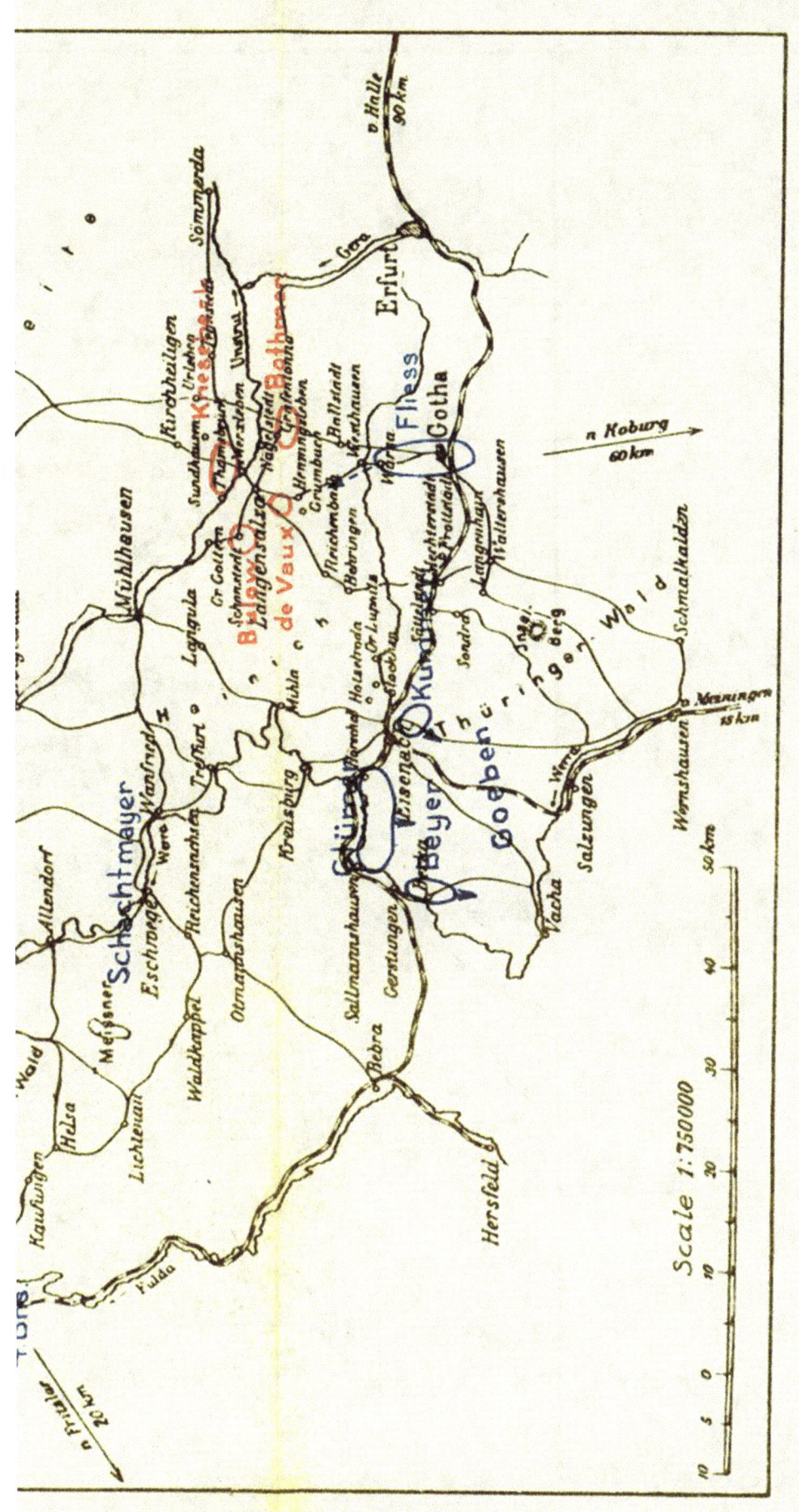

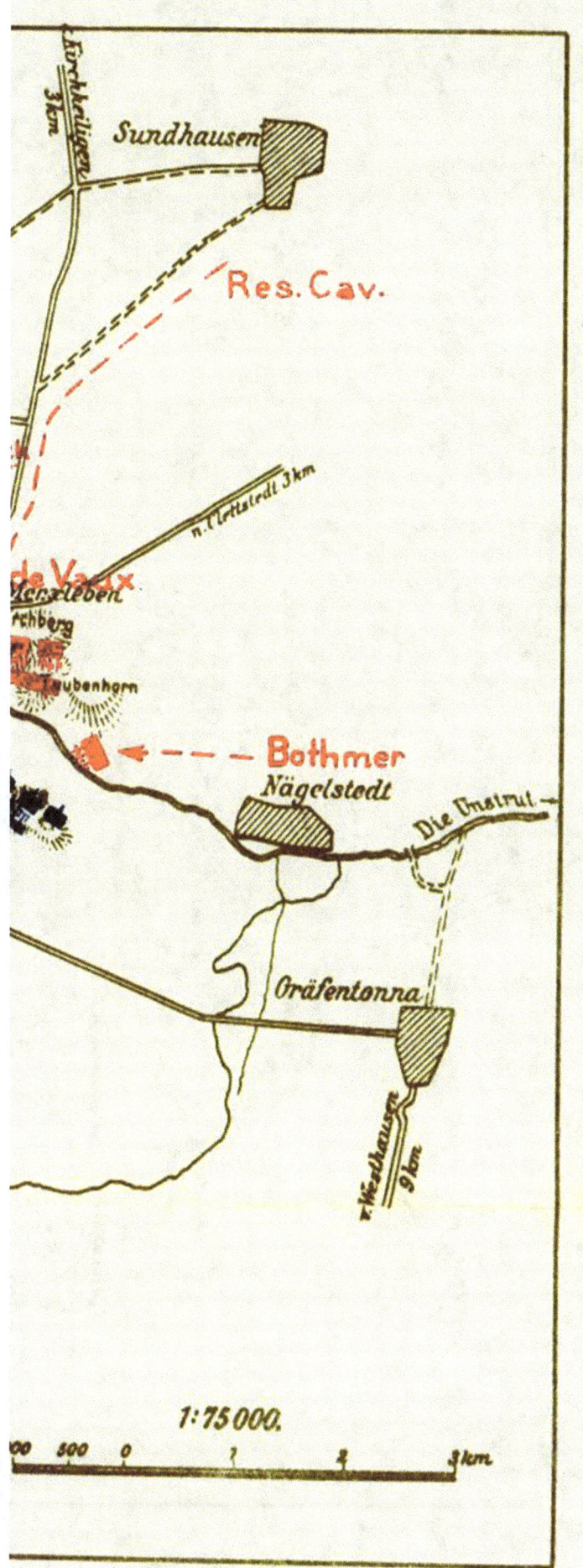

Map 41.

Map 42.

SITUATION ON THE EVENING OF 27 JUNE, 1866

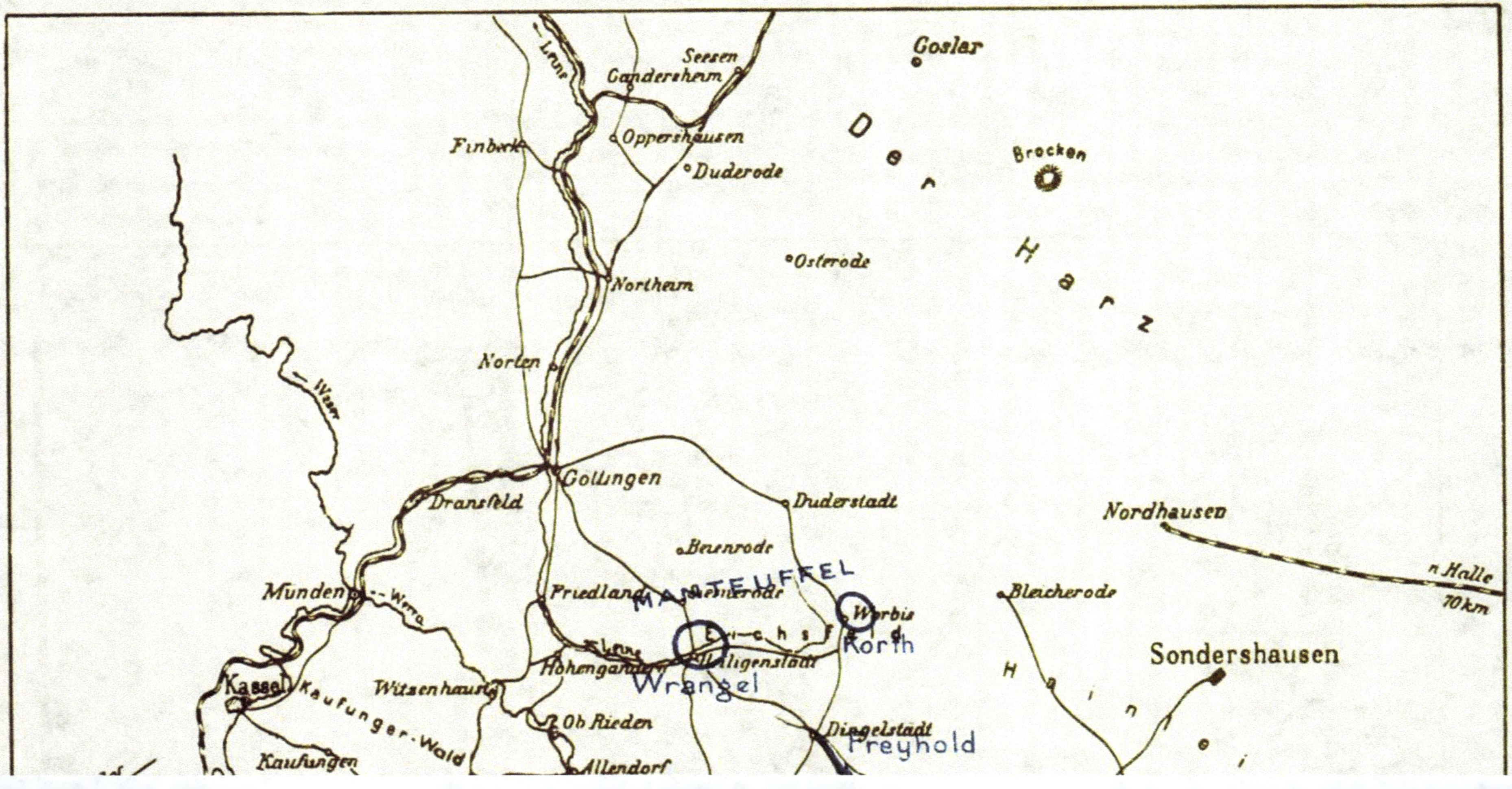

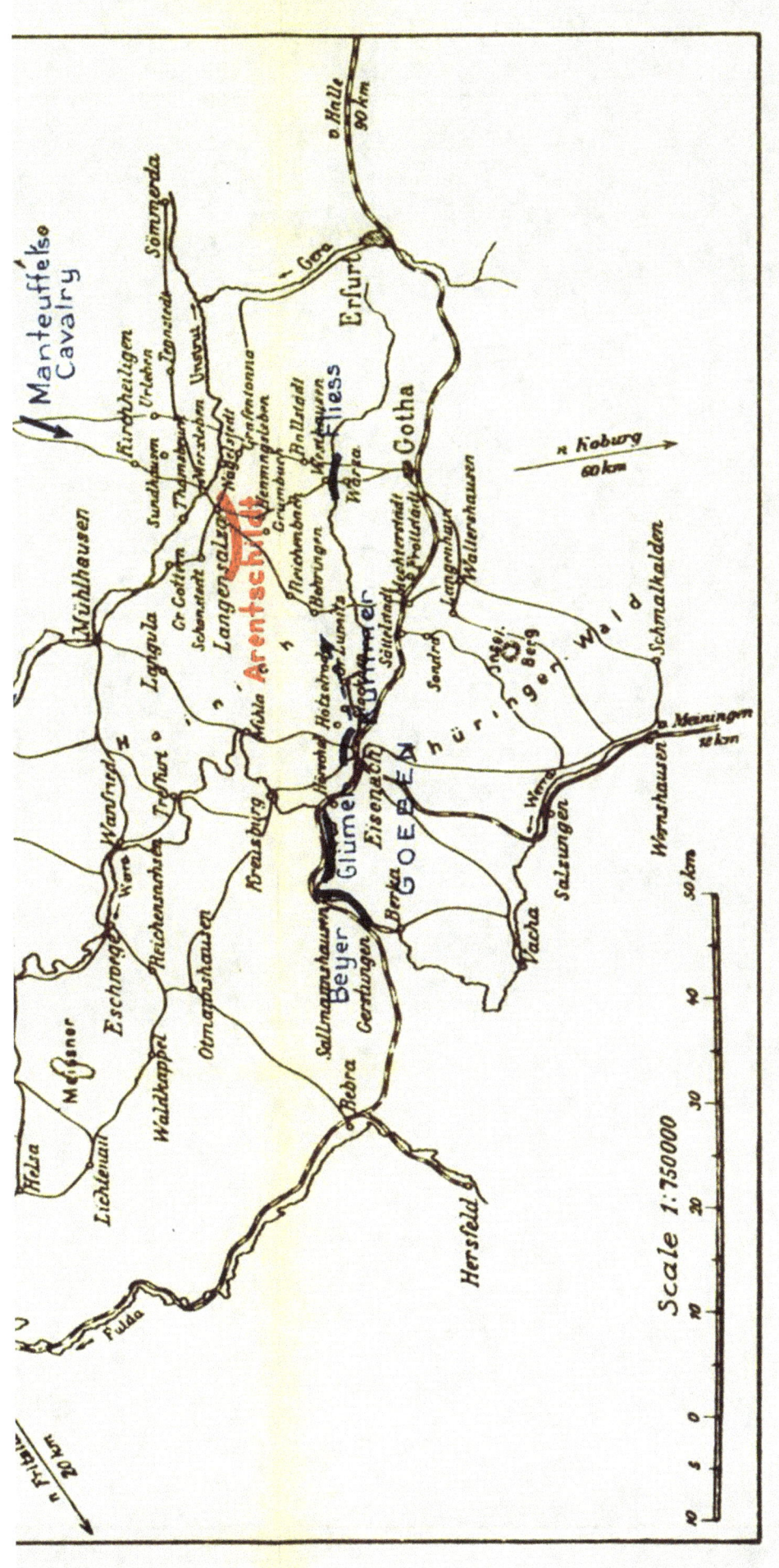

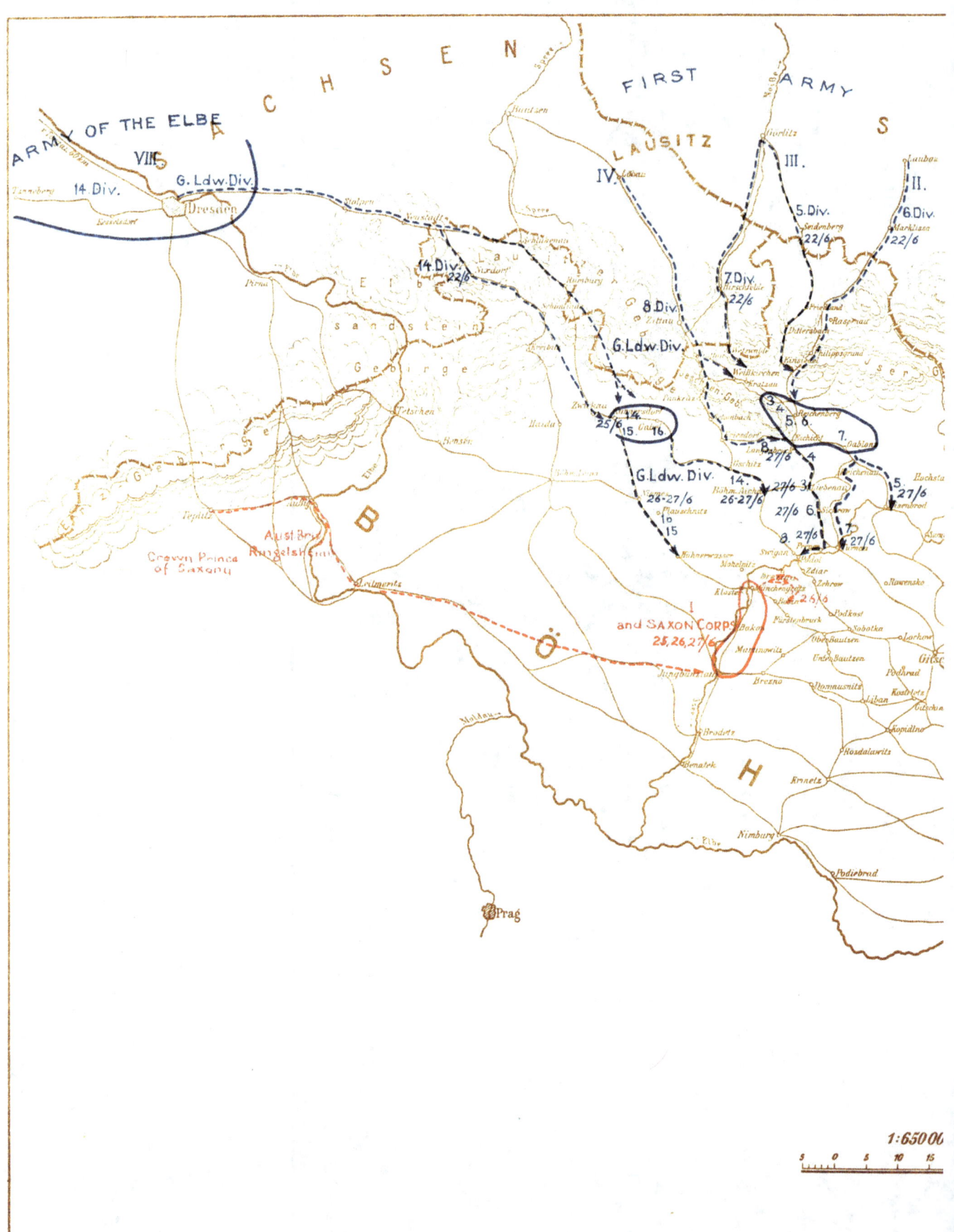

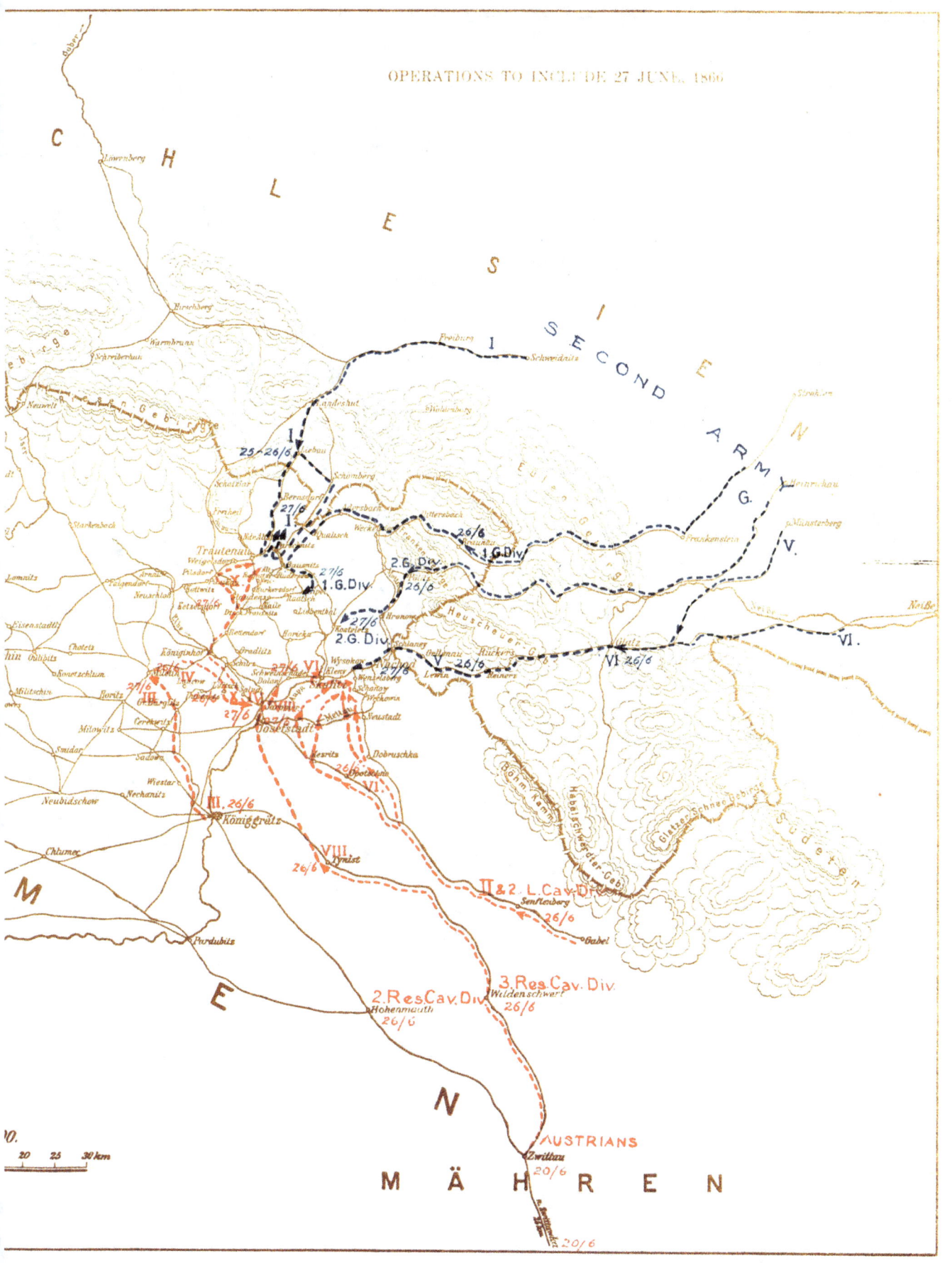

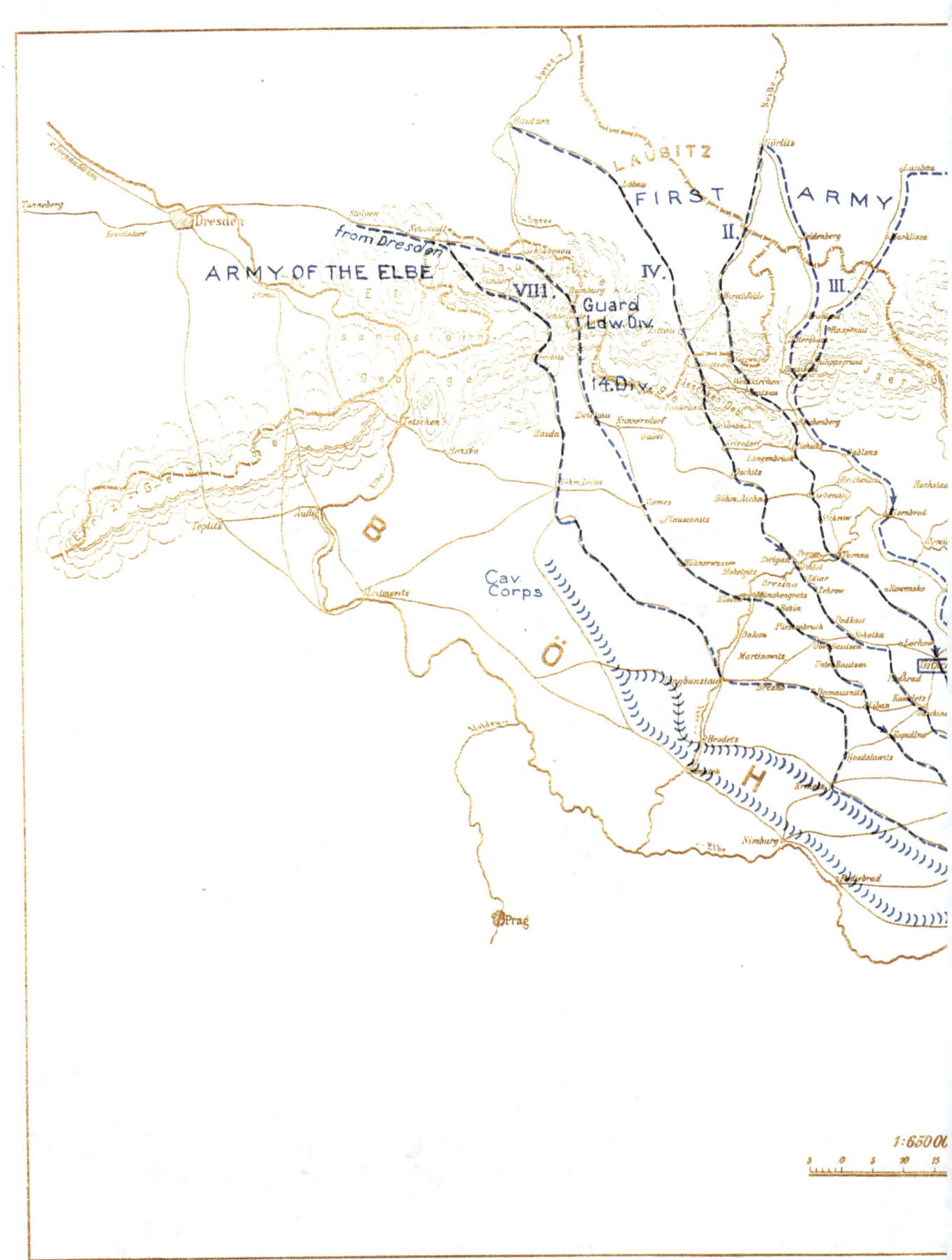

Map 44.

SCHEME FOR THE PRUSSIAN ADVANCE BASED ON
MOLTKE'S PLAN OF CAMPAIGN

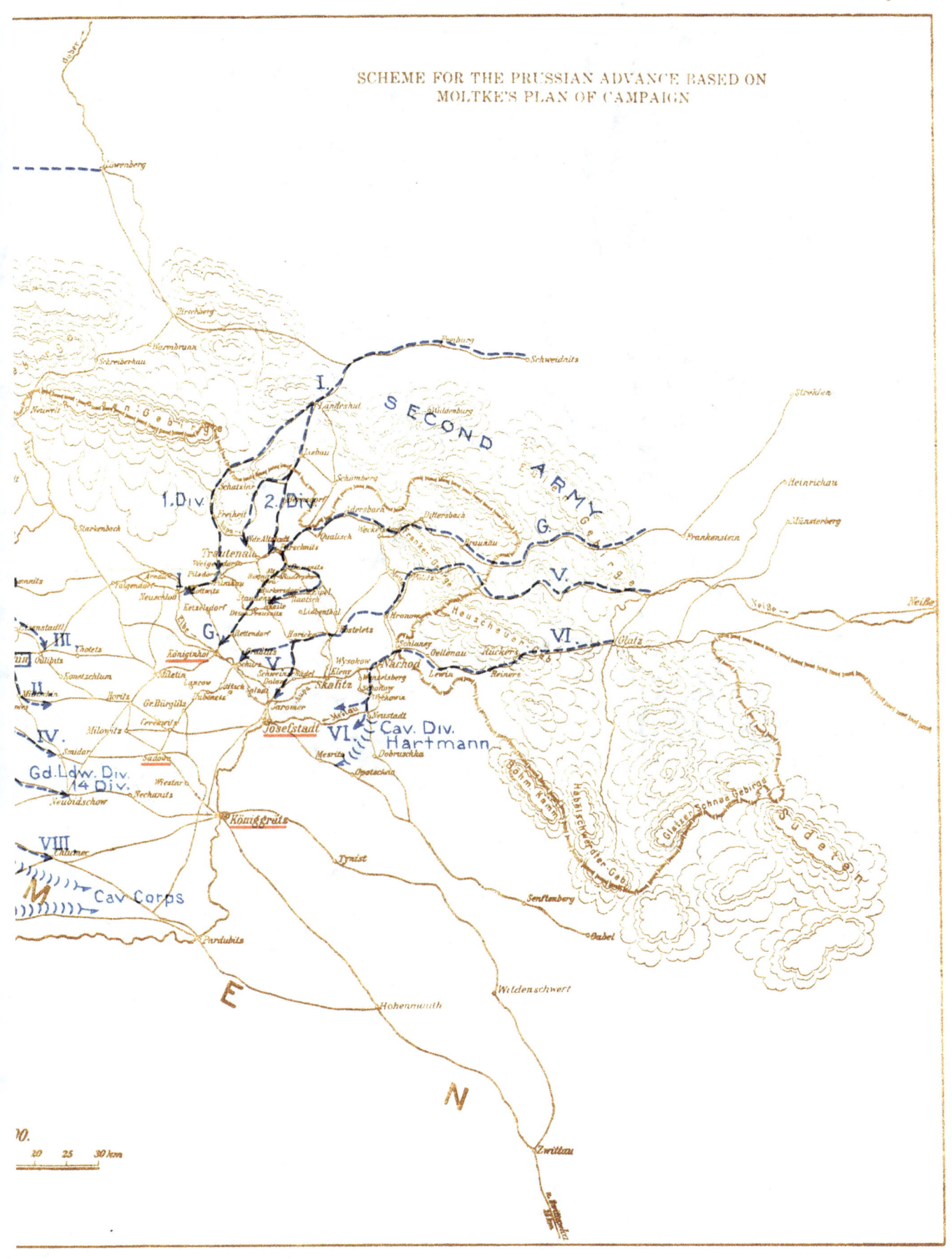

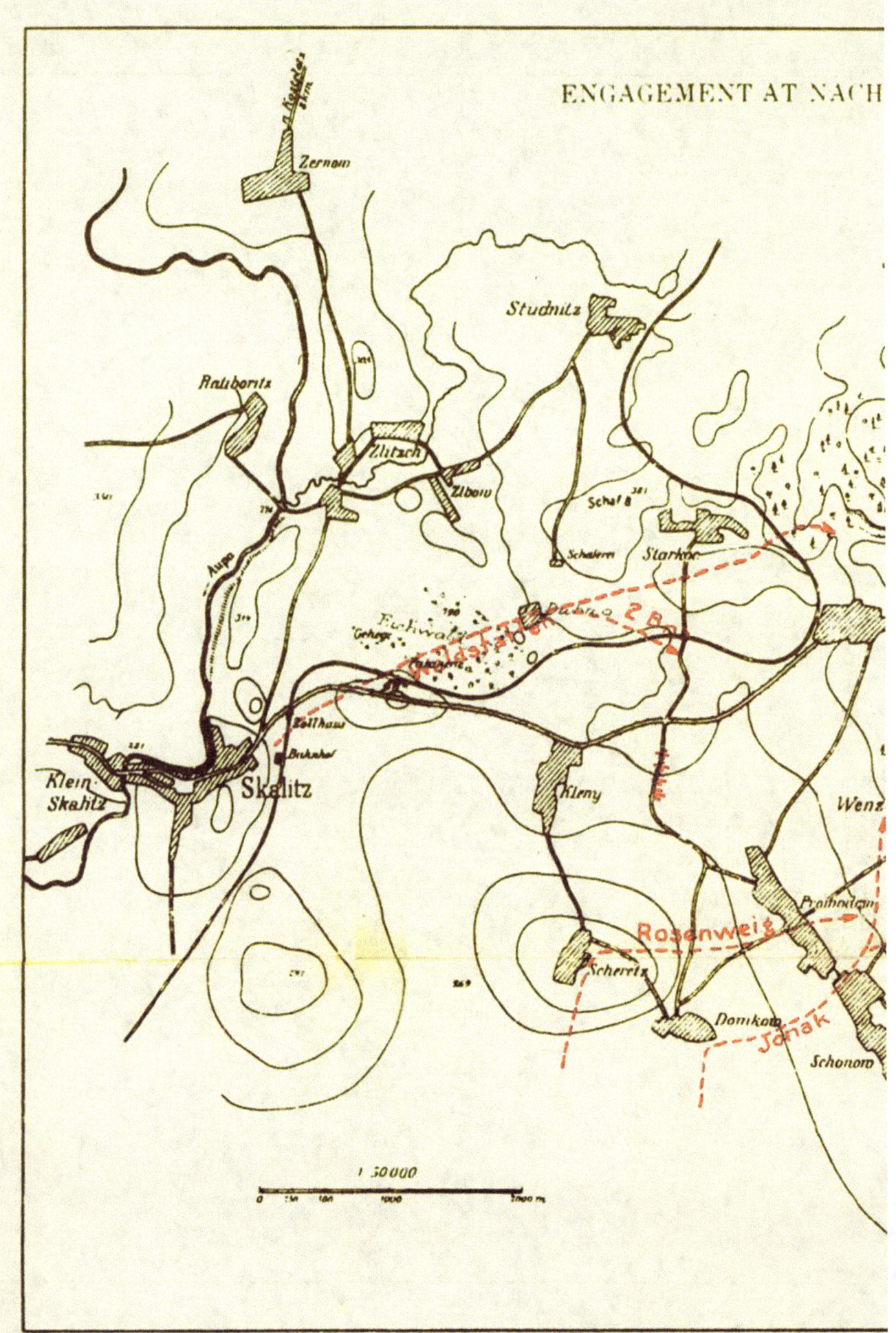

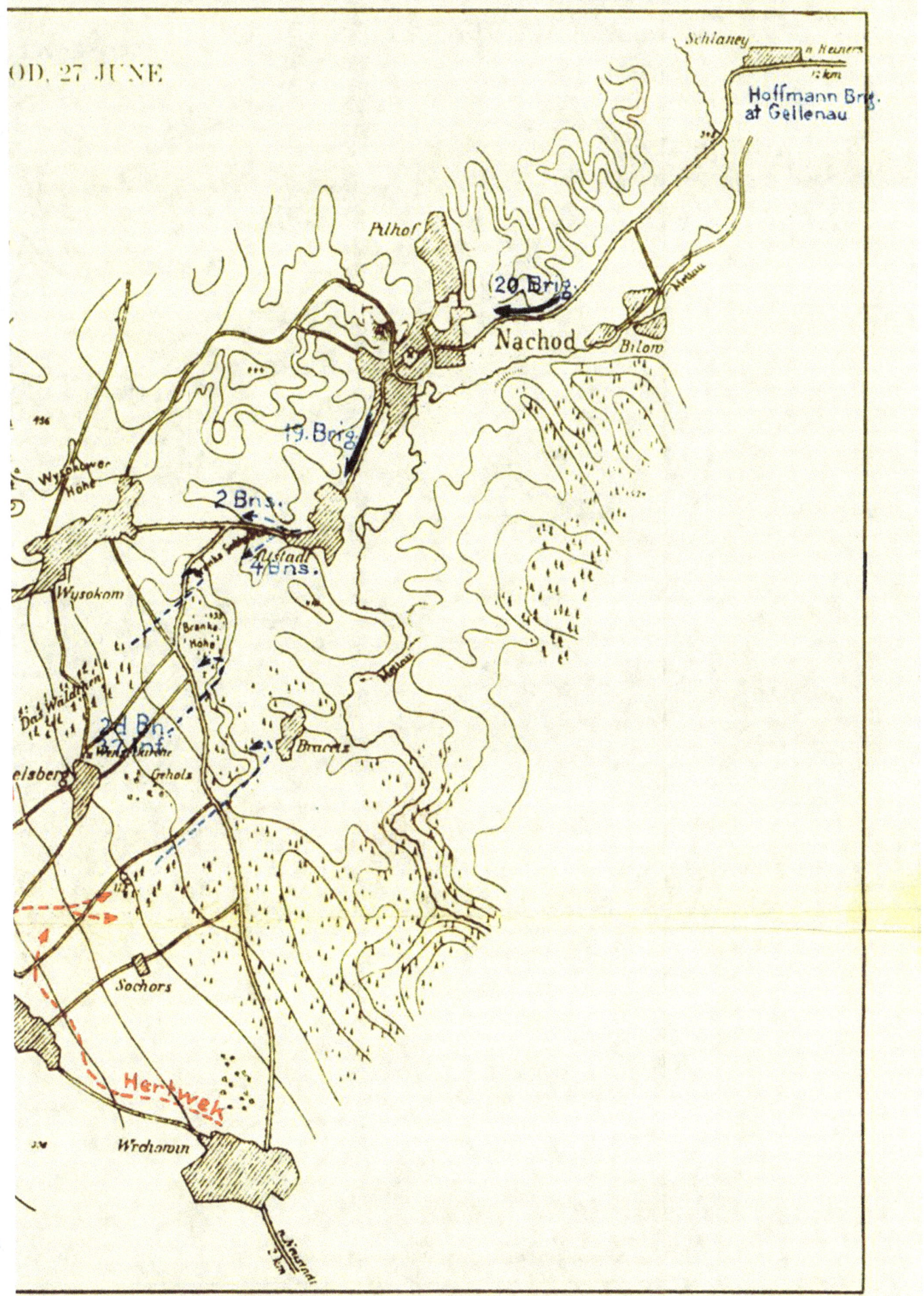

Map 45.

...OD, 27 JUNE

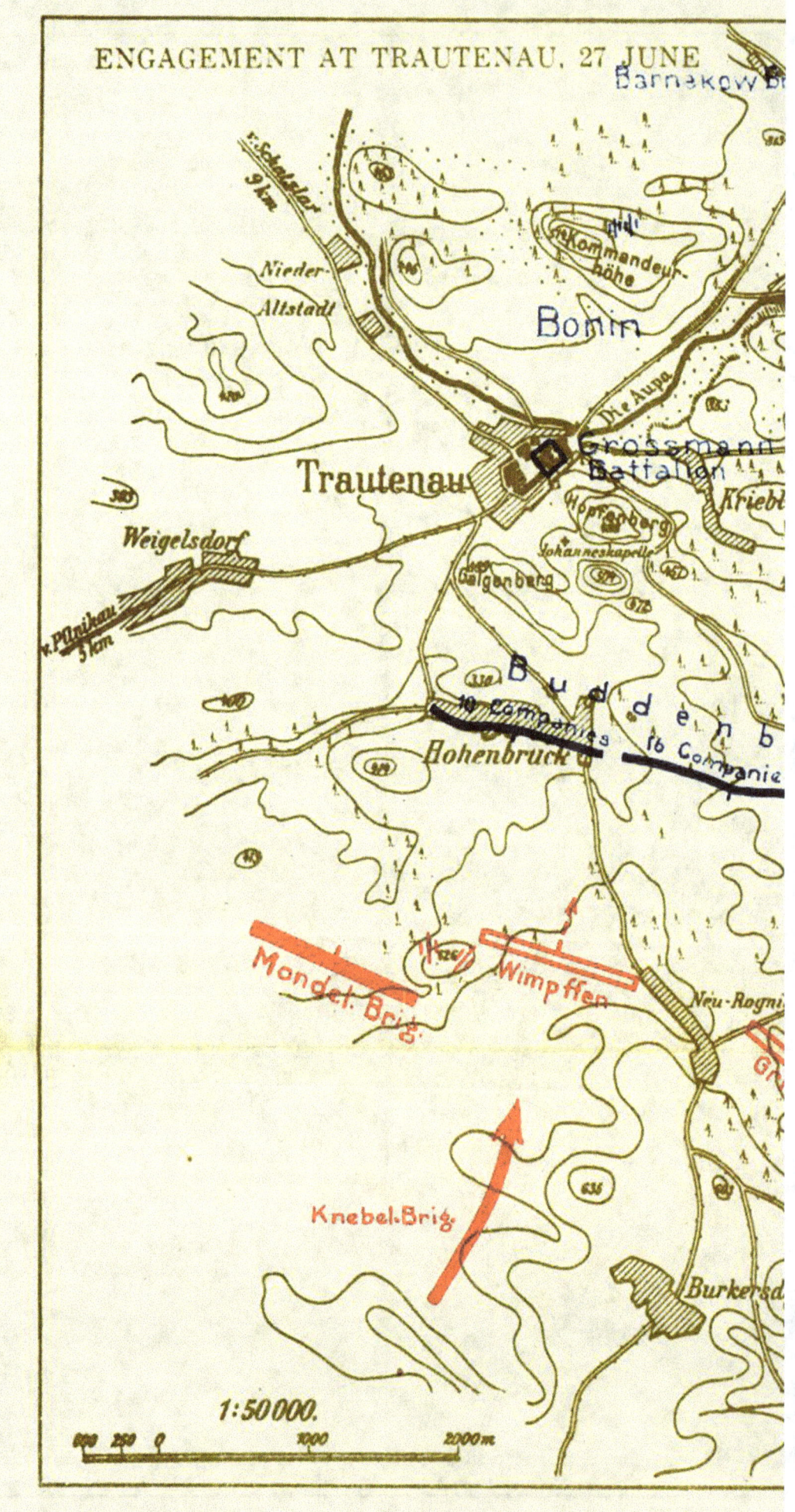

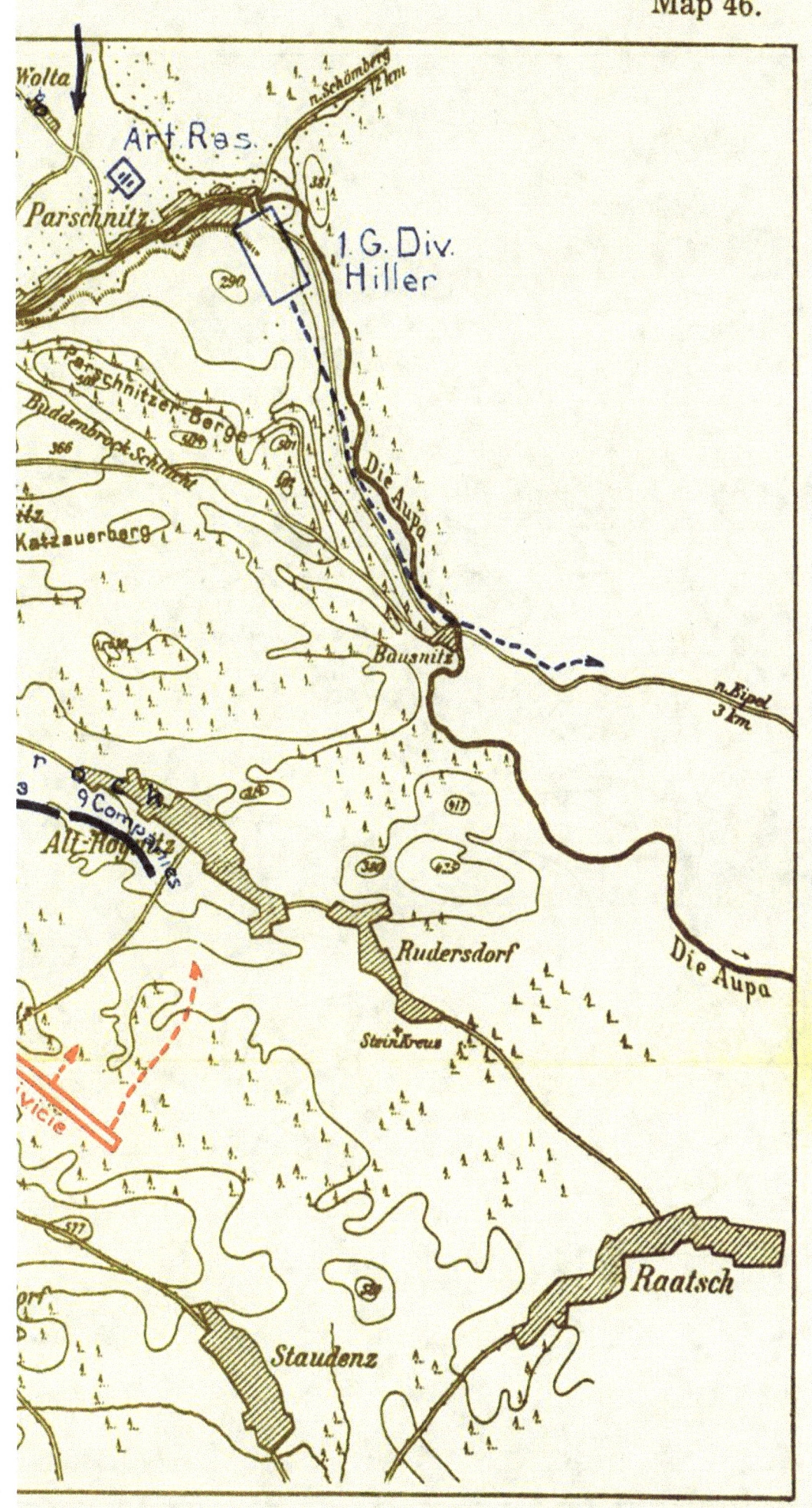

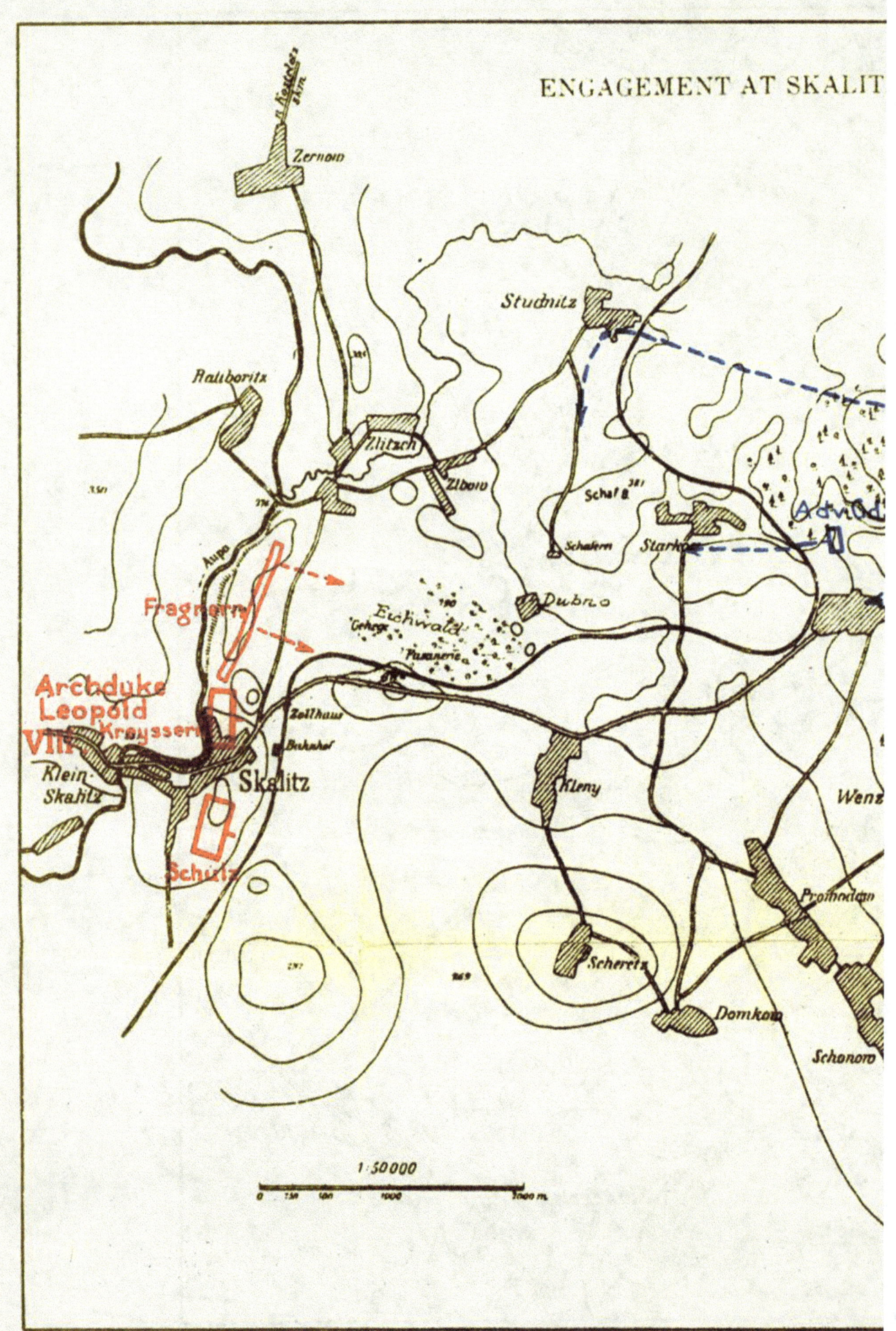

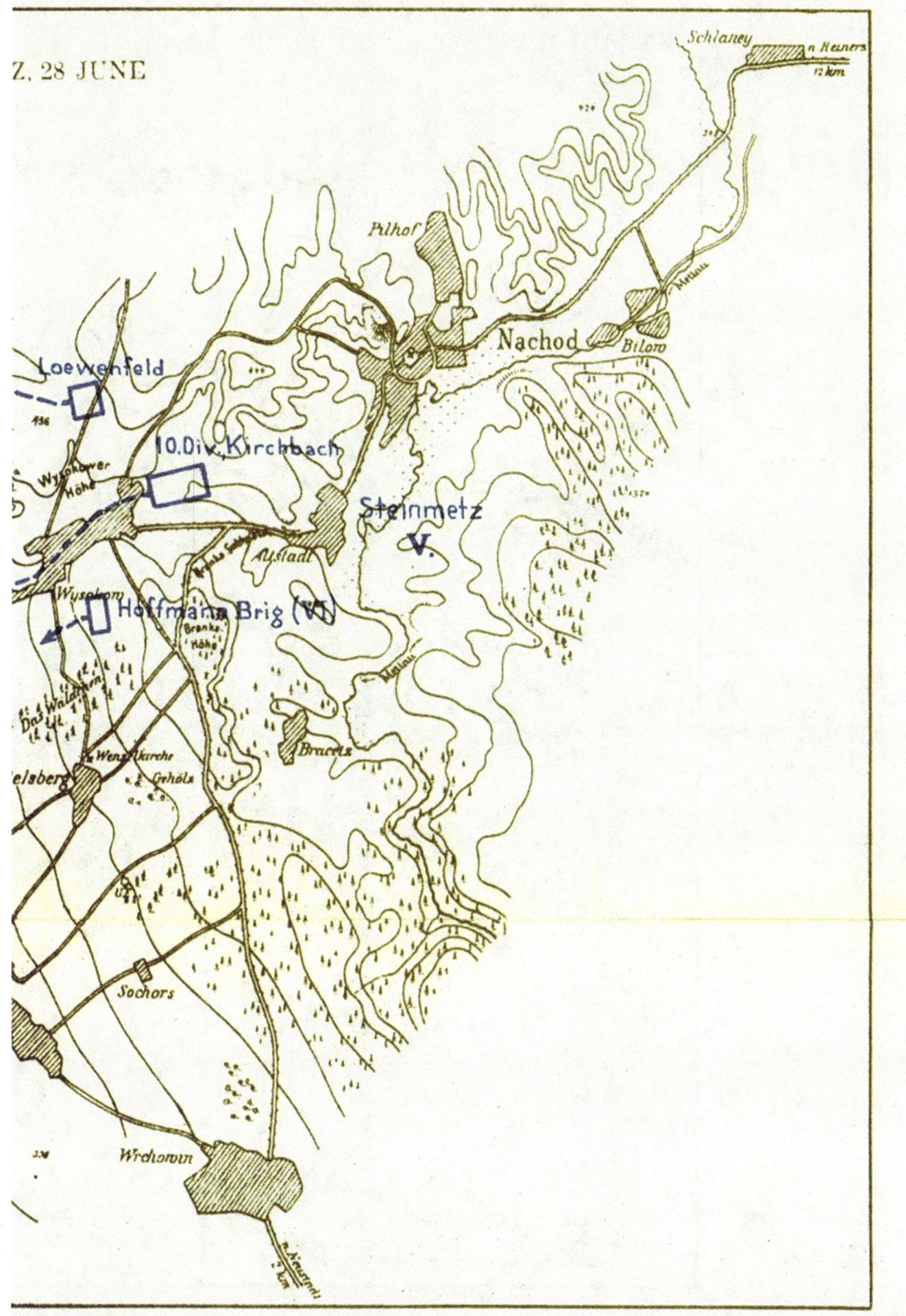

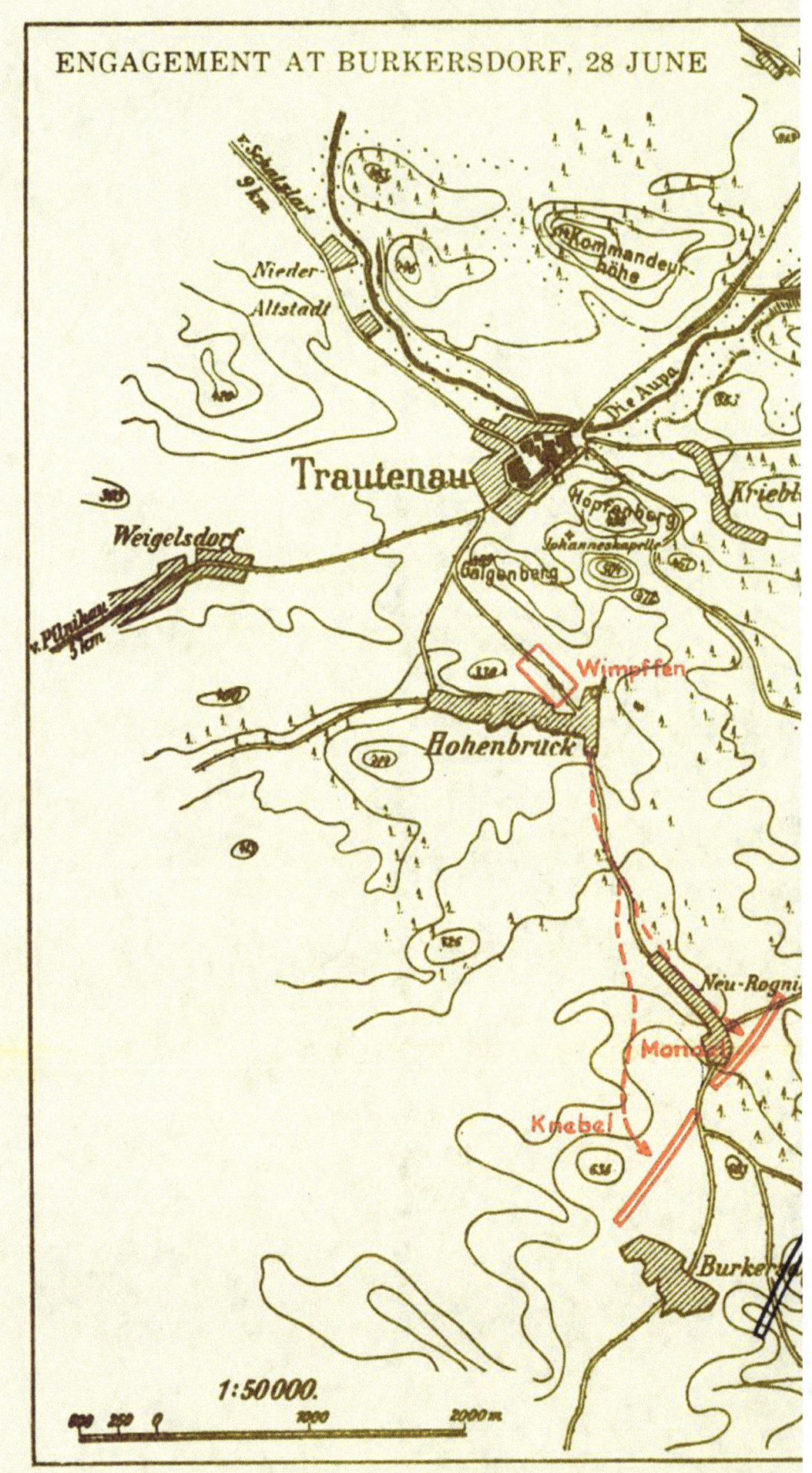

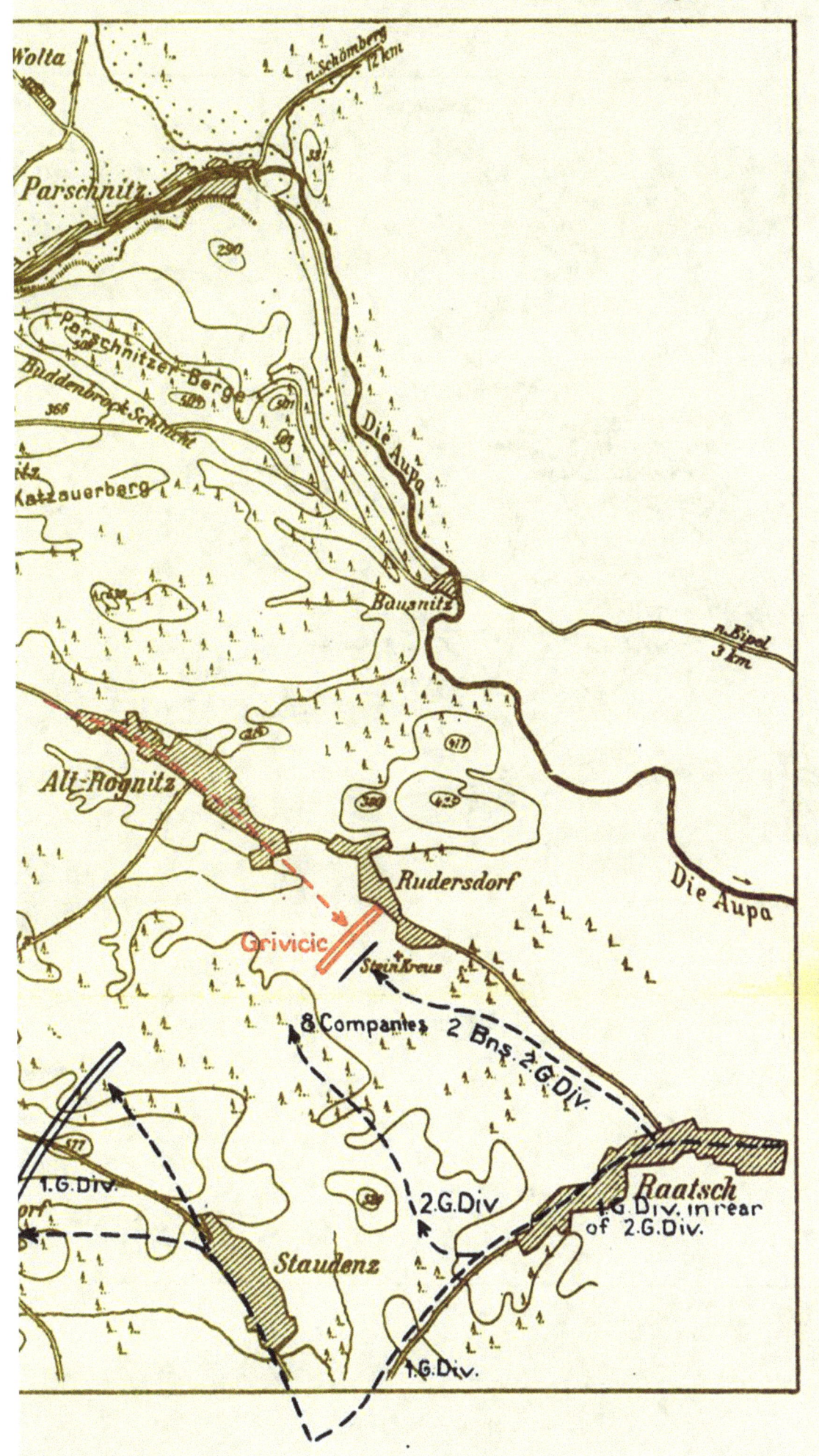

Map 48.

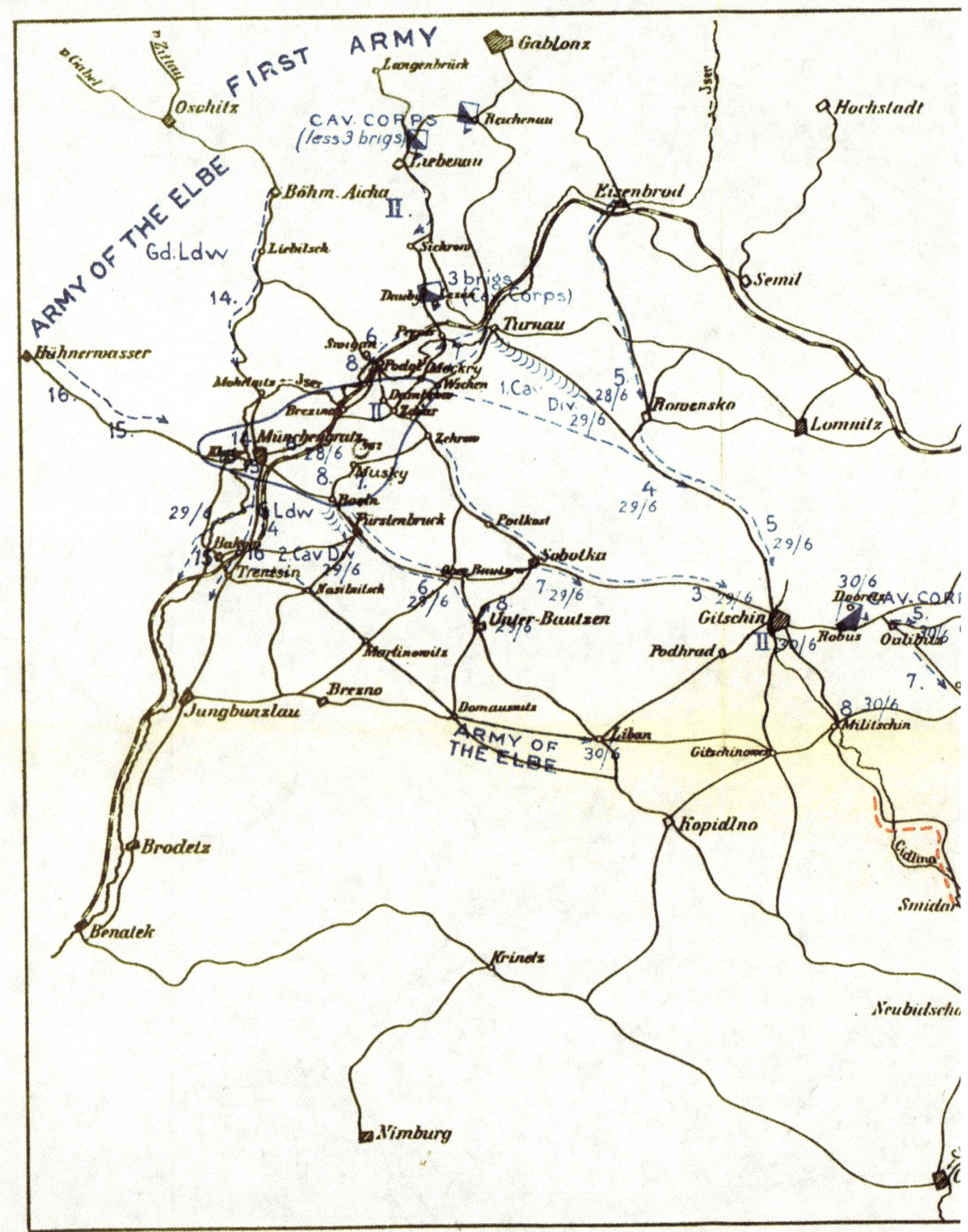

Map 49.

OPERATIONS FROM 28 JUNE TO THE NIGHT OF 30 JUNE

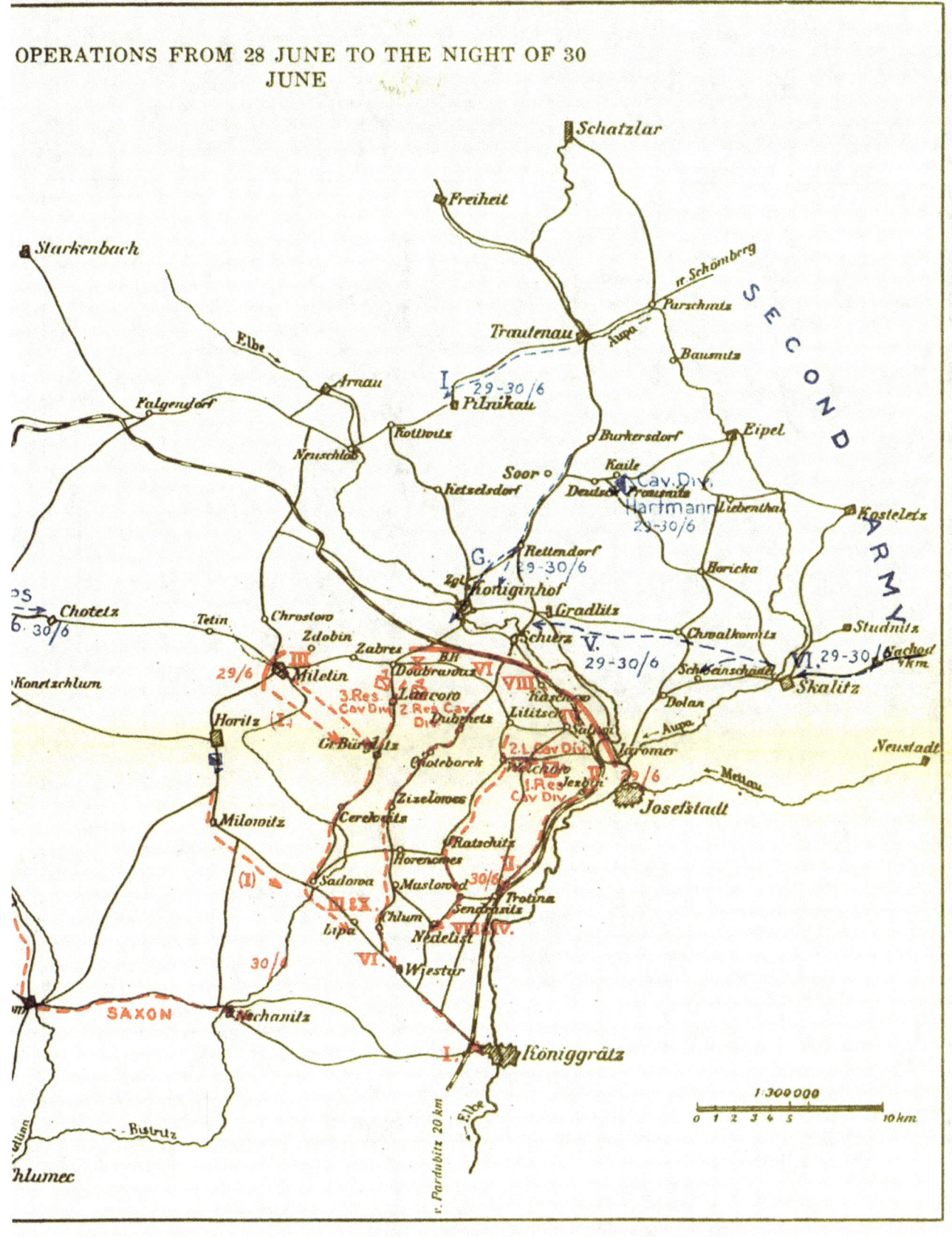

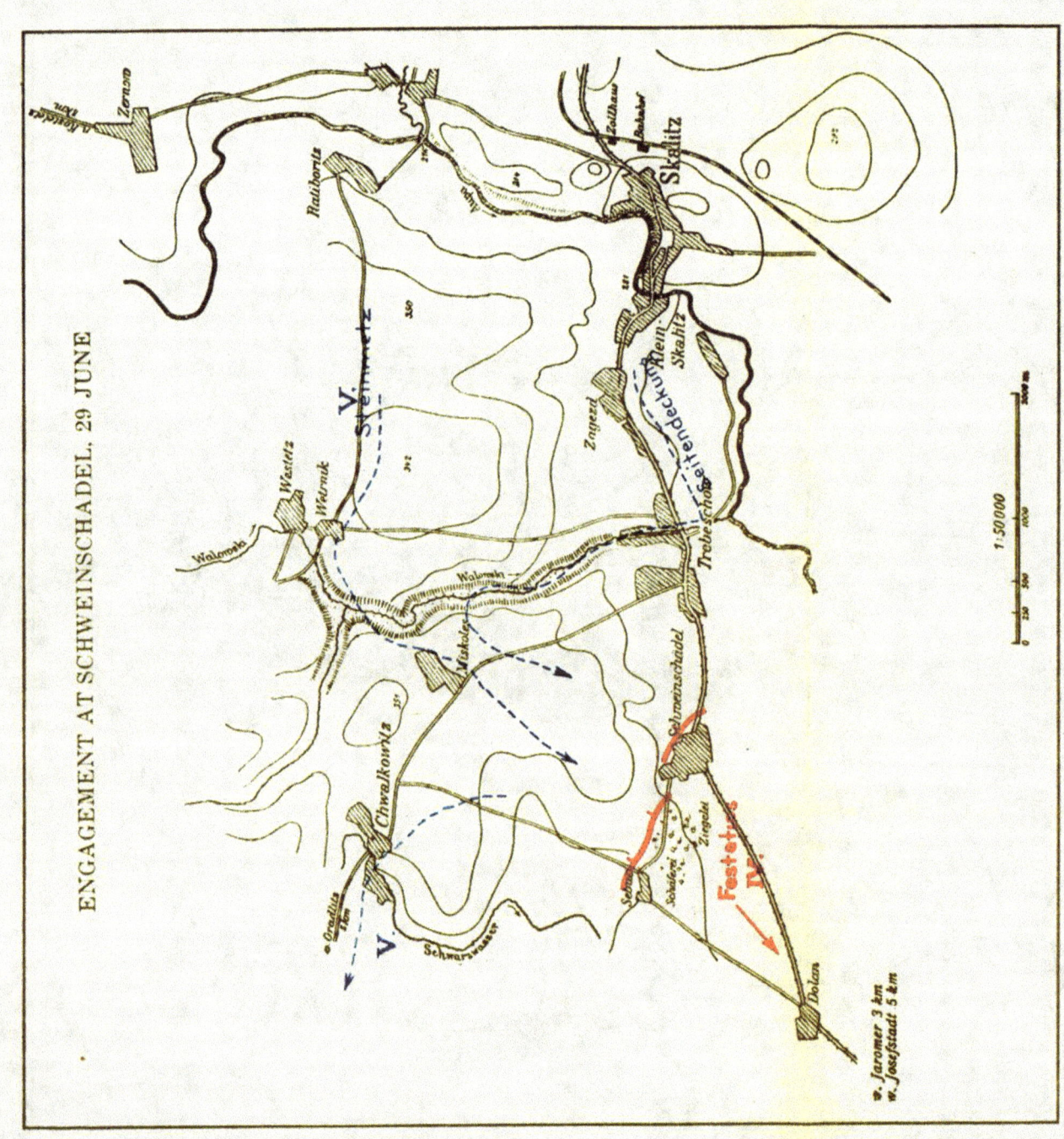

ENGAGEMENT AT GITSCHIN, 29 JUNE

1:50000.

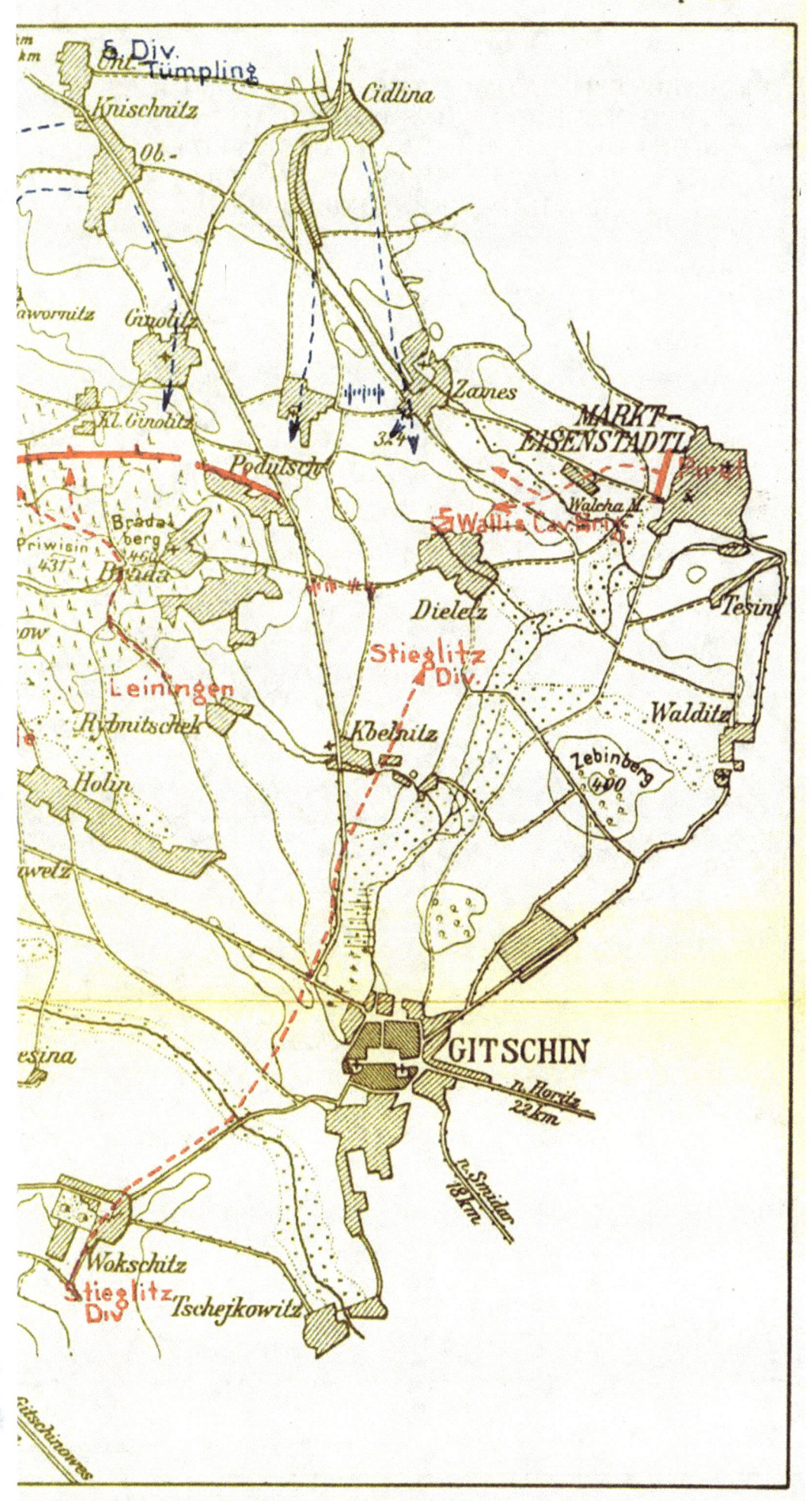

Map 51.

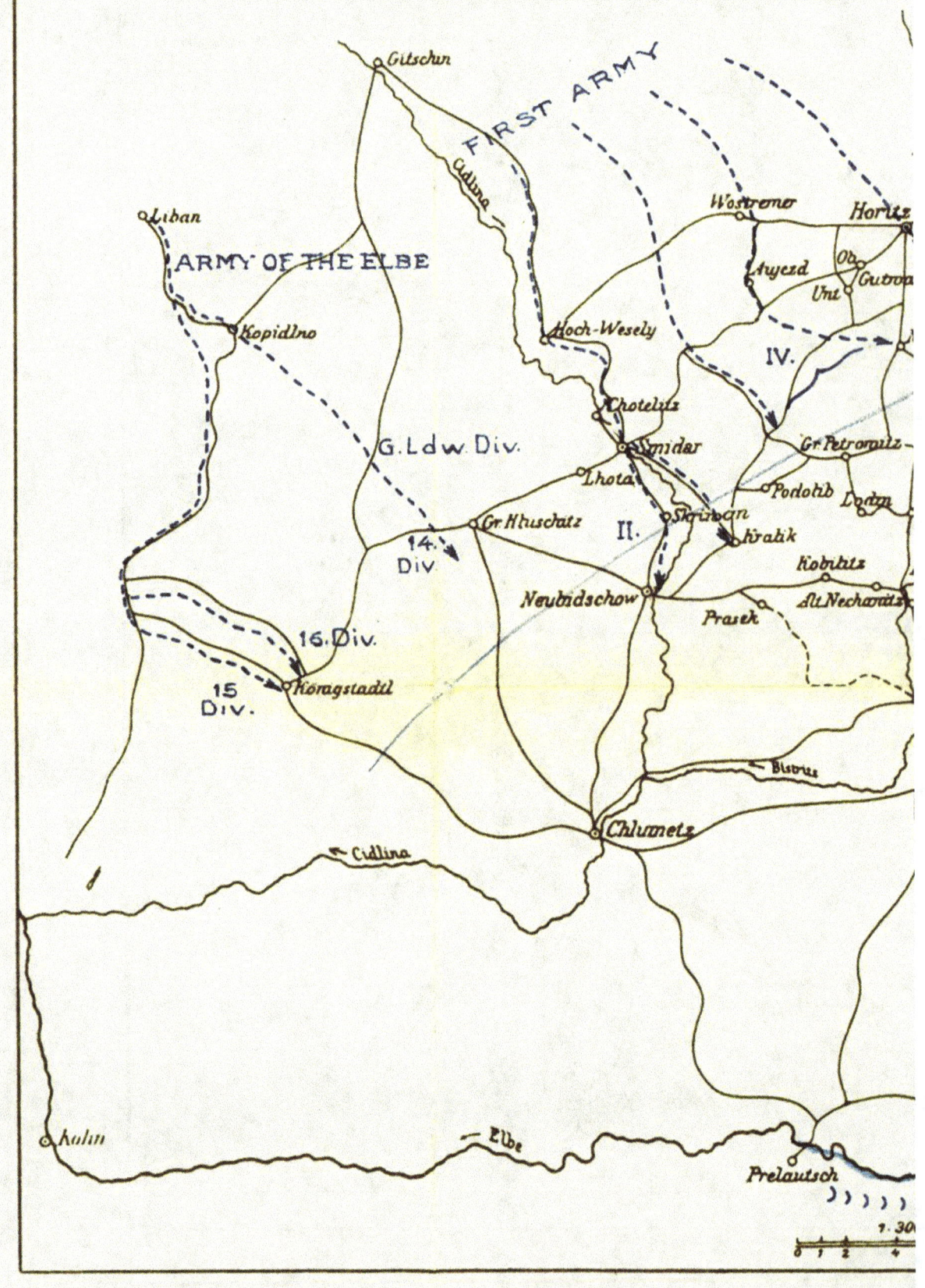

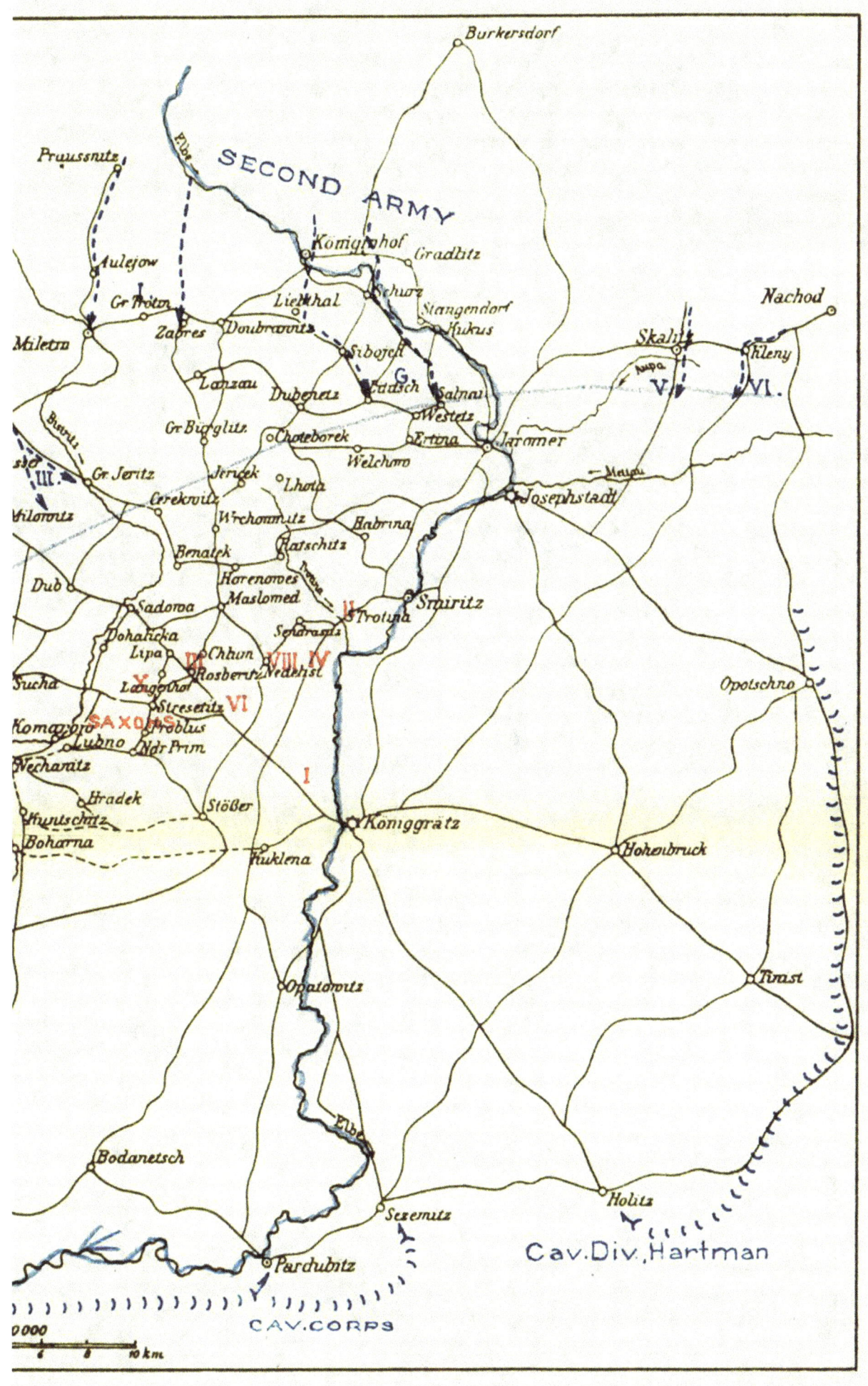

Map 52.

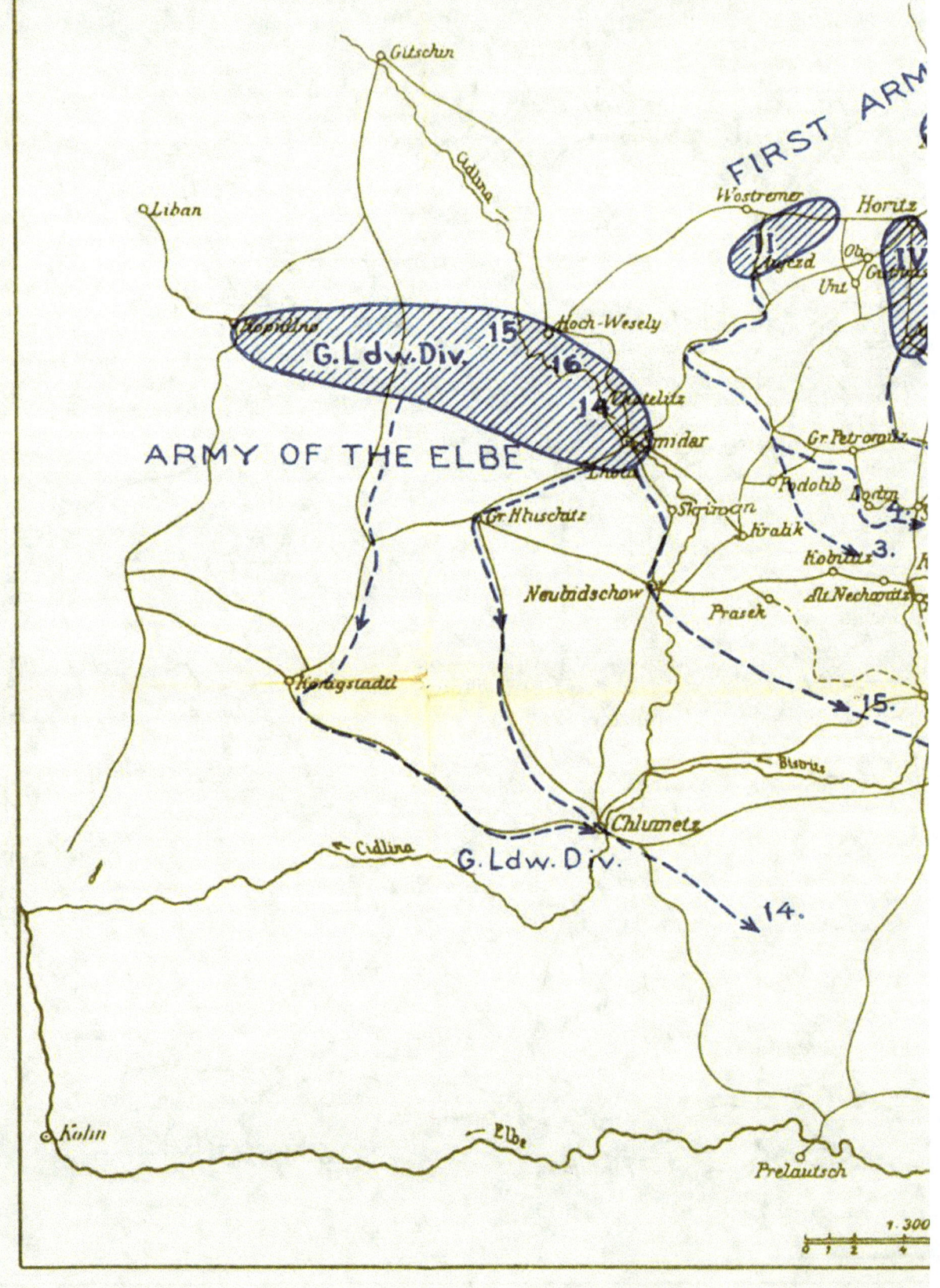

LOCATION OF THE PRUSSIAN ARMIES ON 1-2 JULY. PLAN OF THE PRUSSIAN MOVEMENTS ON 3 JULY, IN ACCORDANCE WITH MOLTKE'S INSTRUCTIONS.

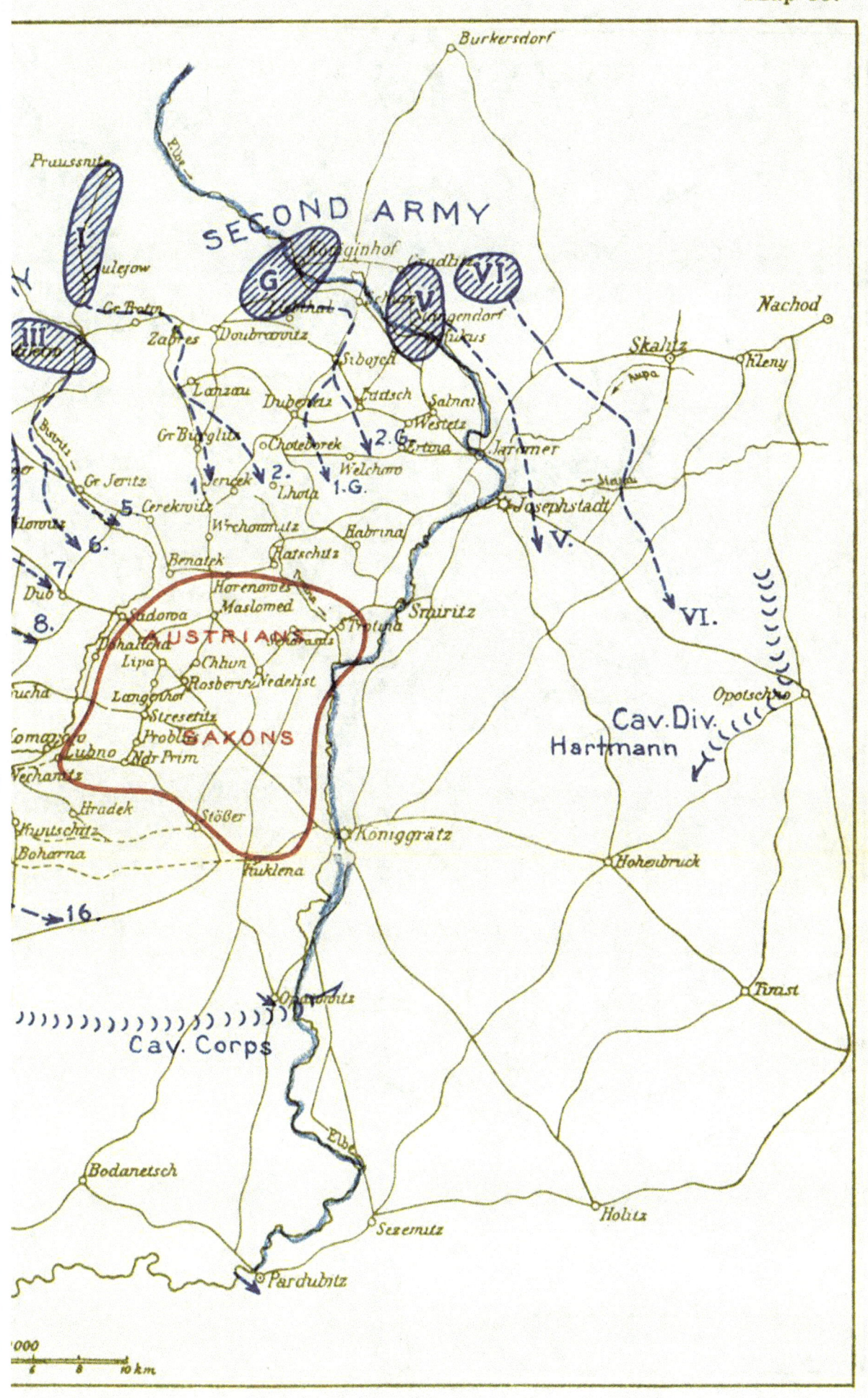

Map 53.

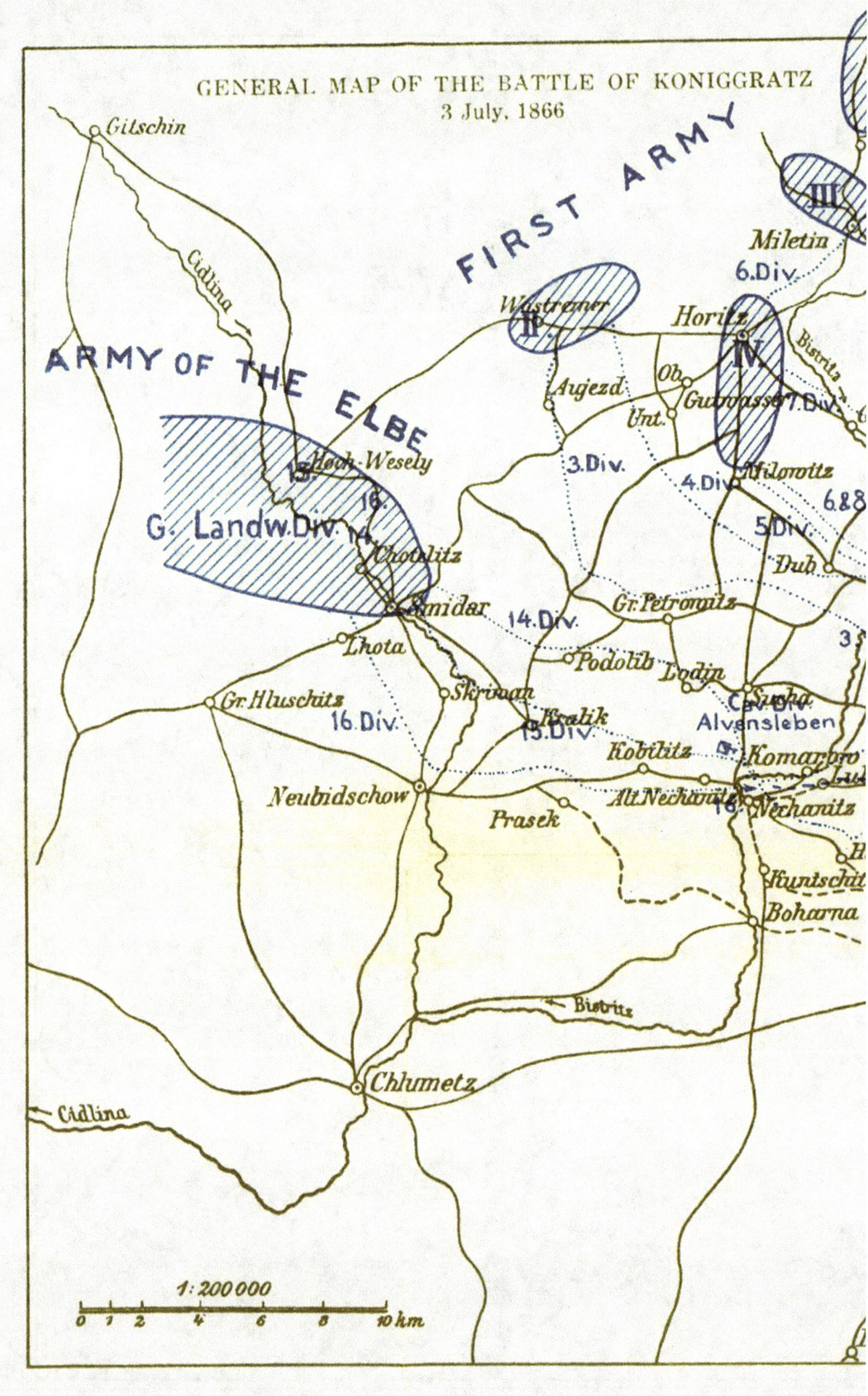

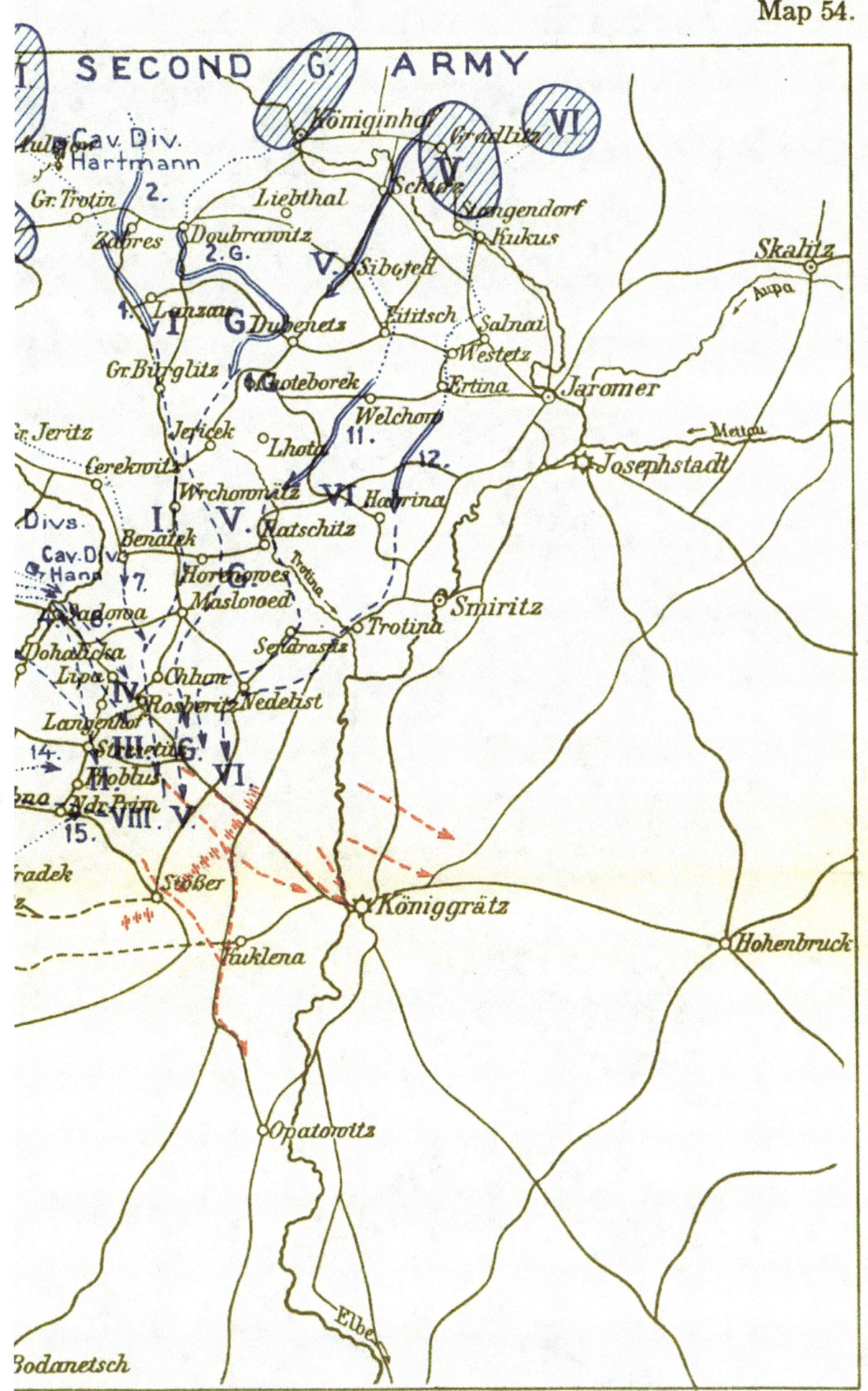

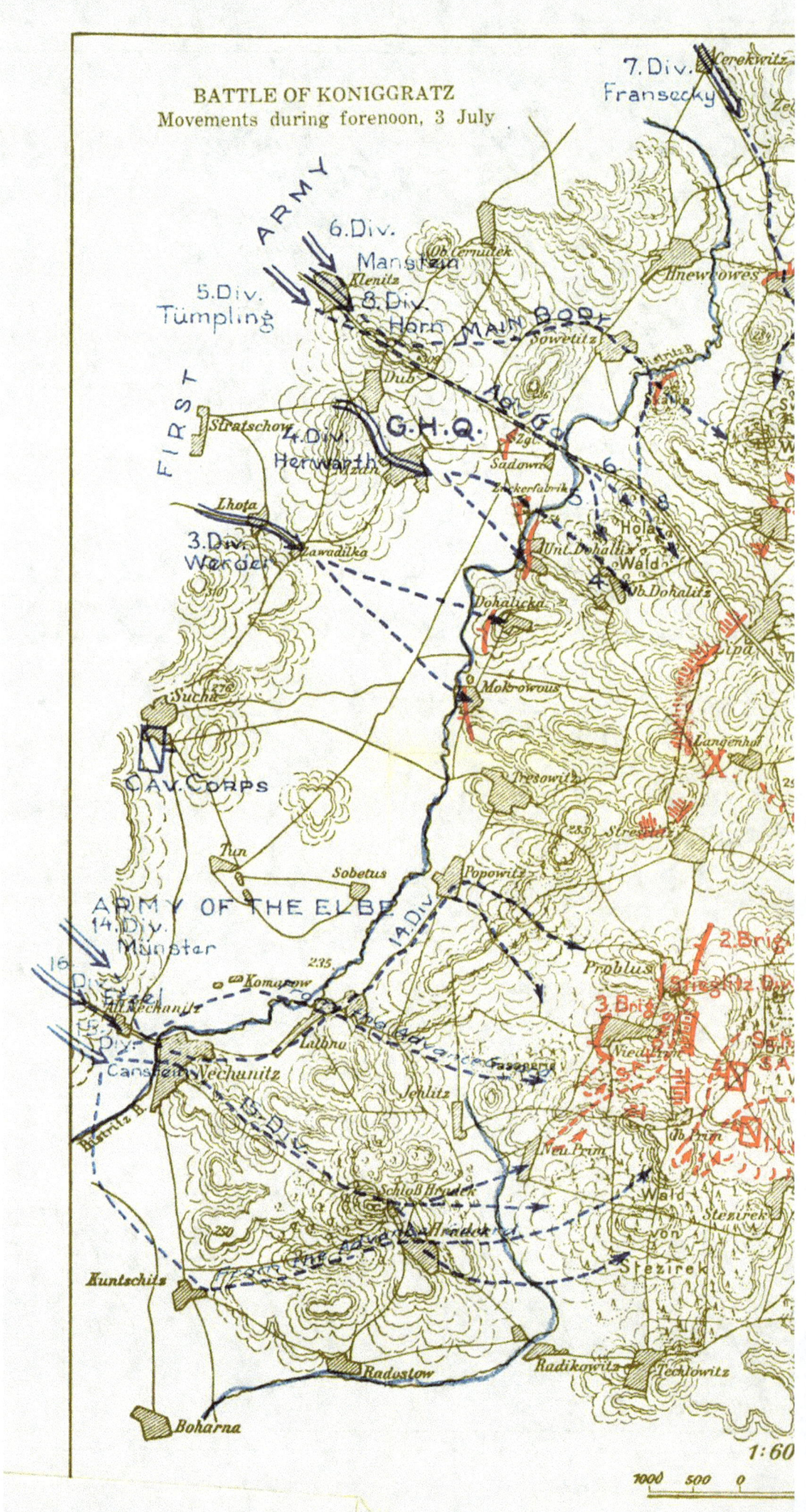

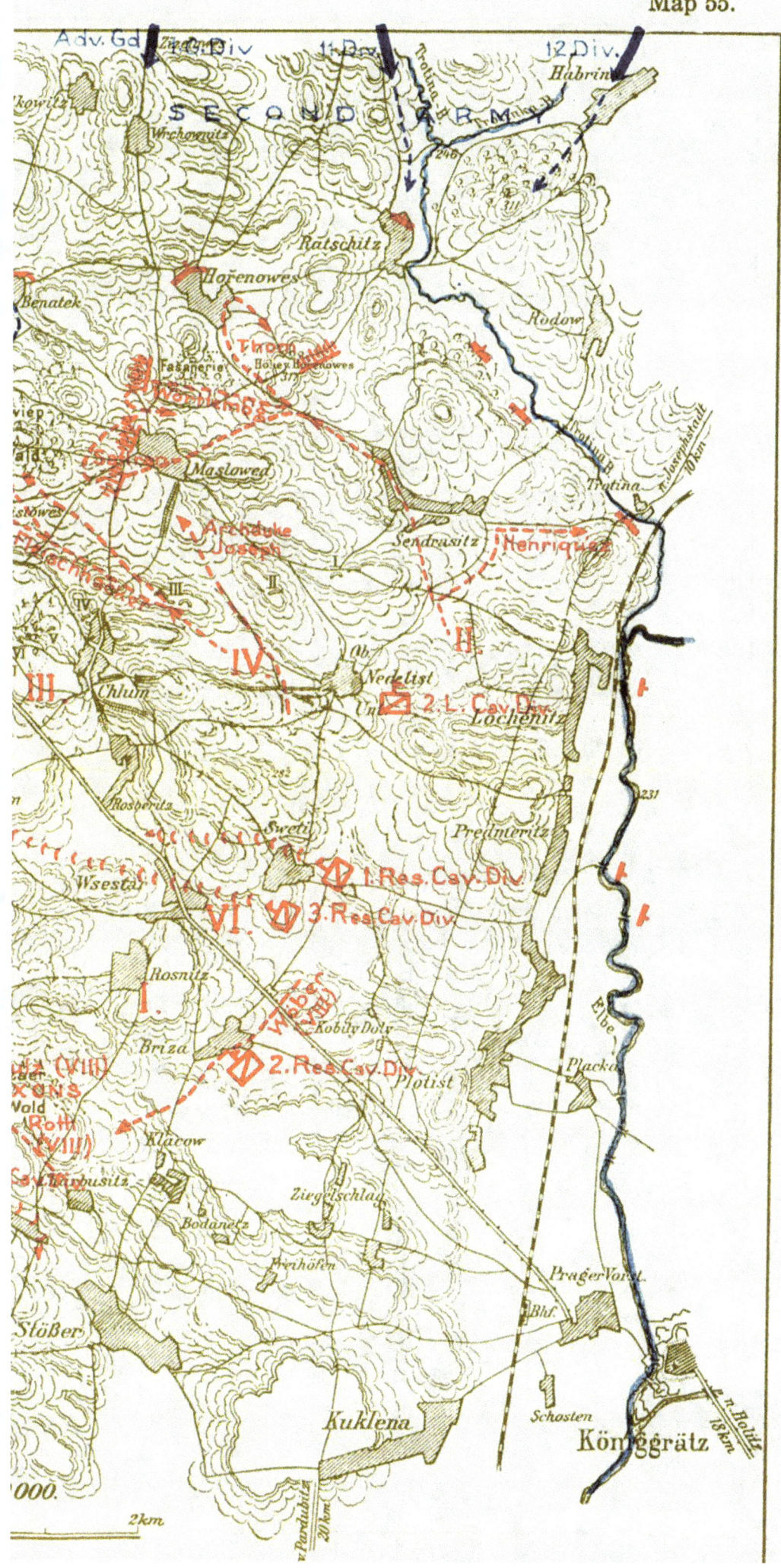

Map 55.

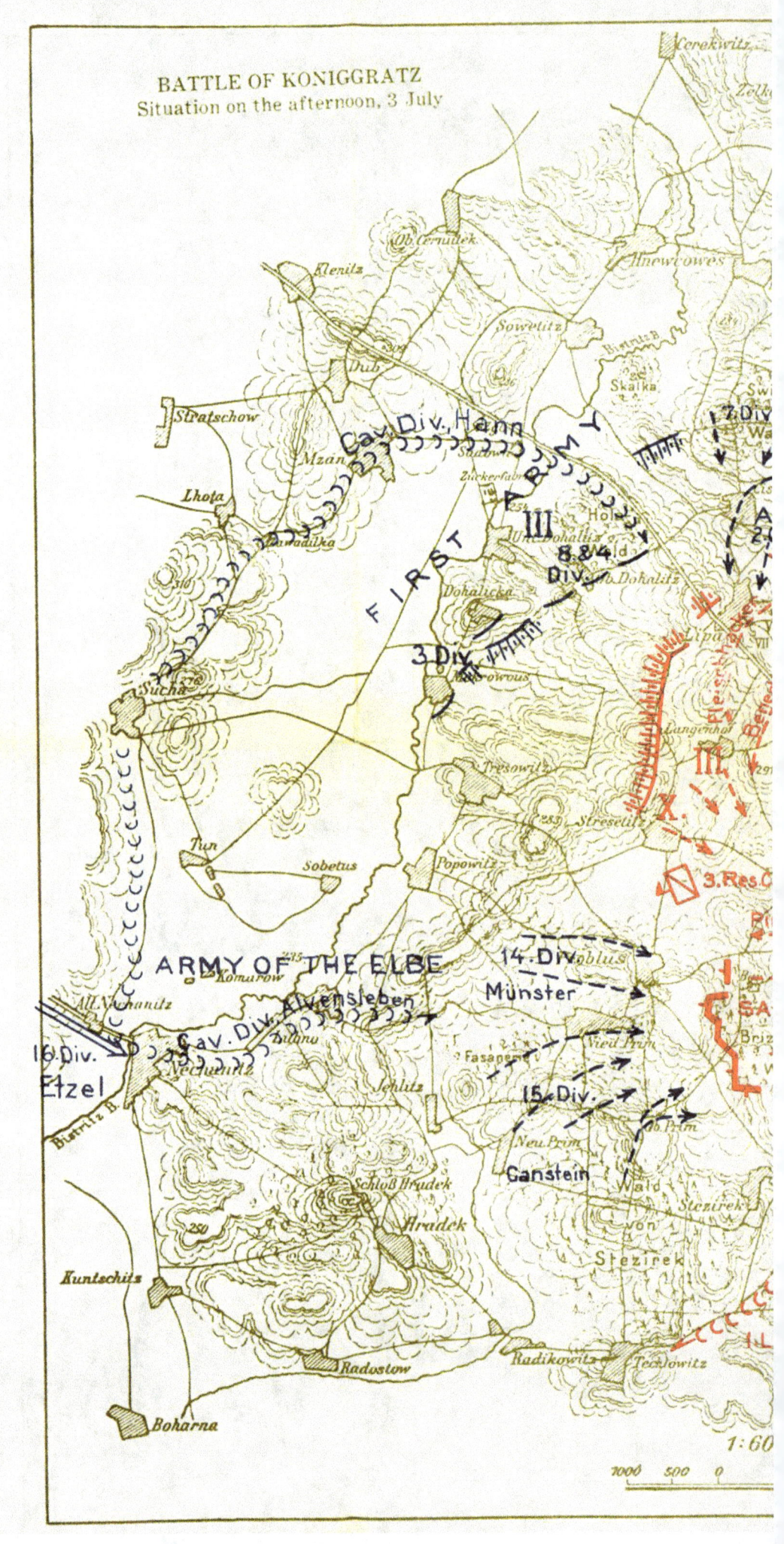

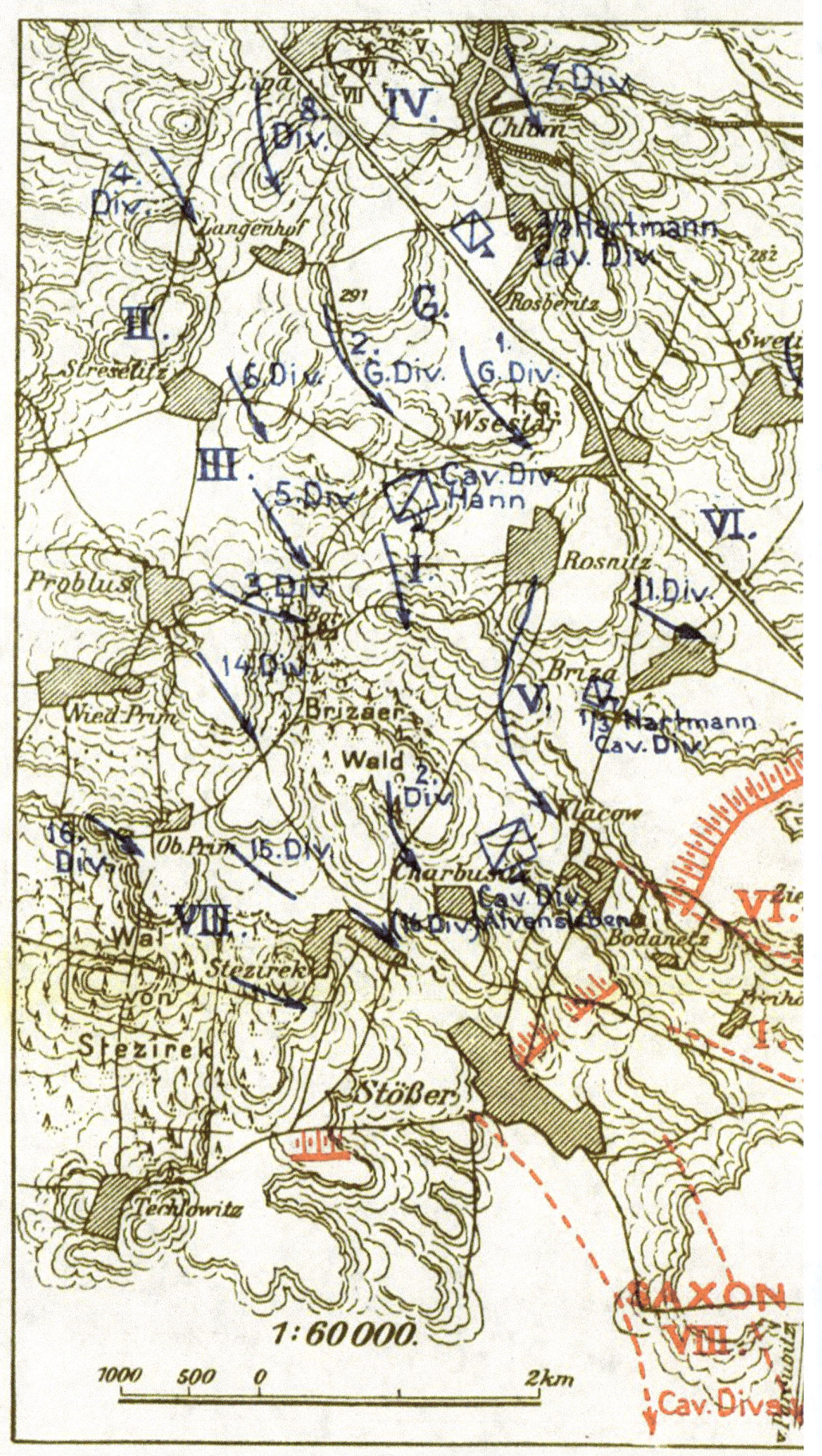

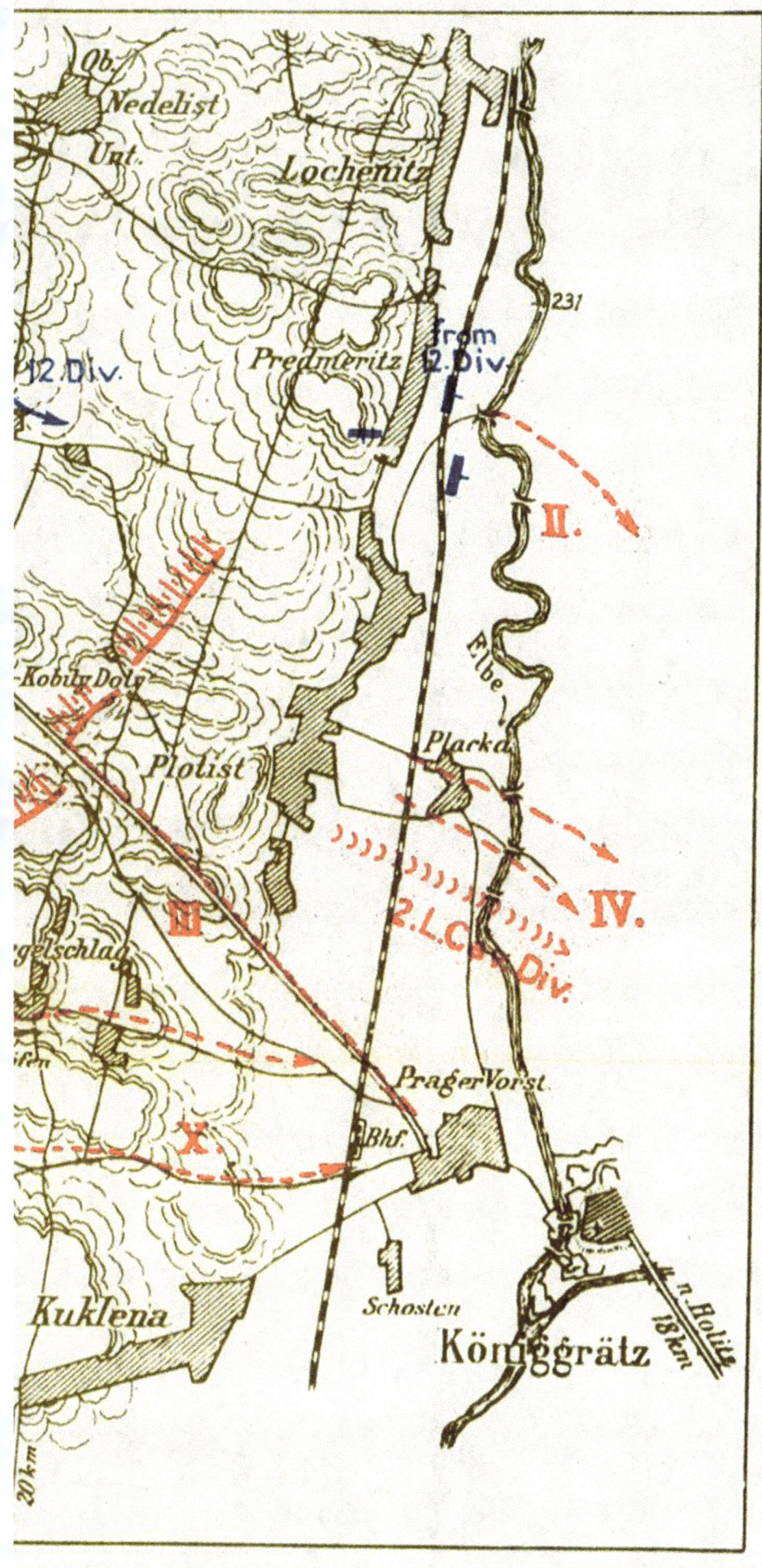

Map 58.

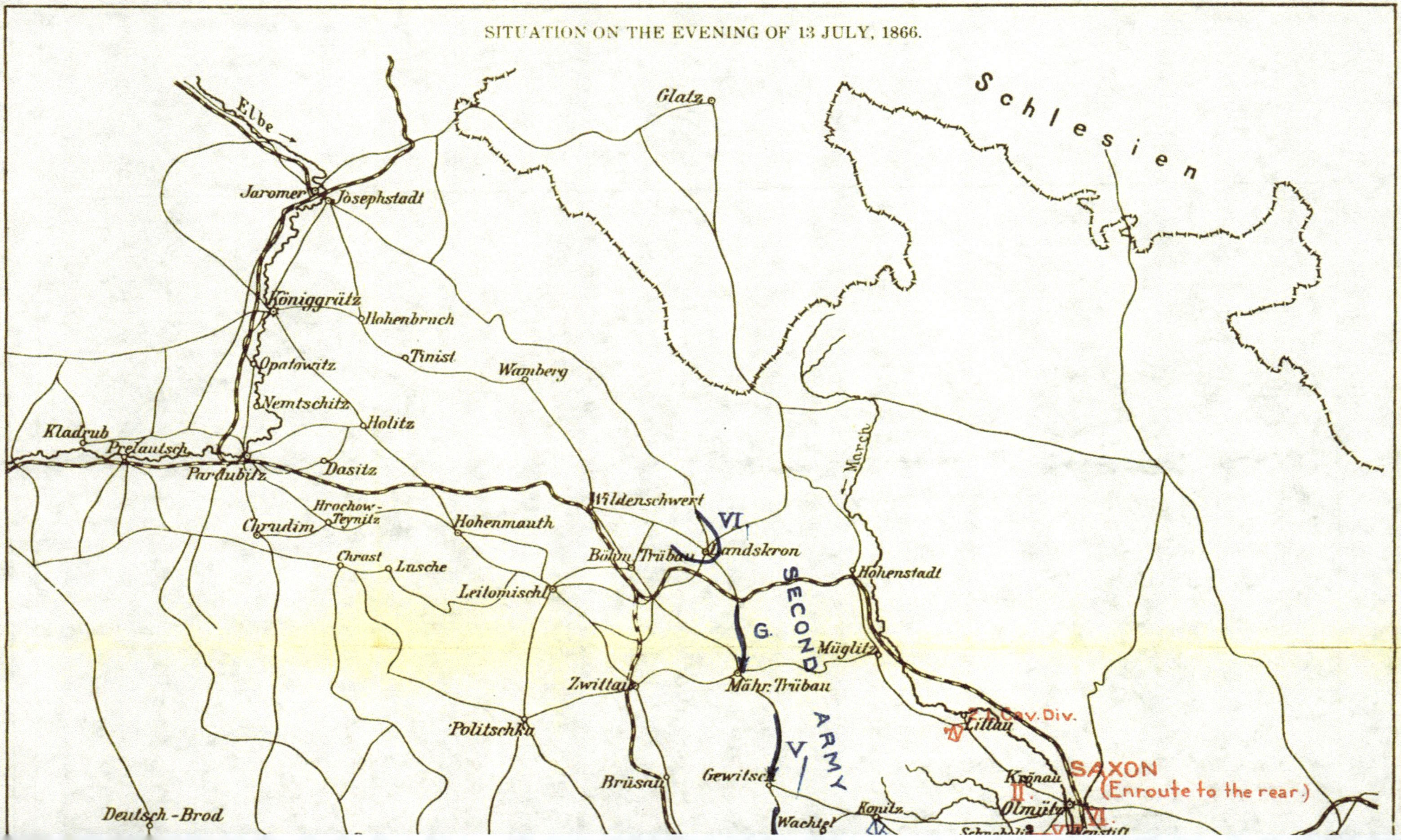
SITUATION ON THE EVENING OF 13 JULY, 1866.
Schlesien
Elbe
Glatz
Jaromer
Josephstadt
Königgrätz
Hohenbruch
Tinist
Wamberg
Opatowitz
Nemtschitz
Holitz
Kladrub
Prelautsch
Pardubitz
Dasitz
Wildenschwert
Hrochow-Teynitz
Chrudim
Hohenmauth
Chrast
Lusche
Böhm. Trübau
Landskron
Hohenstadt
March
Leitomischl
SECOND ARMY
G.
VI.
V.
Müglitz
Zwittau
Mähr. Trübau
Politschka
Littau
Cav. Div.
SAXON
(Enroute to the rear.)
Krönau
Olmütz
Brüsau
Gewitsch
Konitz
Wachtel
Deutsch-Brod

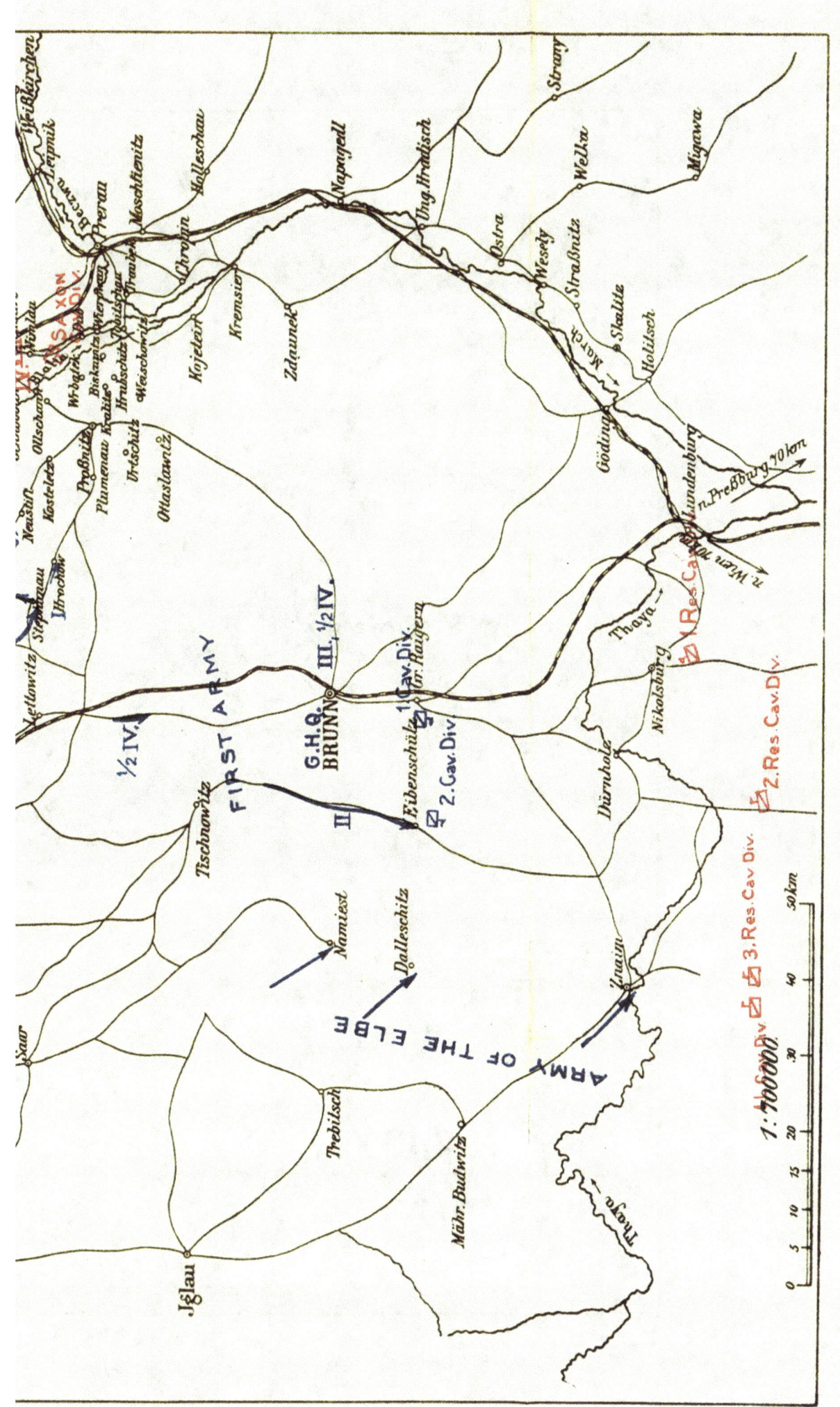

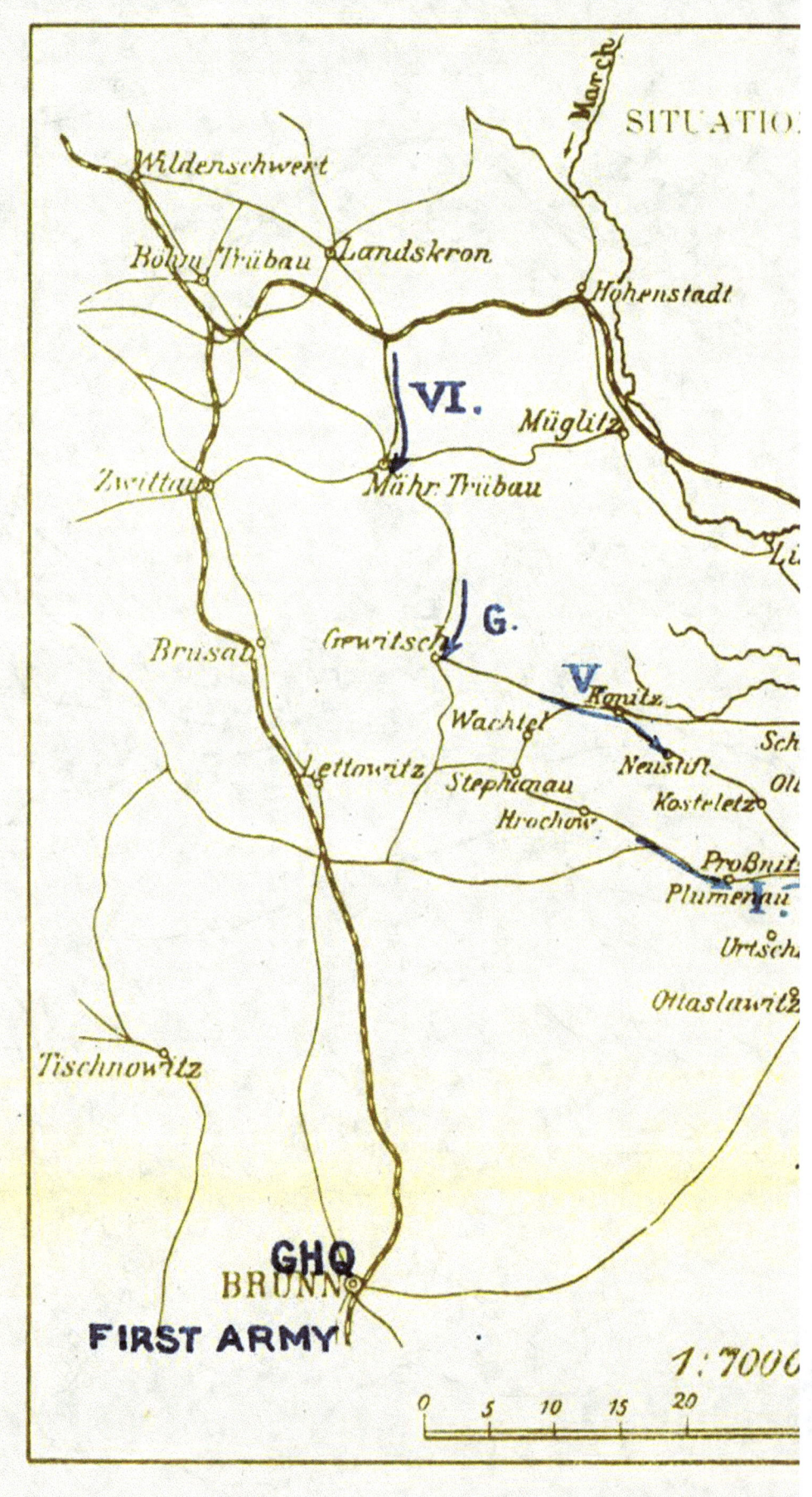

Map 59.

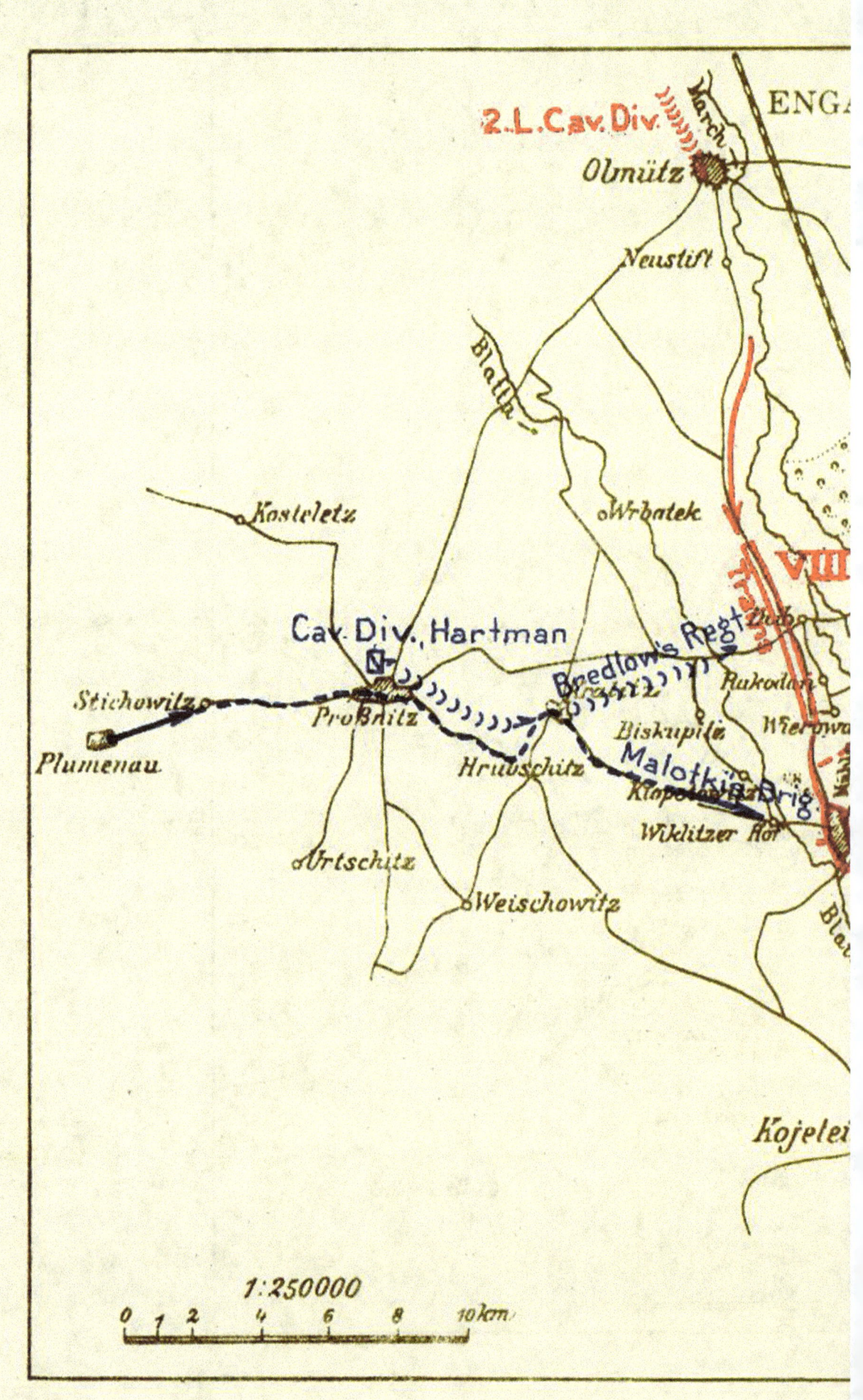

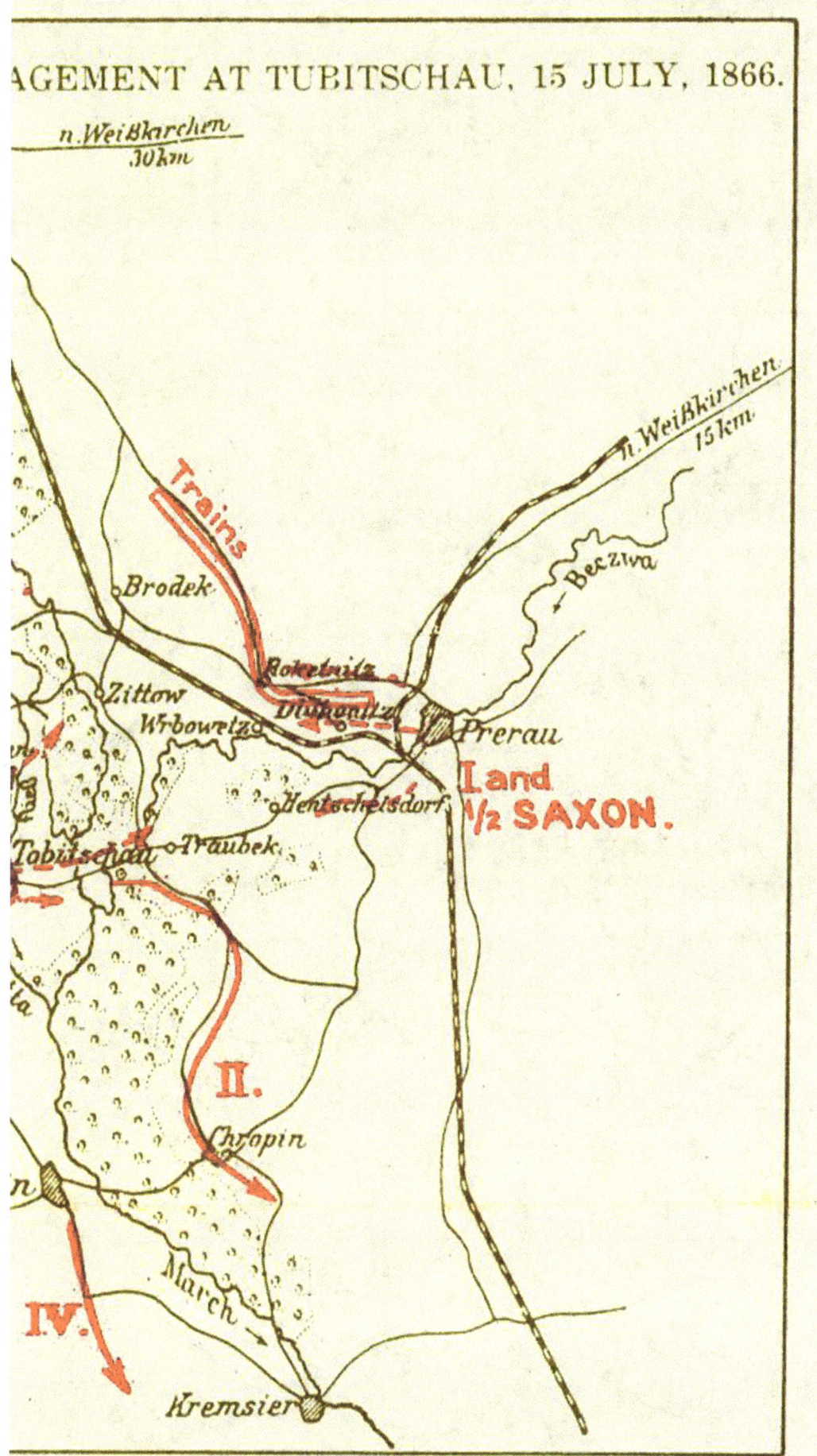

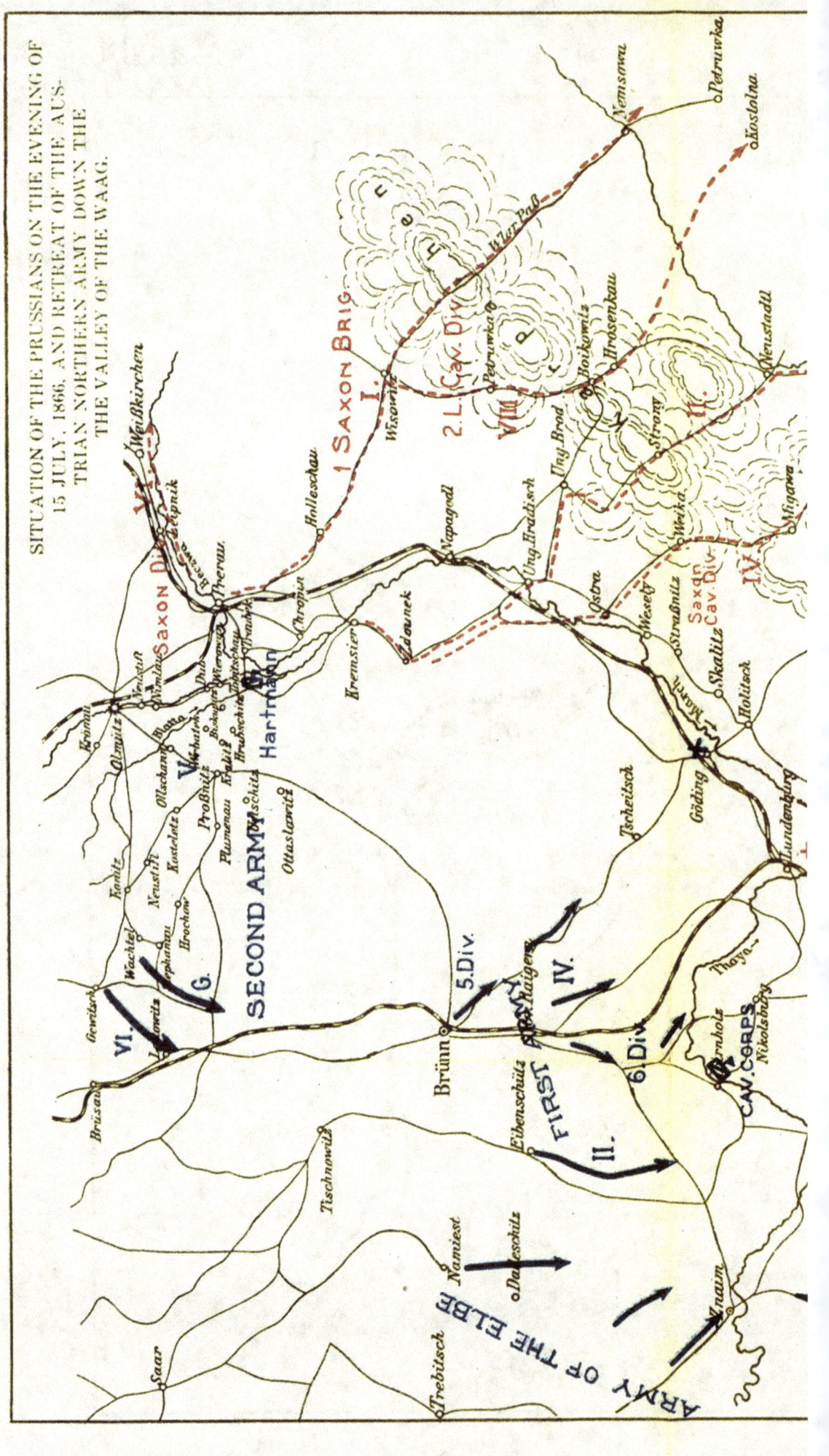

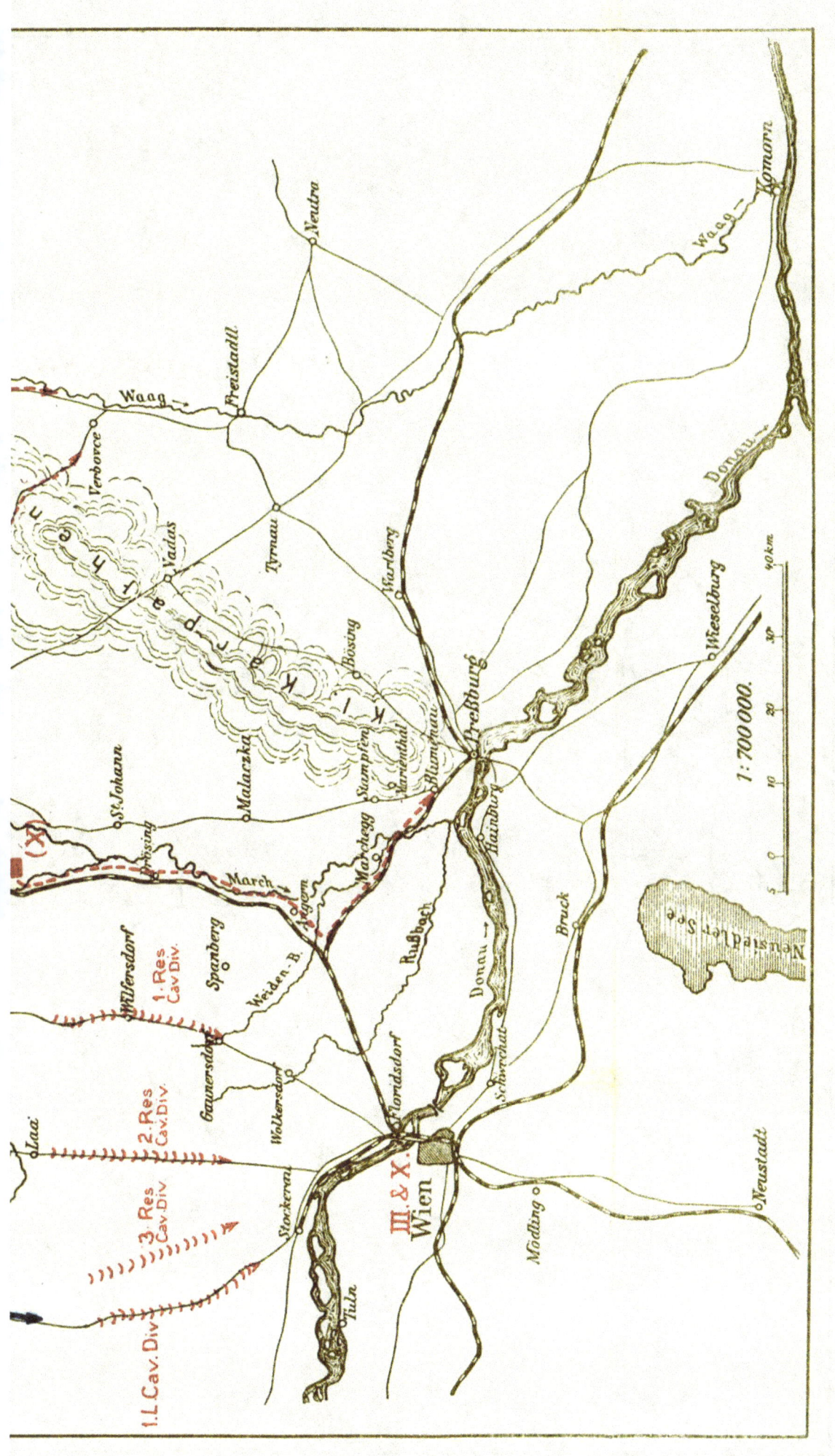

Map 62.

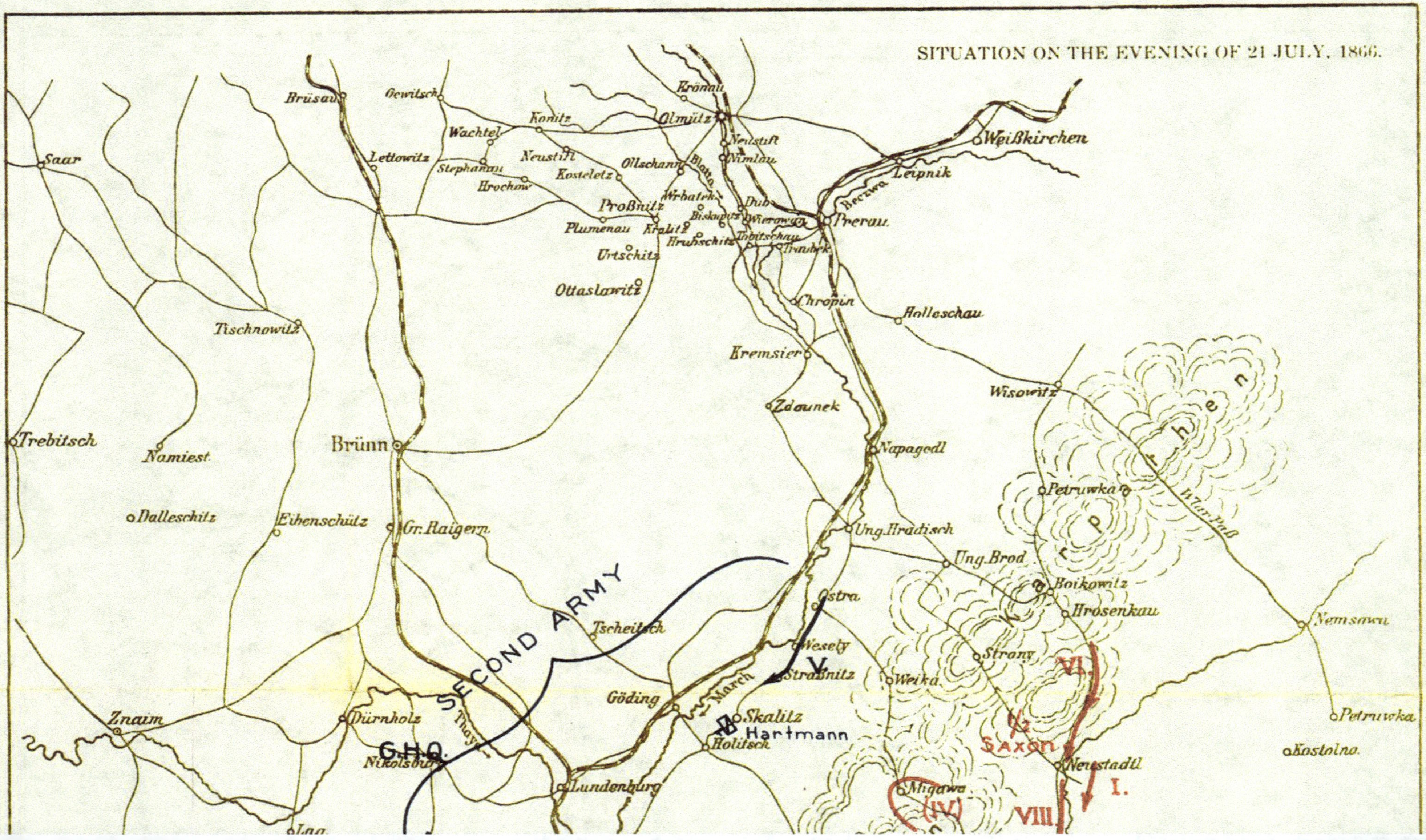
SITUATION ON THE EVENING OF 21 JULY, 1866.
Brüsau
Gewitsch
Saar
Lettowitz
Wachtel
Konitz
Olmütz
Krönau
Neustift
Nimlau
Weißkirchen
Leipnik
Beczwa
Prerau
Stephanau
Hrochow
Kostelelz
Ollschann
Blatta
Wrbatek
Proßnitz
Plumenau
Kralitz
Biskupitz
Dub
Wierowan
Tobitschau
Hruschitz
Traubek
Urtschitz
Ottaslawitz
Chropin
Holleschau
Tischnowitz
Kremsier
Wisowitz
Zdaunek
Trebitsch
Namiest
Brünn
Napagedl
Petruwka
Wlar Paß
Dalleschitz
Eibenschütz
Gr. Raigern
Ung. Hradisch
Ung. Brod
Boikowitz
Hrosenkau
SECOND ARMY
Tscheitsch
Ostra
Nemsowa
Wesely
V
Straßnitz
March
Weika
Strany
VI.
Göding
Skalitz
Hartmann
Holitsch
Znaim
Dürnholz
Thaya
G.H.Q.
Nikolsburg
Saxon
Neustadtl
Petruwka
Kostolna
Lundenburg
Migawa
(IV)
VIII
I.

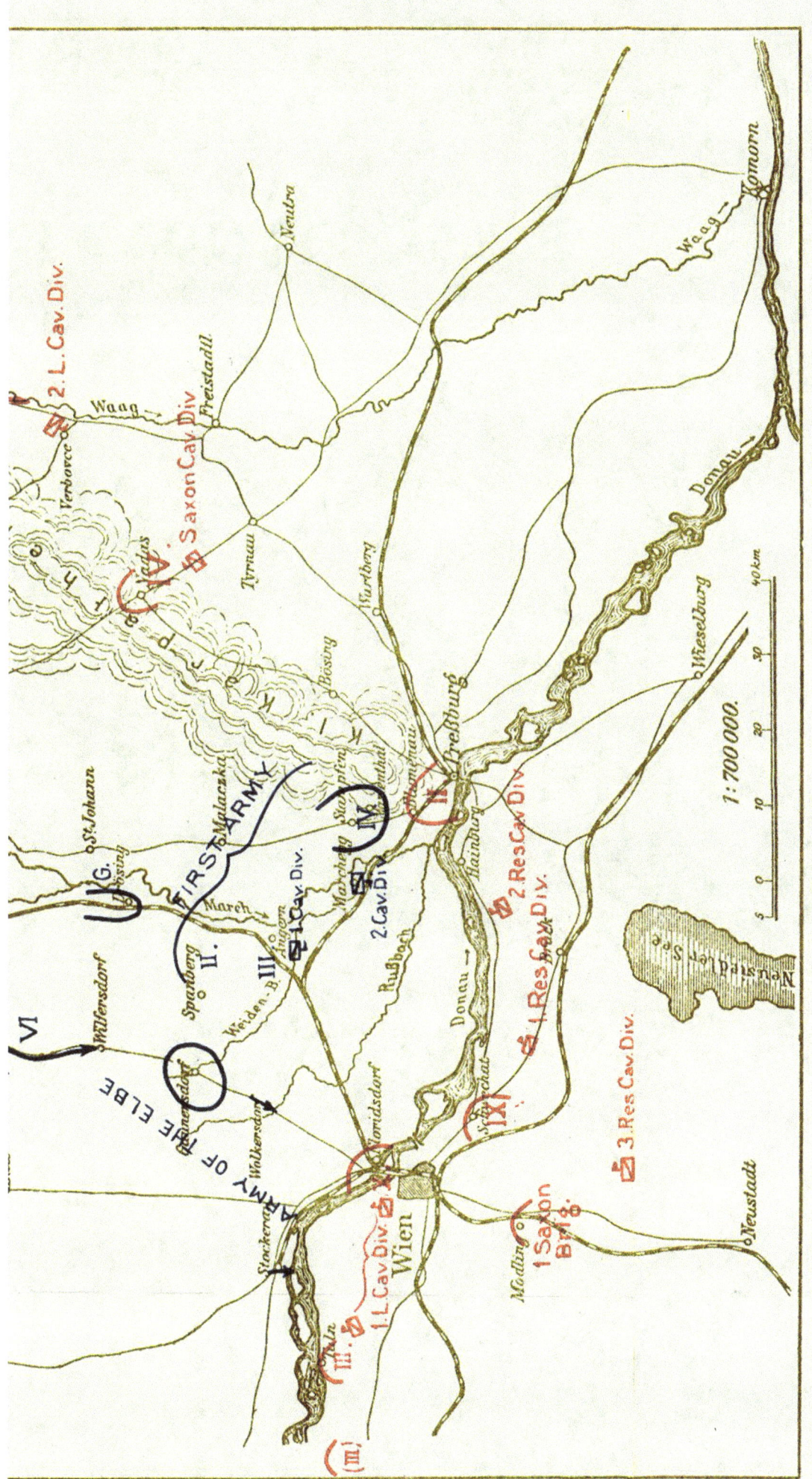

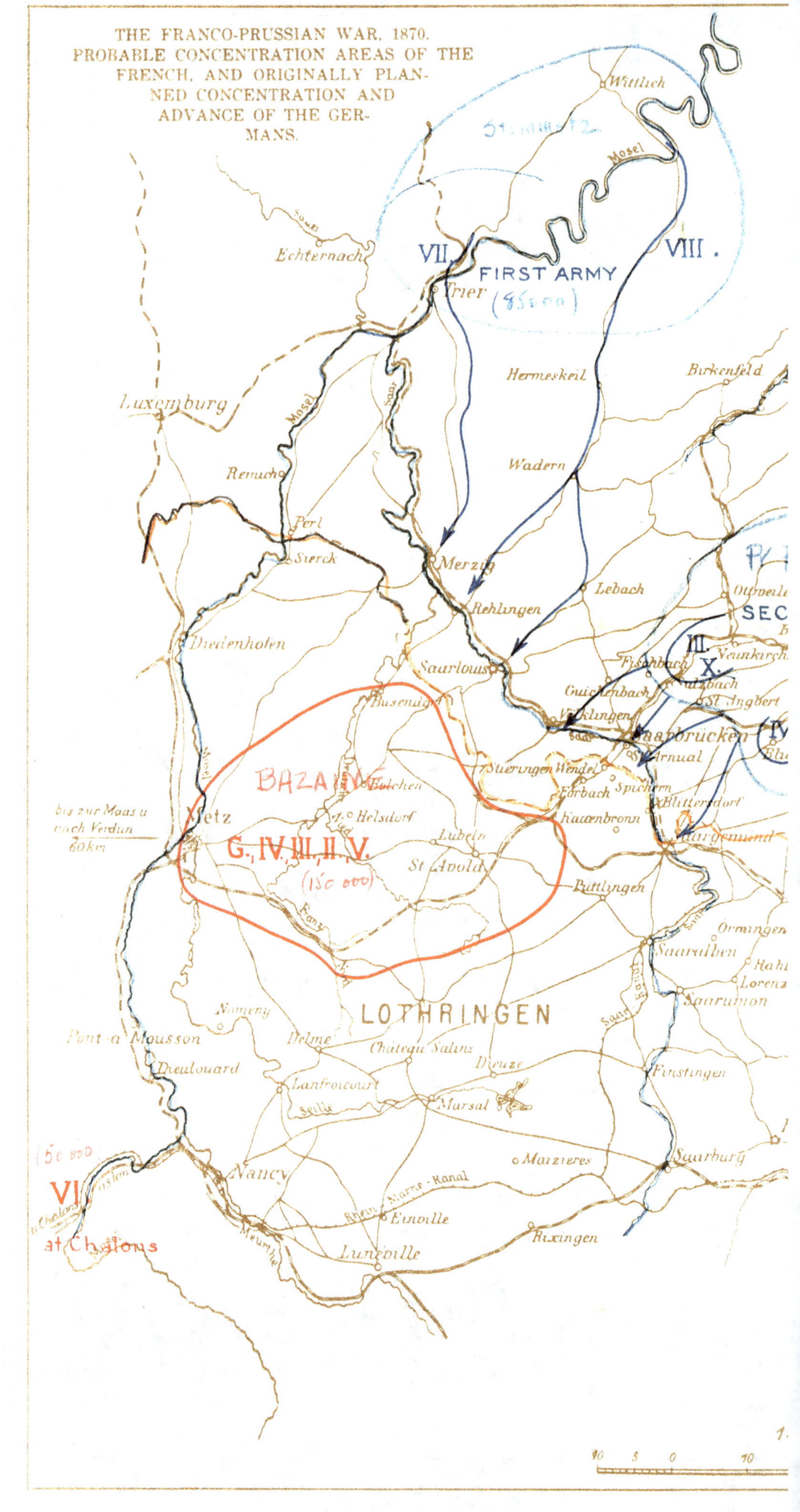

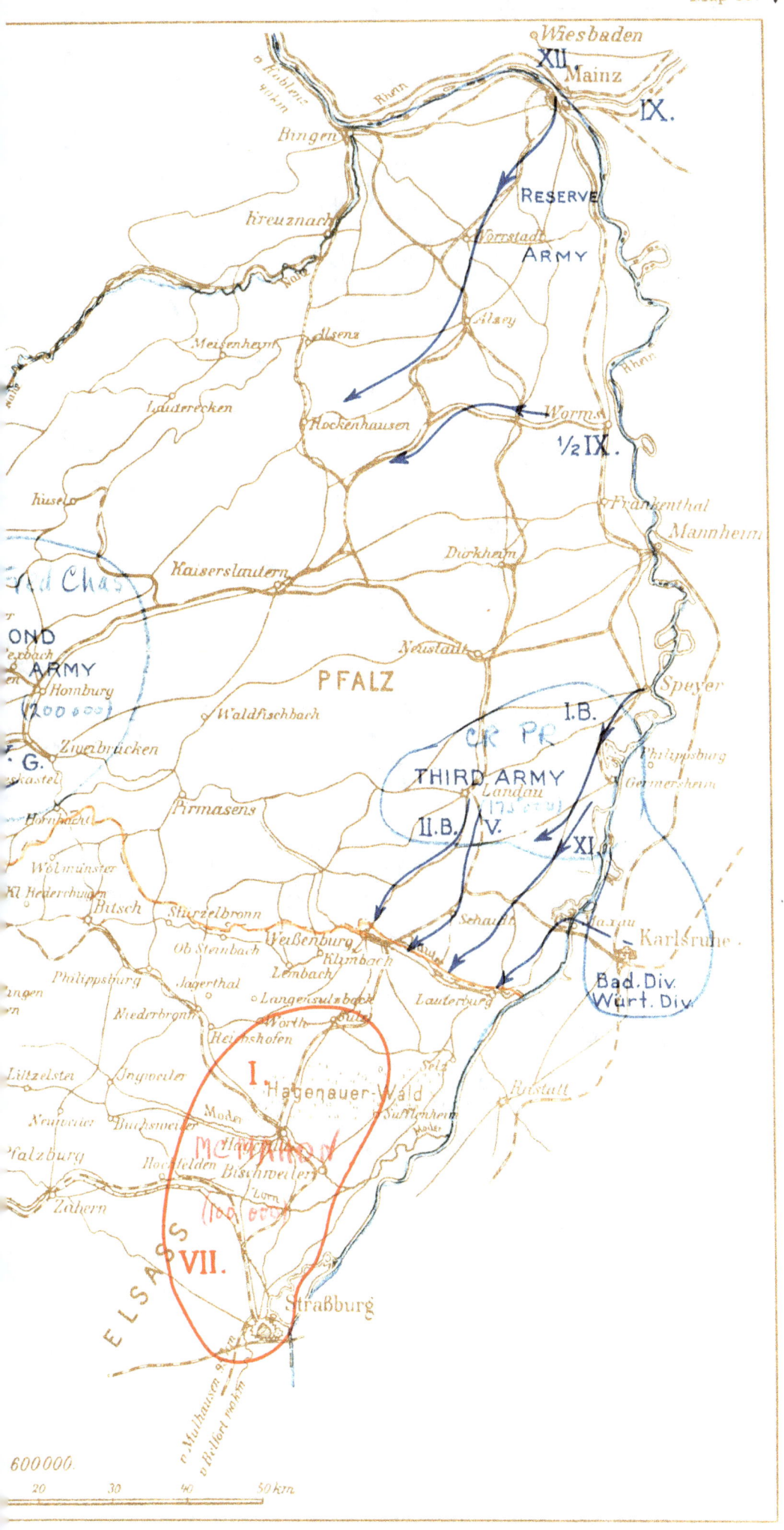

Map 63.

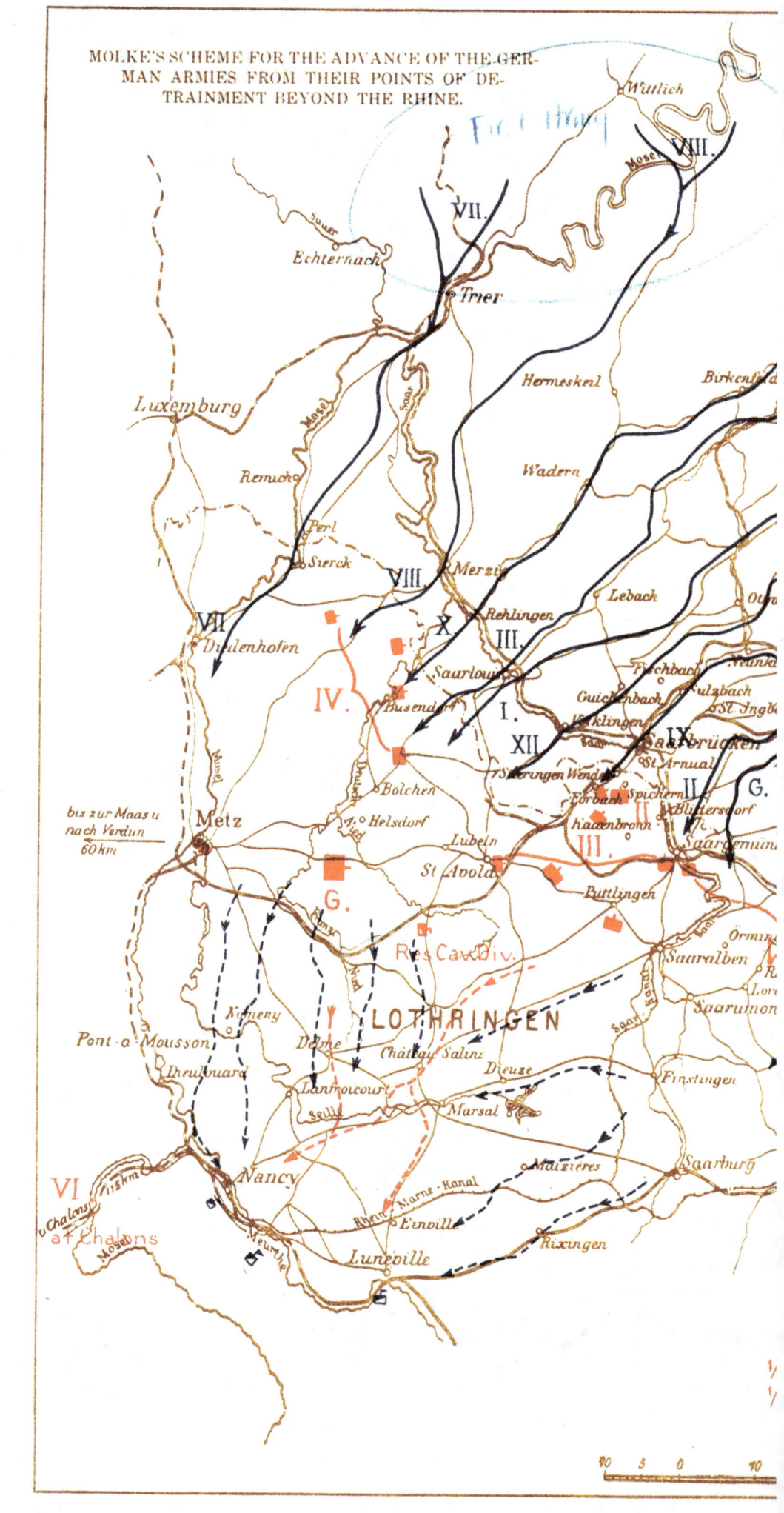

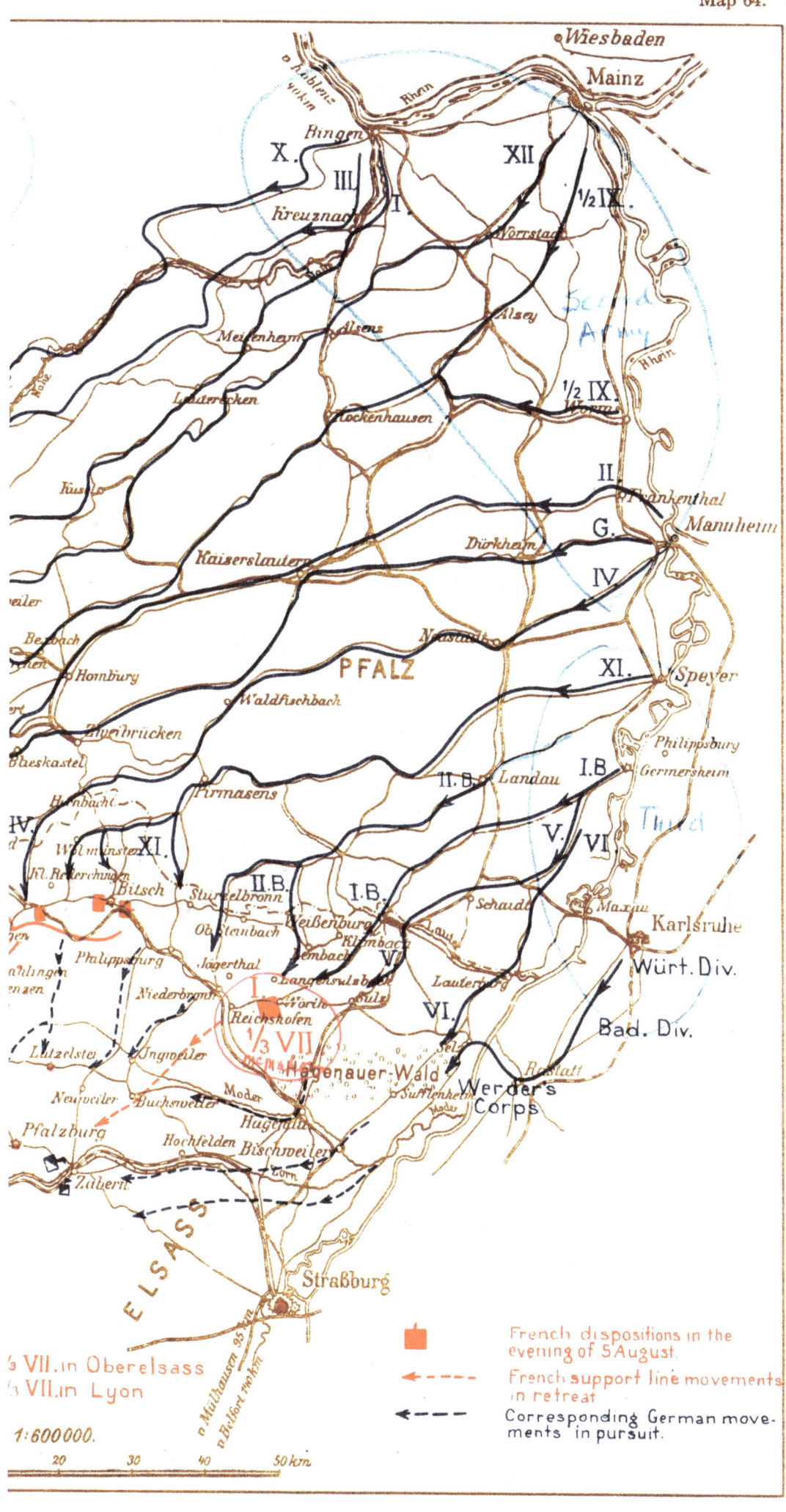

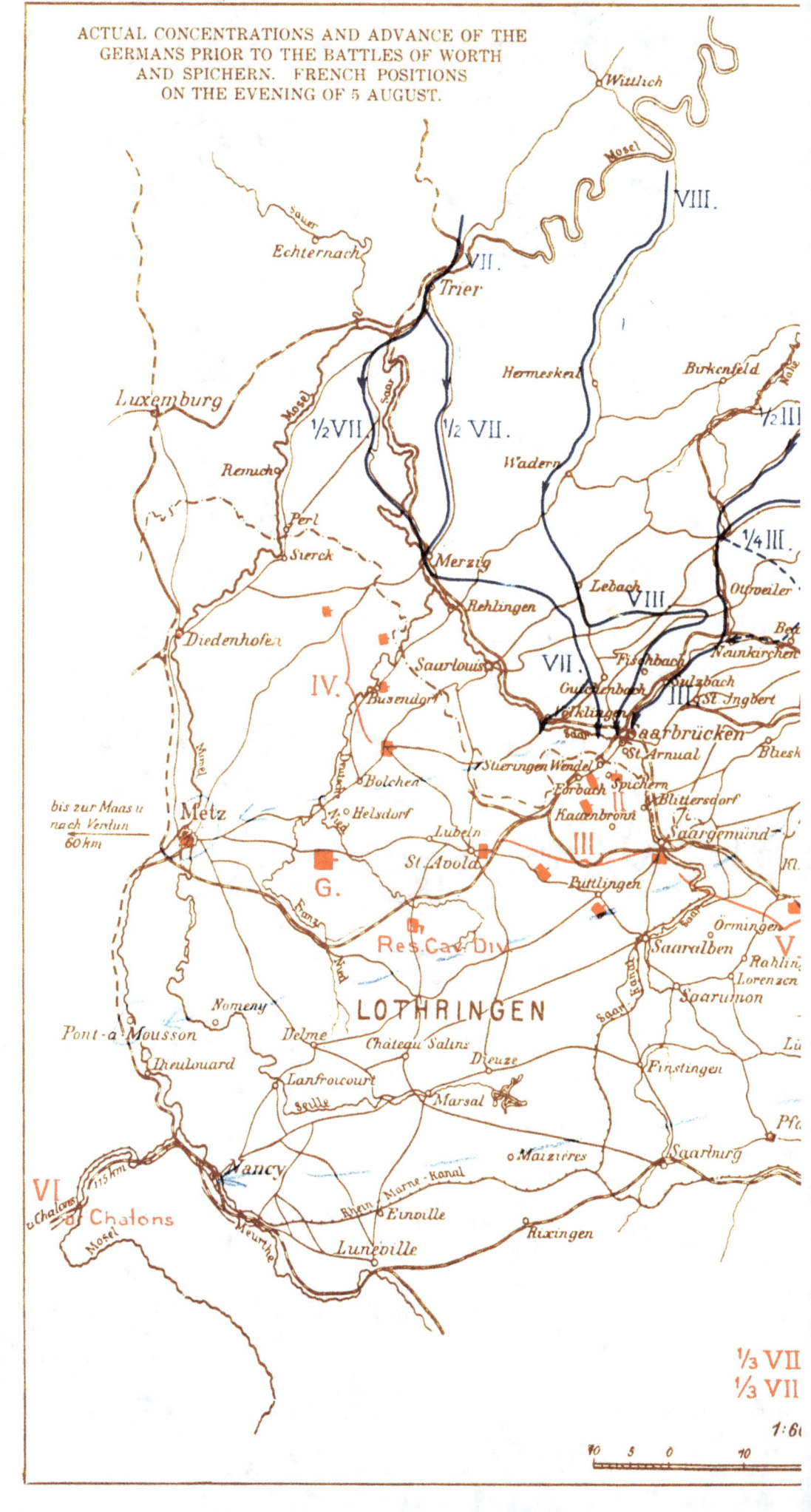

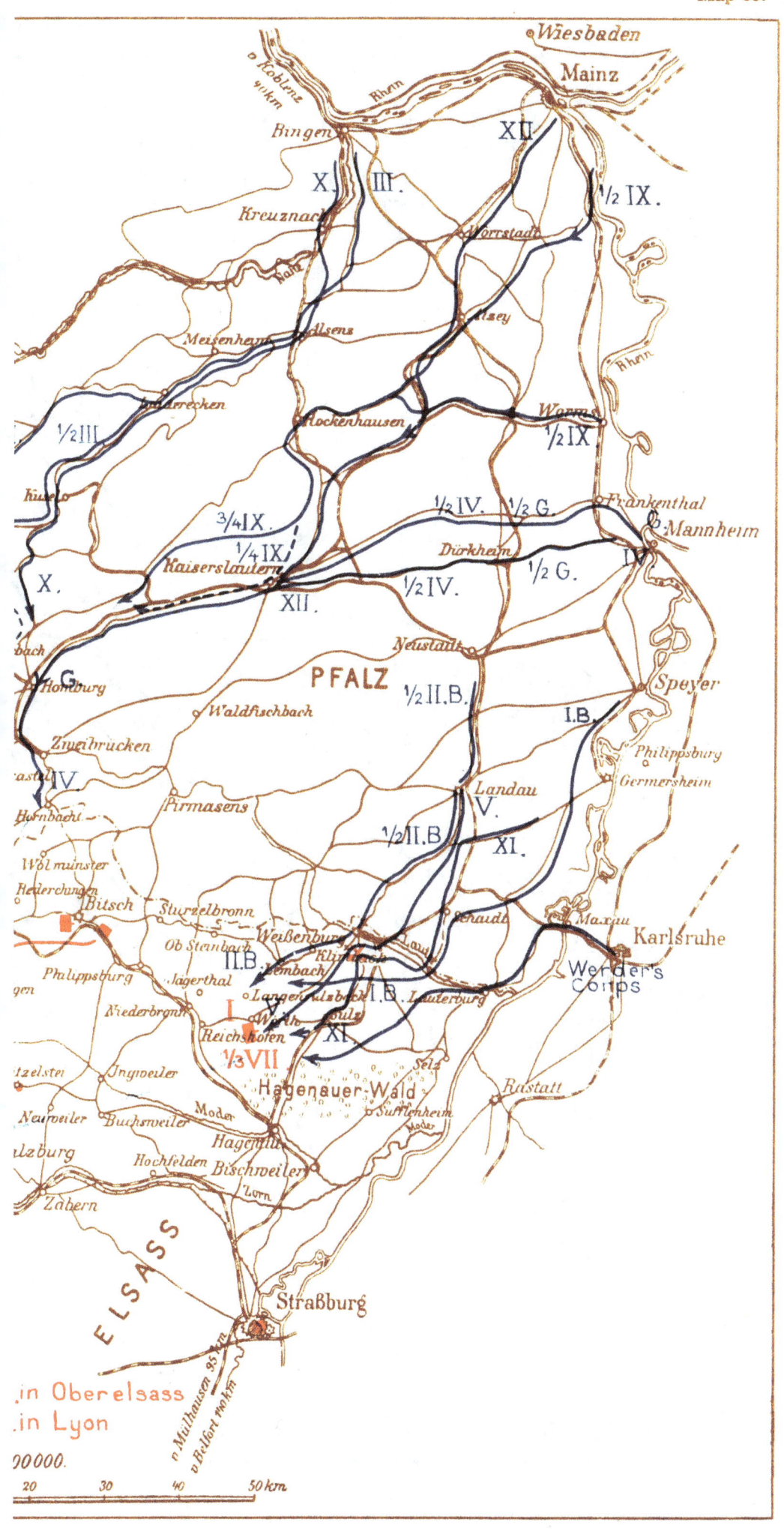

Map 65.

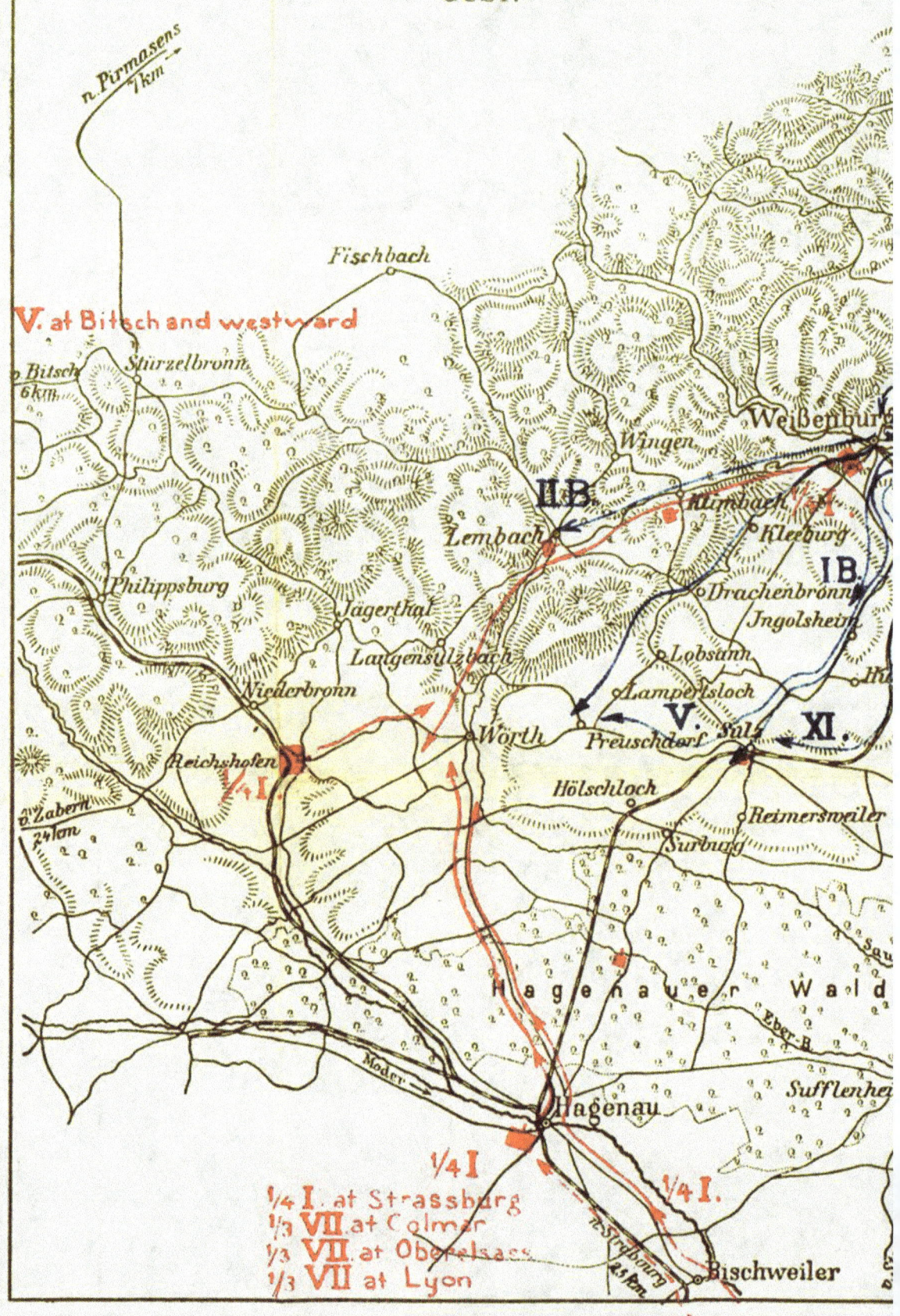

MOVEMENTS OF THE THIRD ARMY AND OF MacMAHON'S TROOPS FROM THE EVENING OF 3 AUGUST TO THE EVENING OF 5 AUGUST.

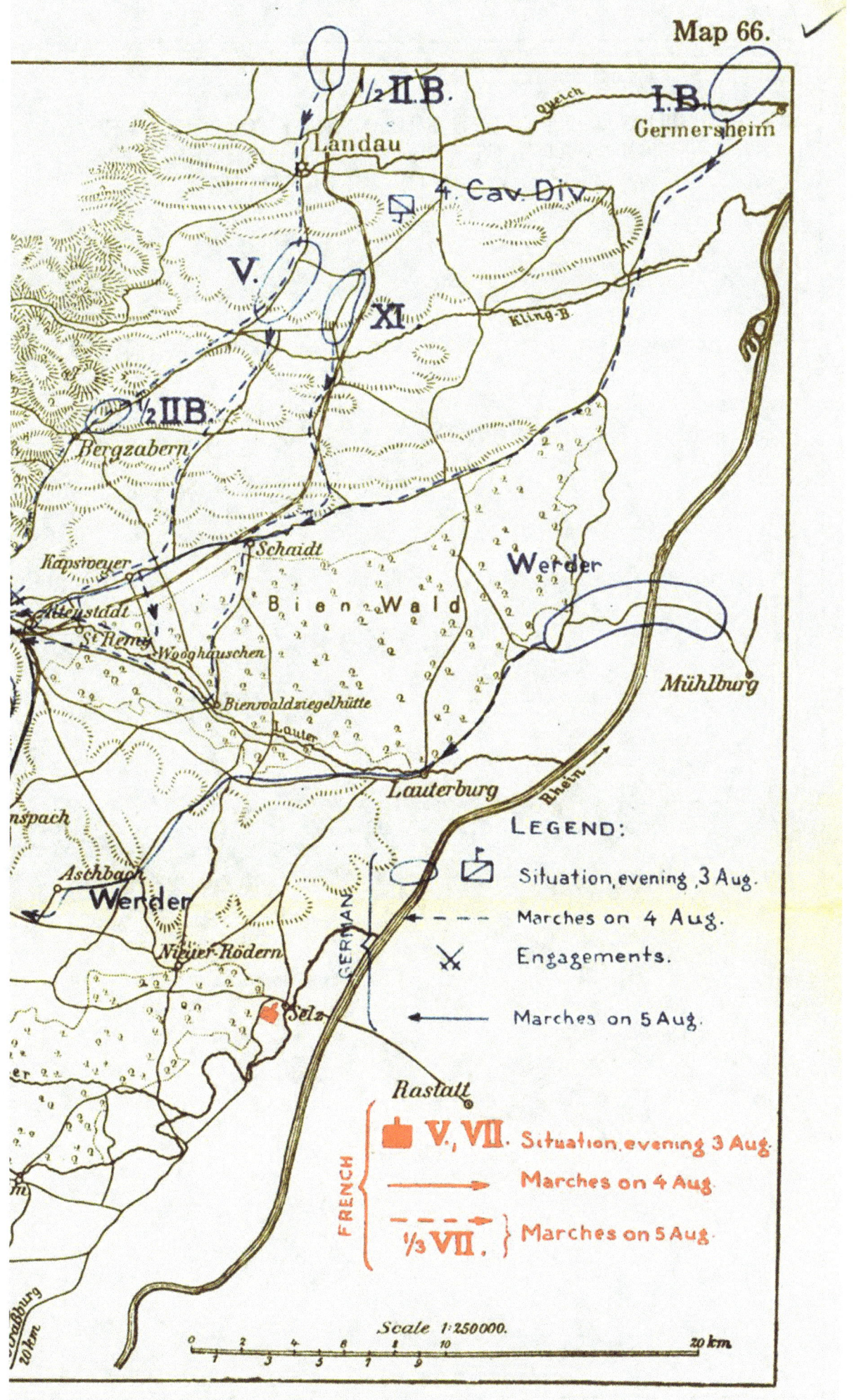

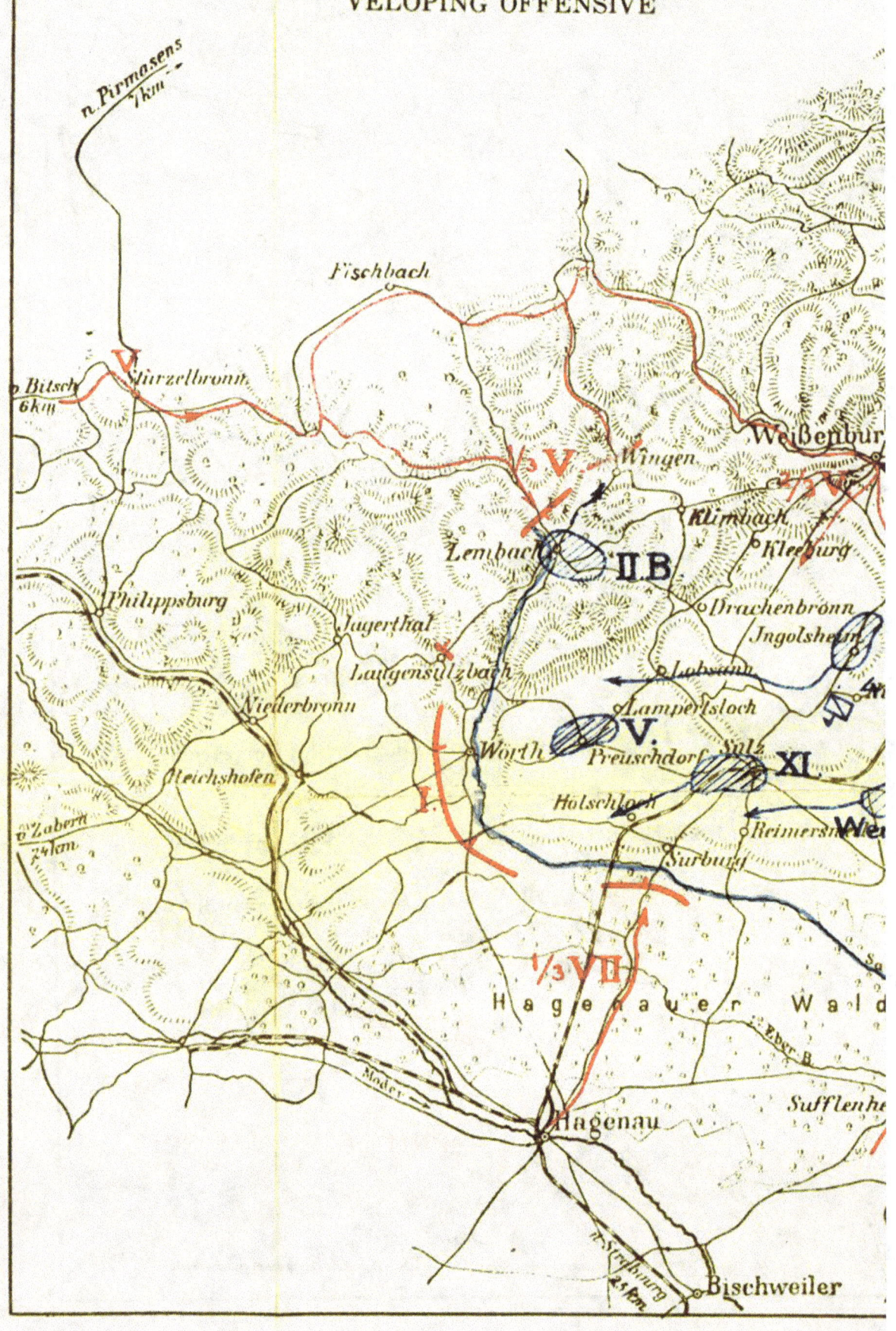

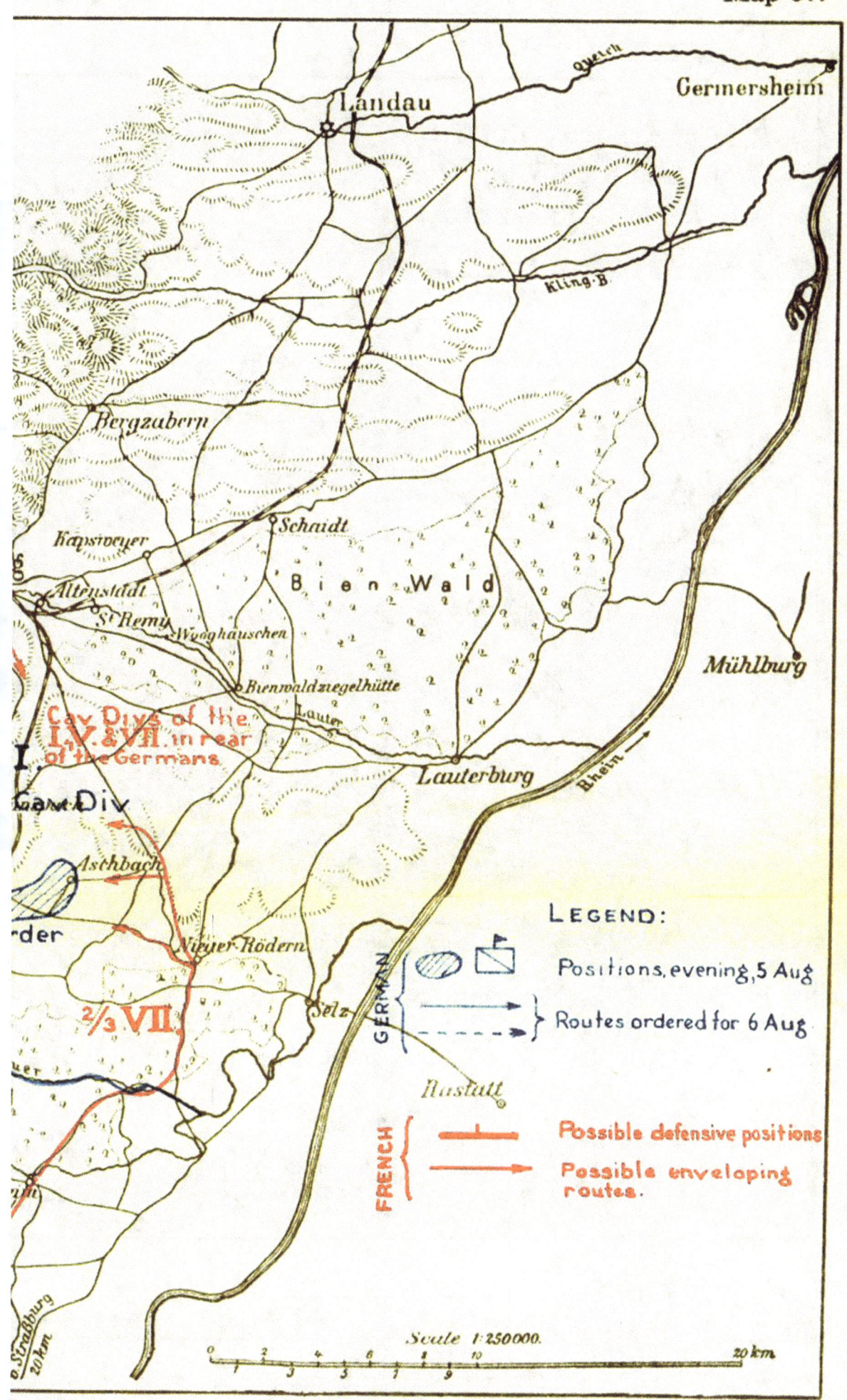

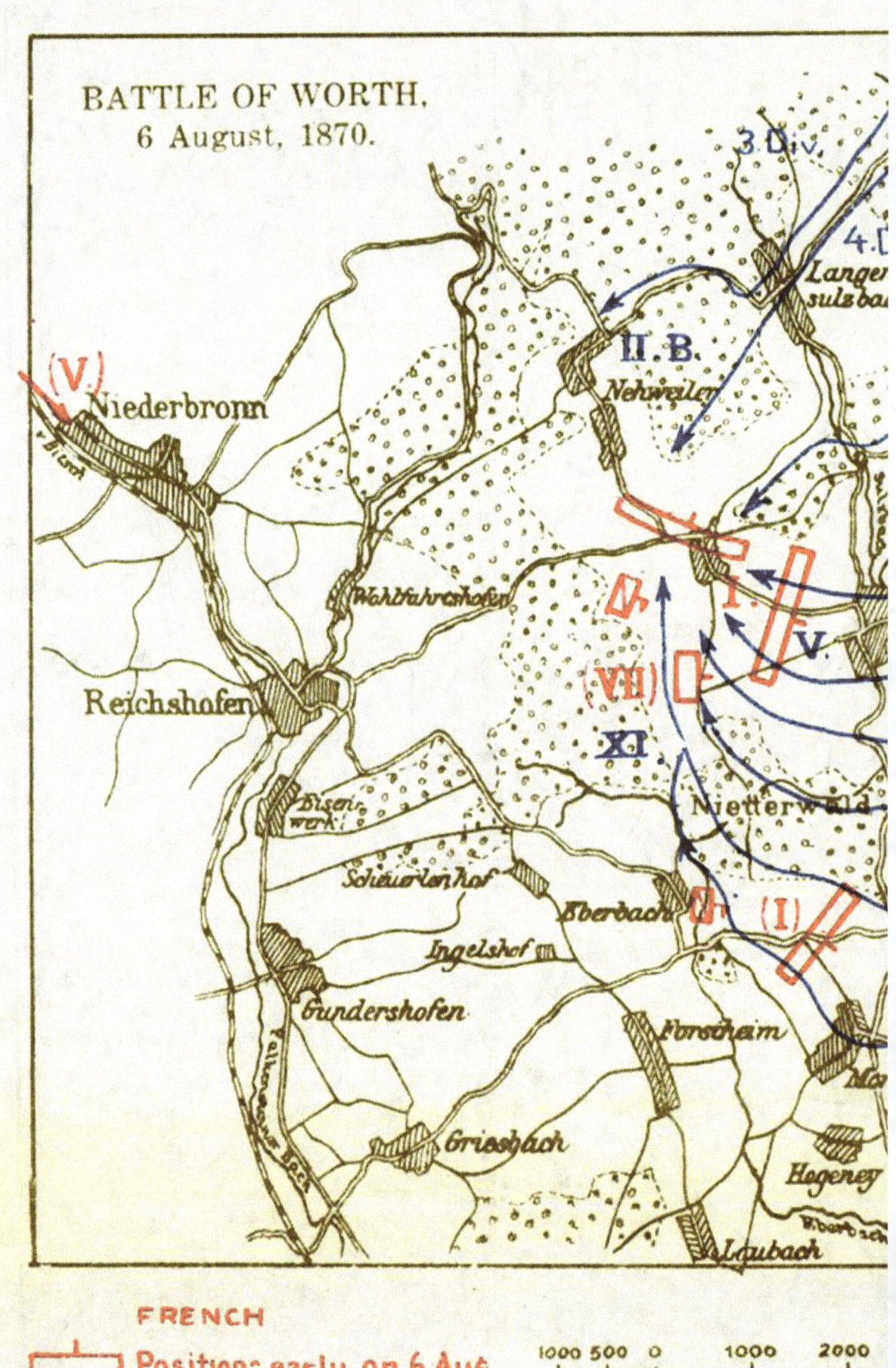

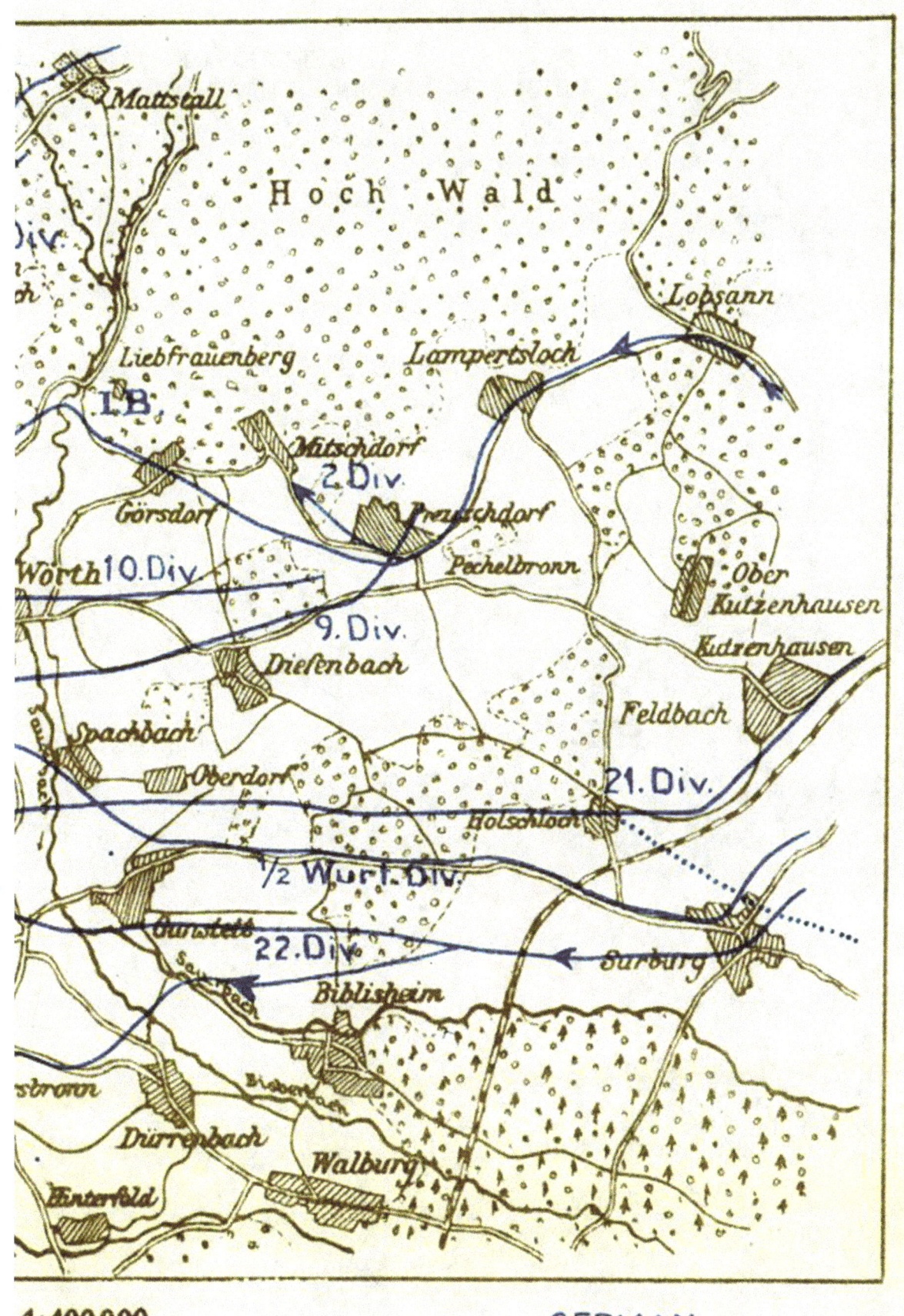

Map 68.

1:100 000

GERMAN
.... Outposts night 5 & 6 Aug
⟵ Marches and combats up until noon.

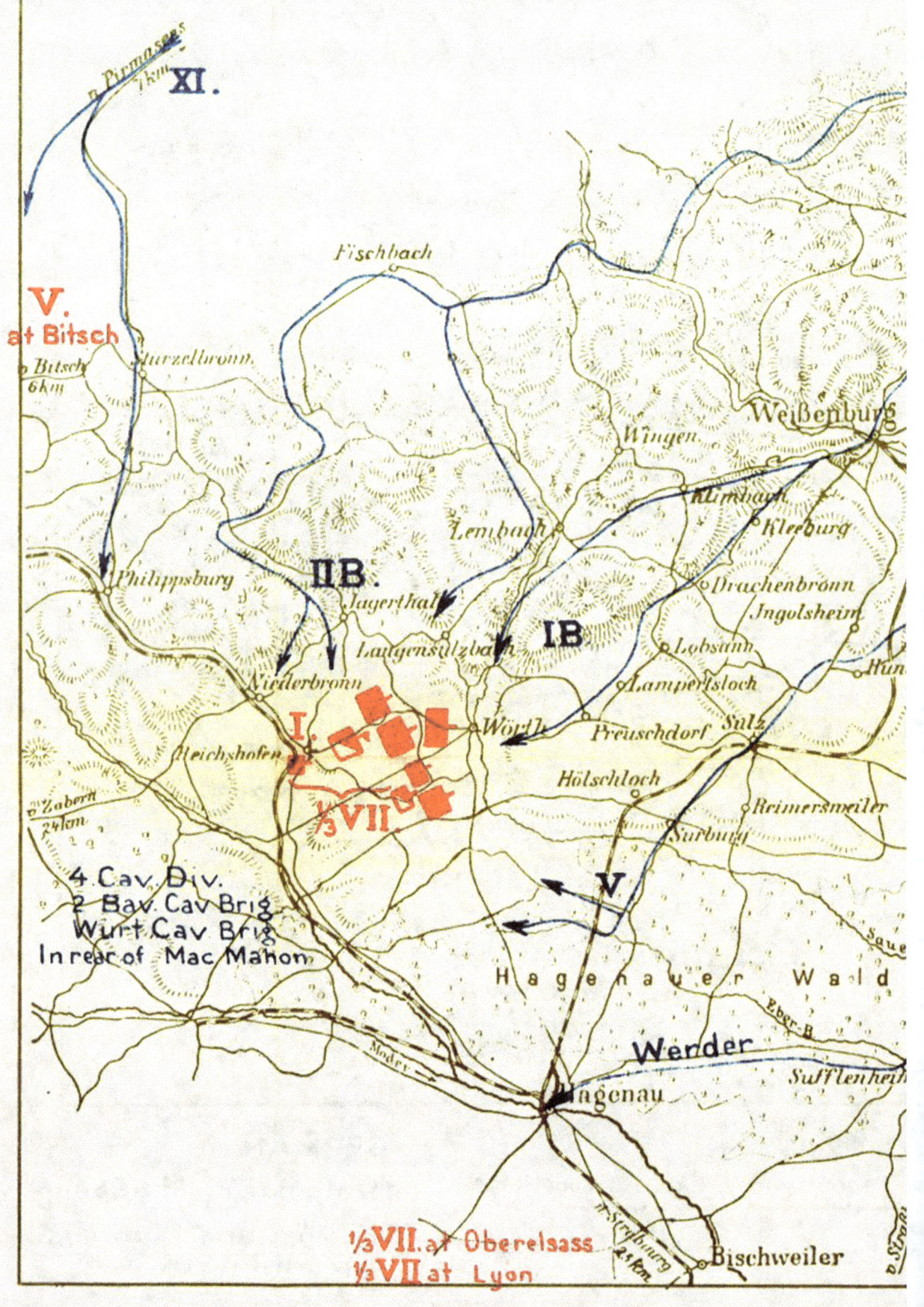

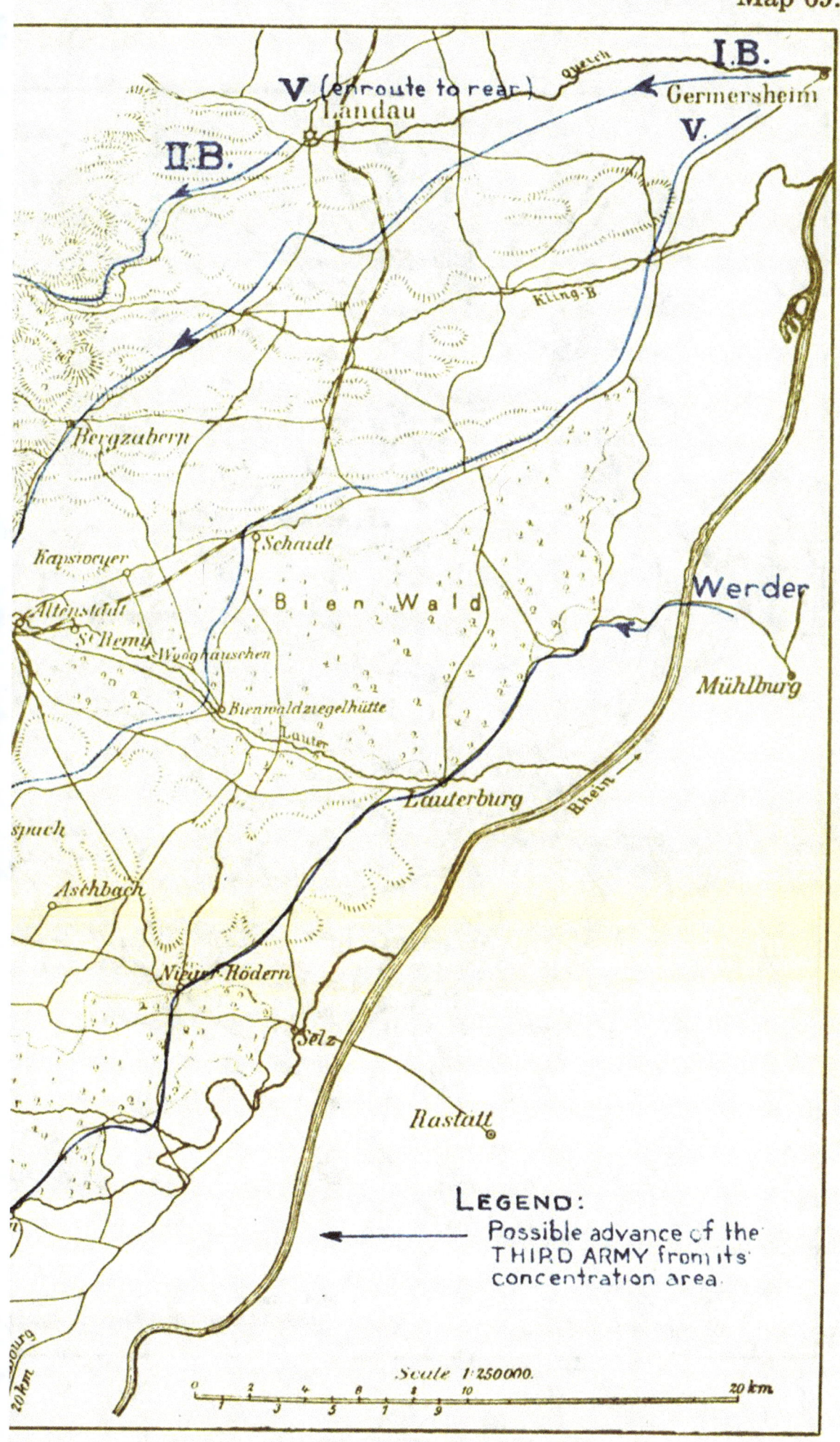

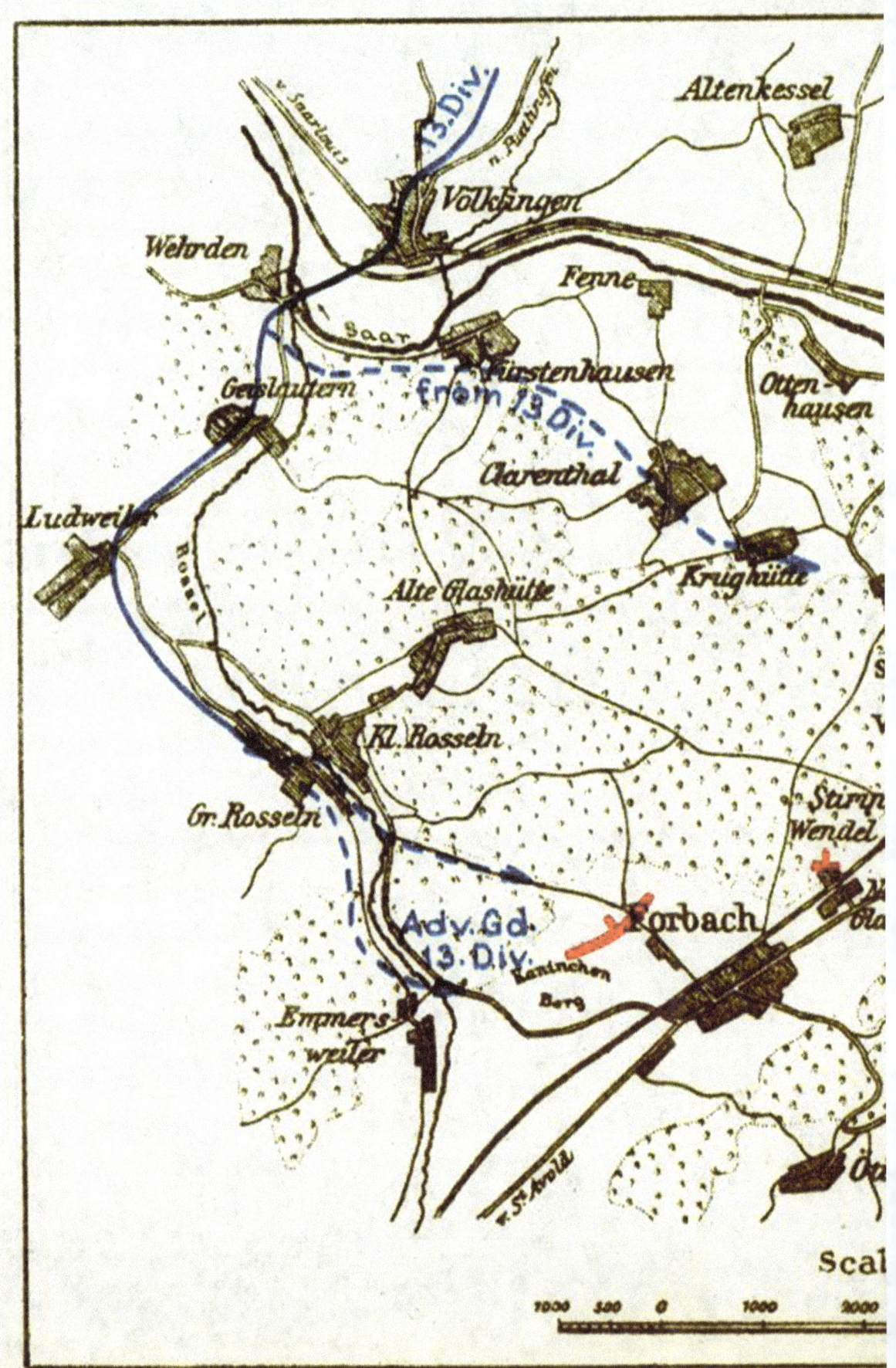

SPICHERN.   Map 70.

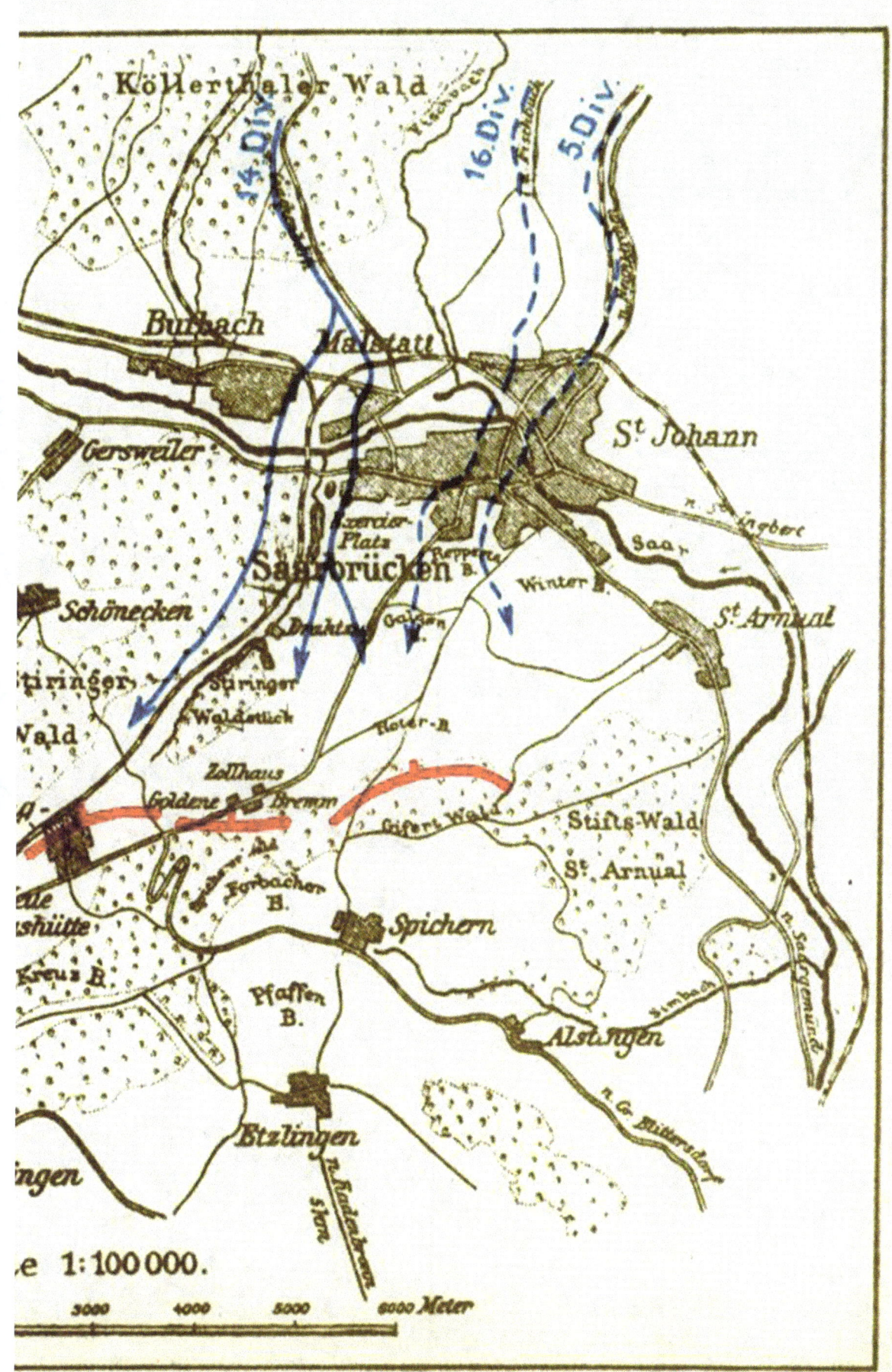

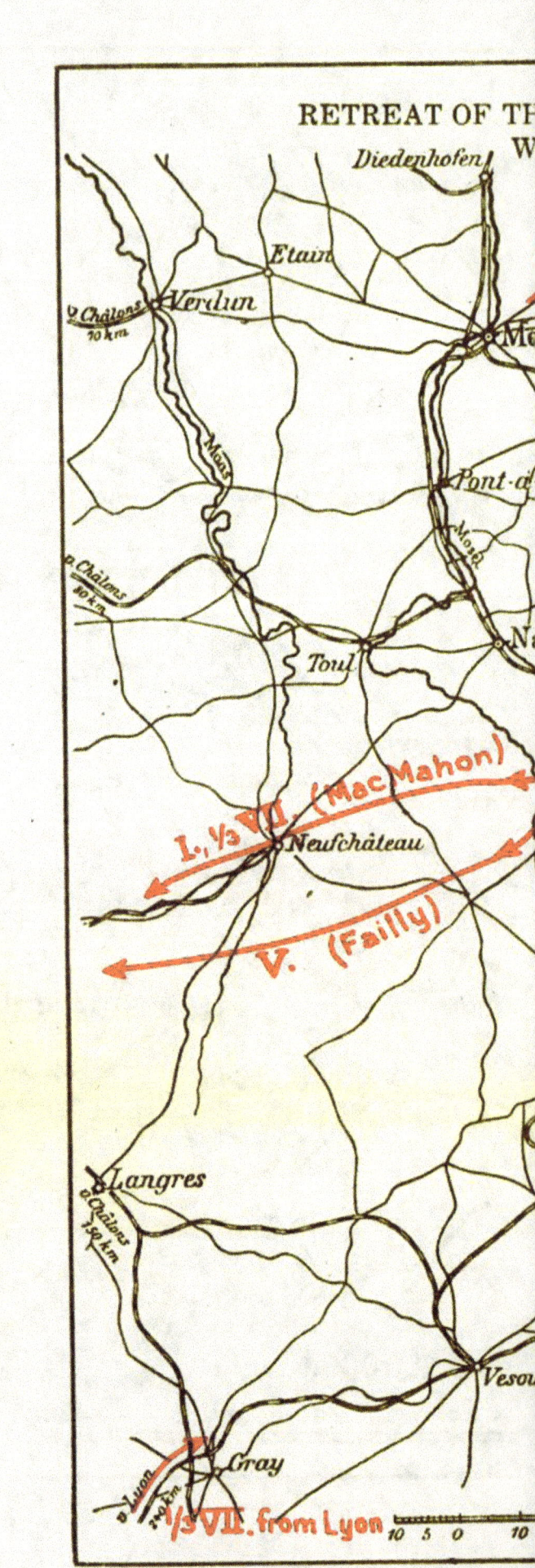

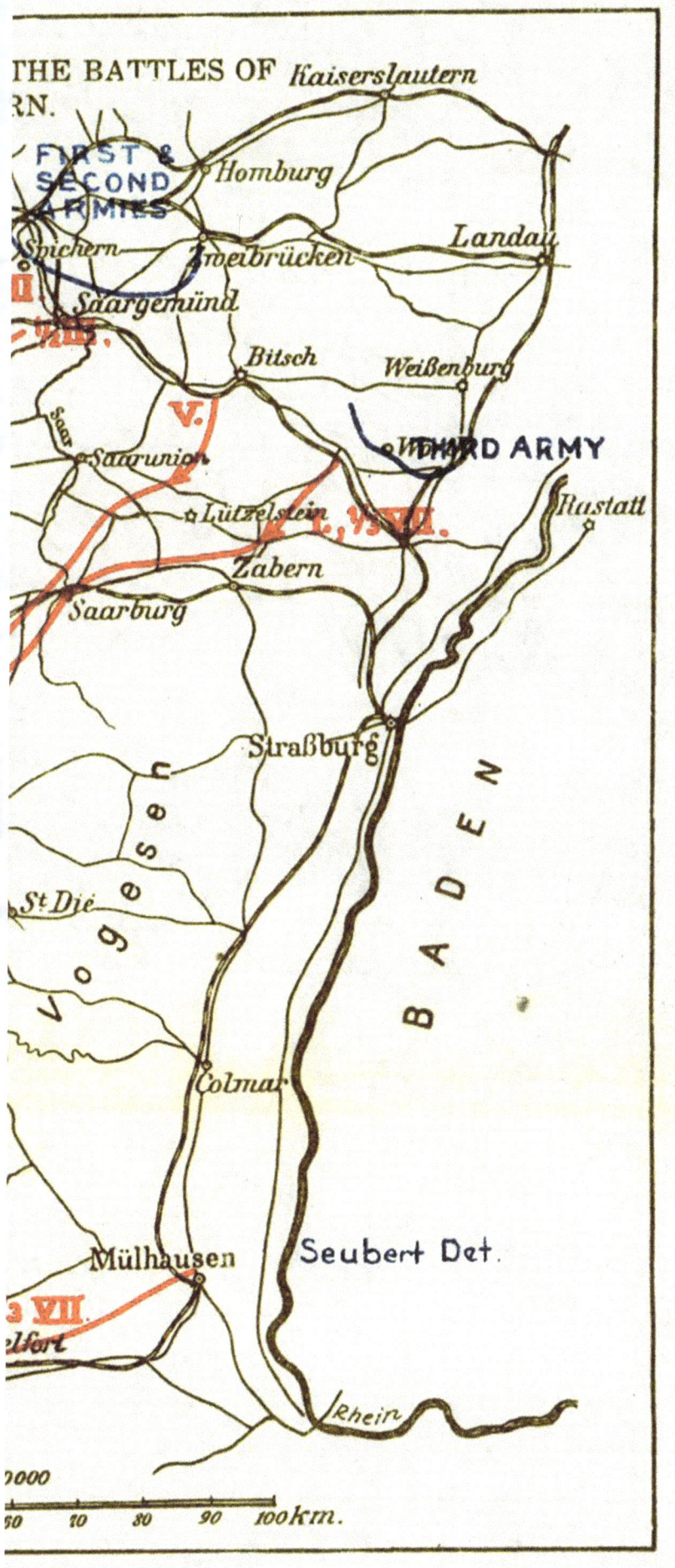

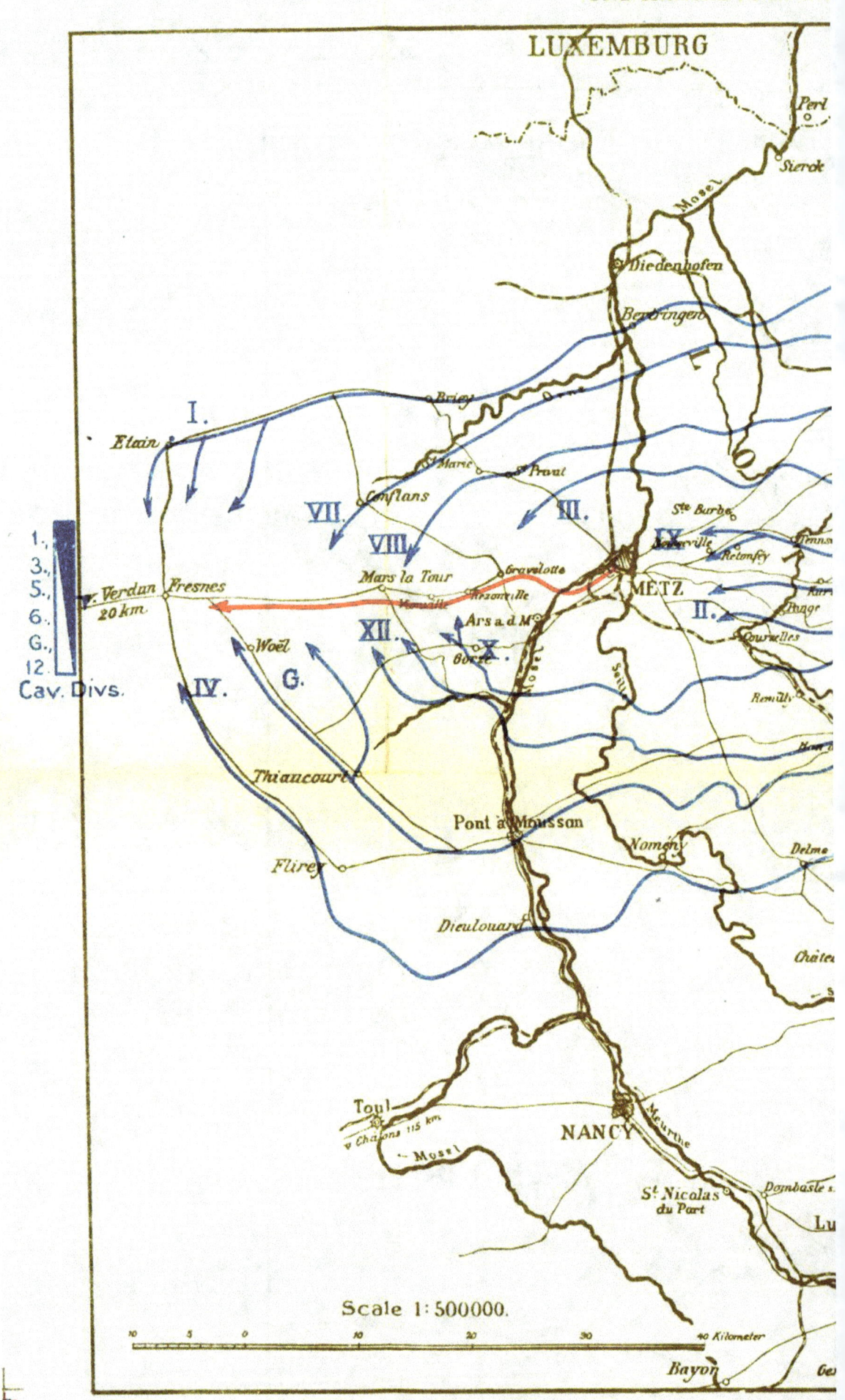

OF THE FIRST AND SEC-
BEYOND THE MOSELLE

Map 72.

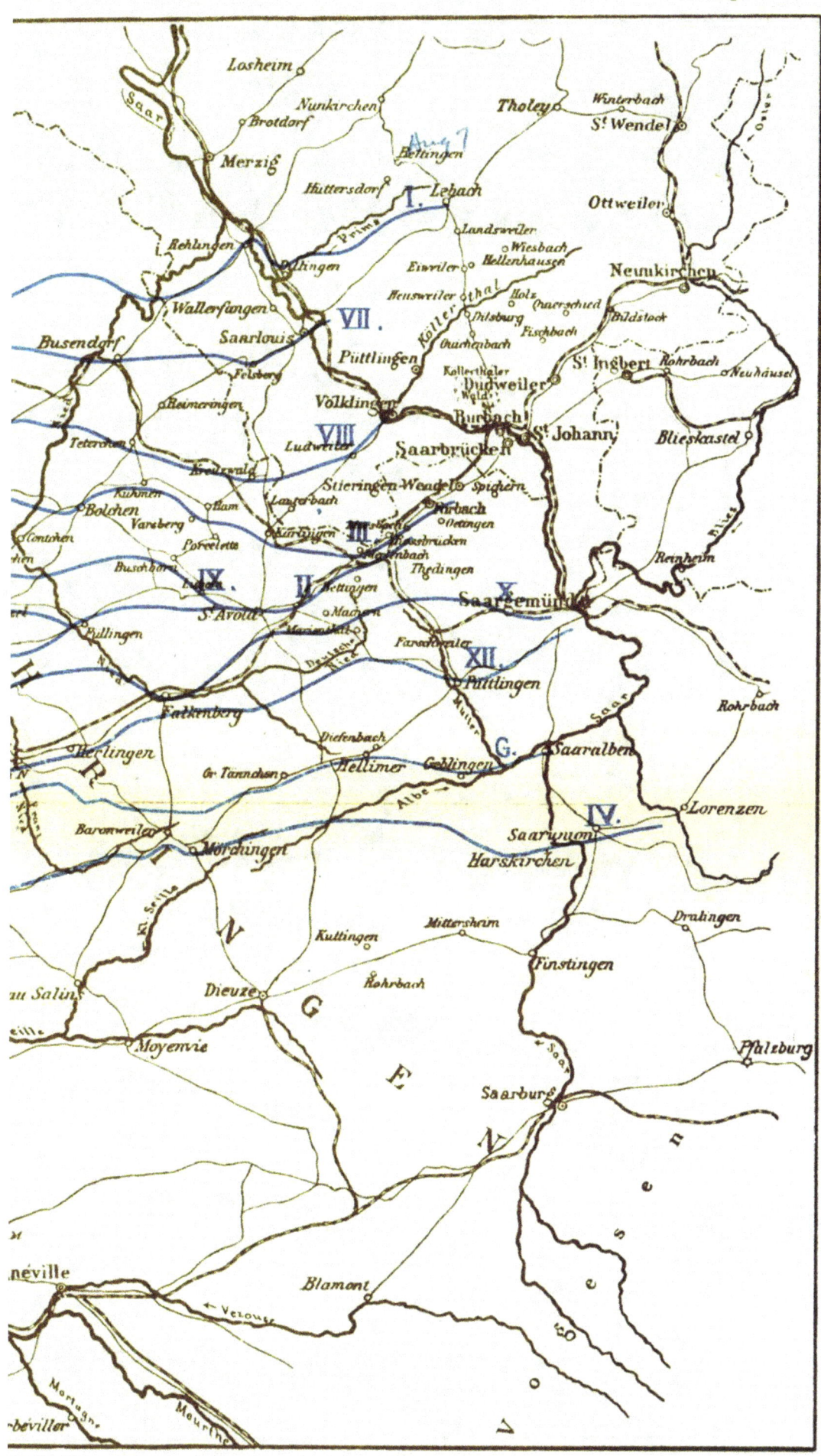

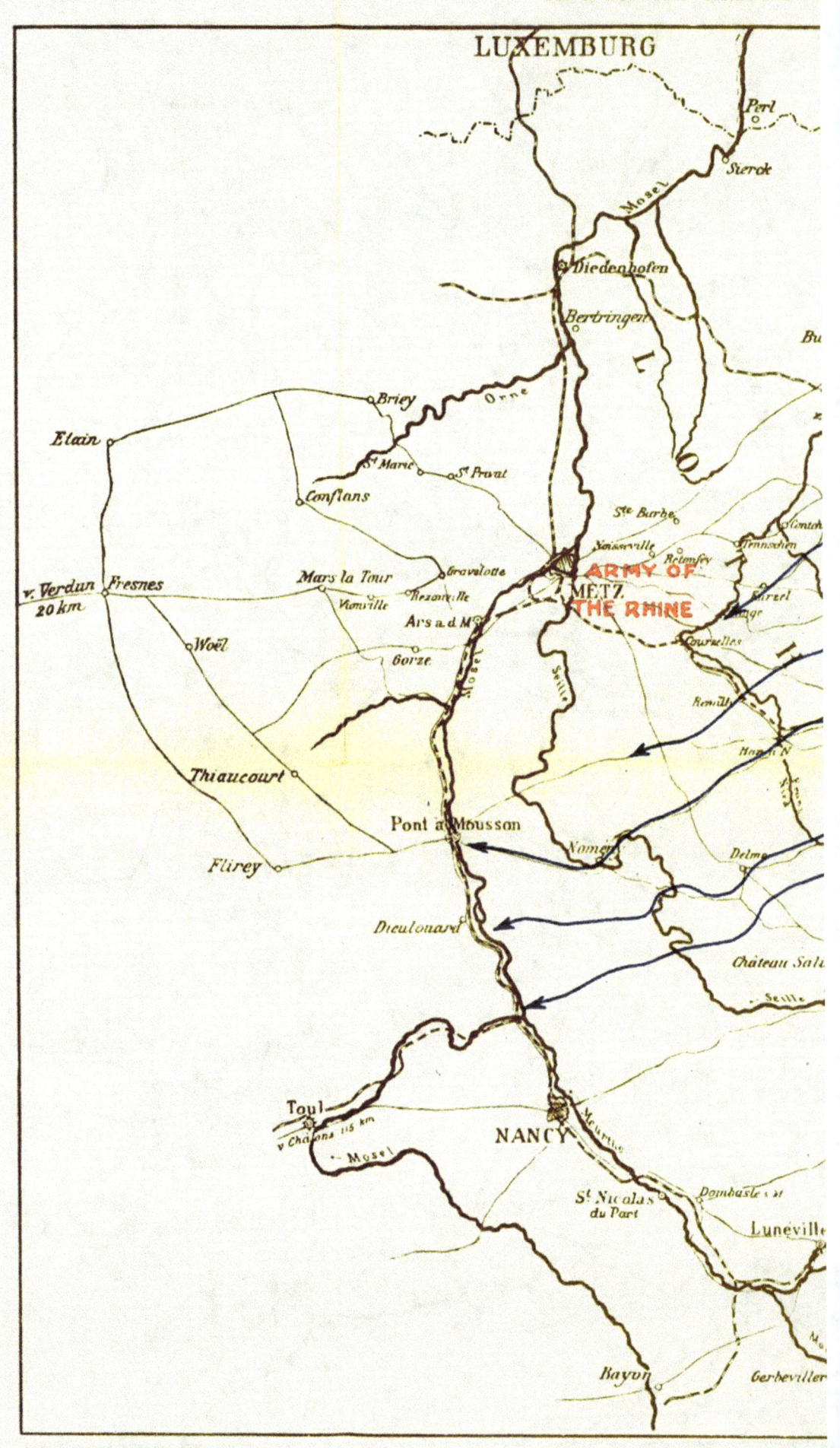

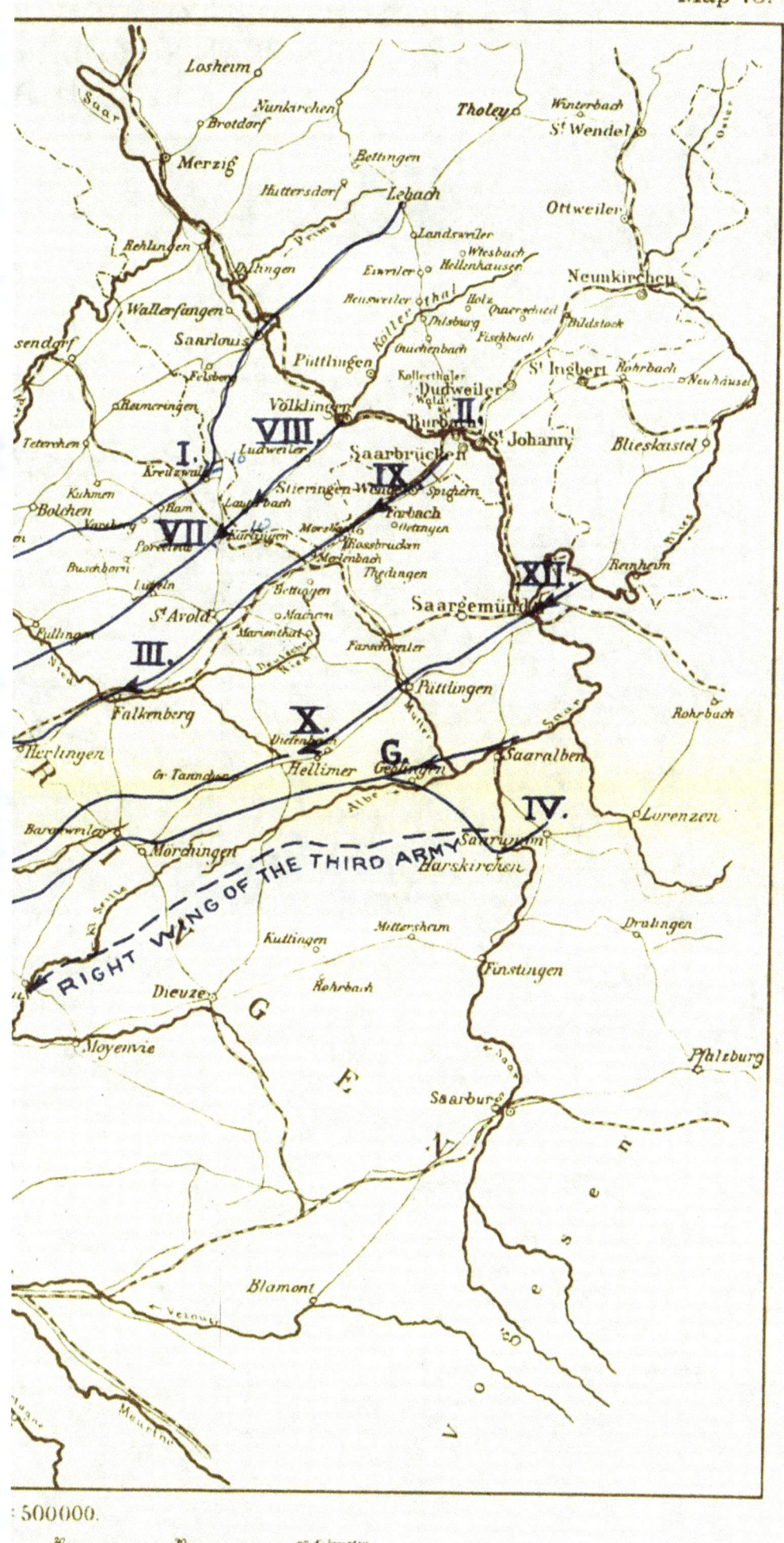

ANCE OF THE FIRST
THE MOSELLE.

Map 73.

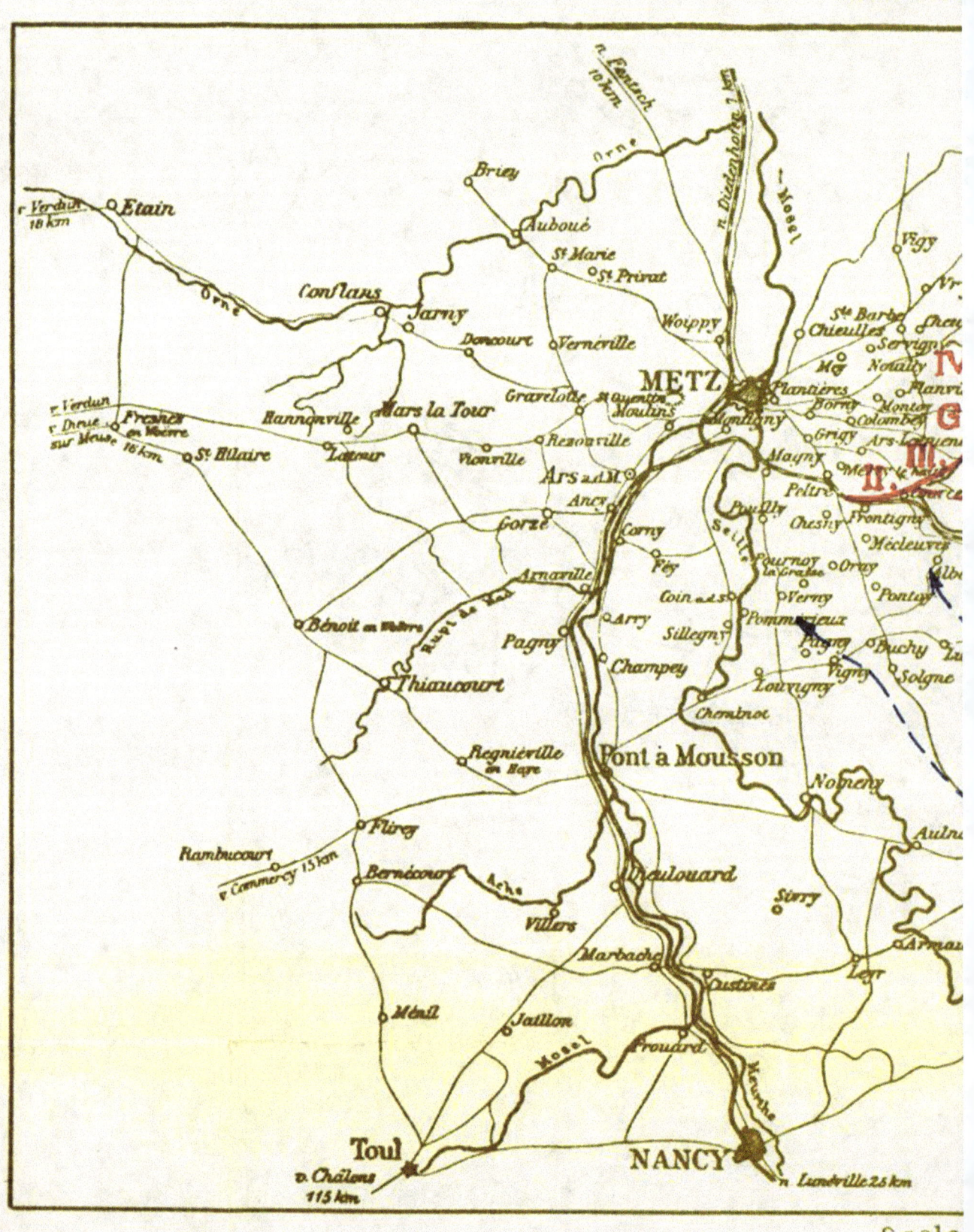

FRENCH POSITIONS ON 10
TERS' PLAN FOR OPER
OND A

AUGUST. HEADQUAR-
ATIONS BY THE SEC-
RMY.

Map 74.

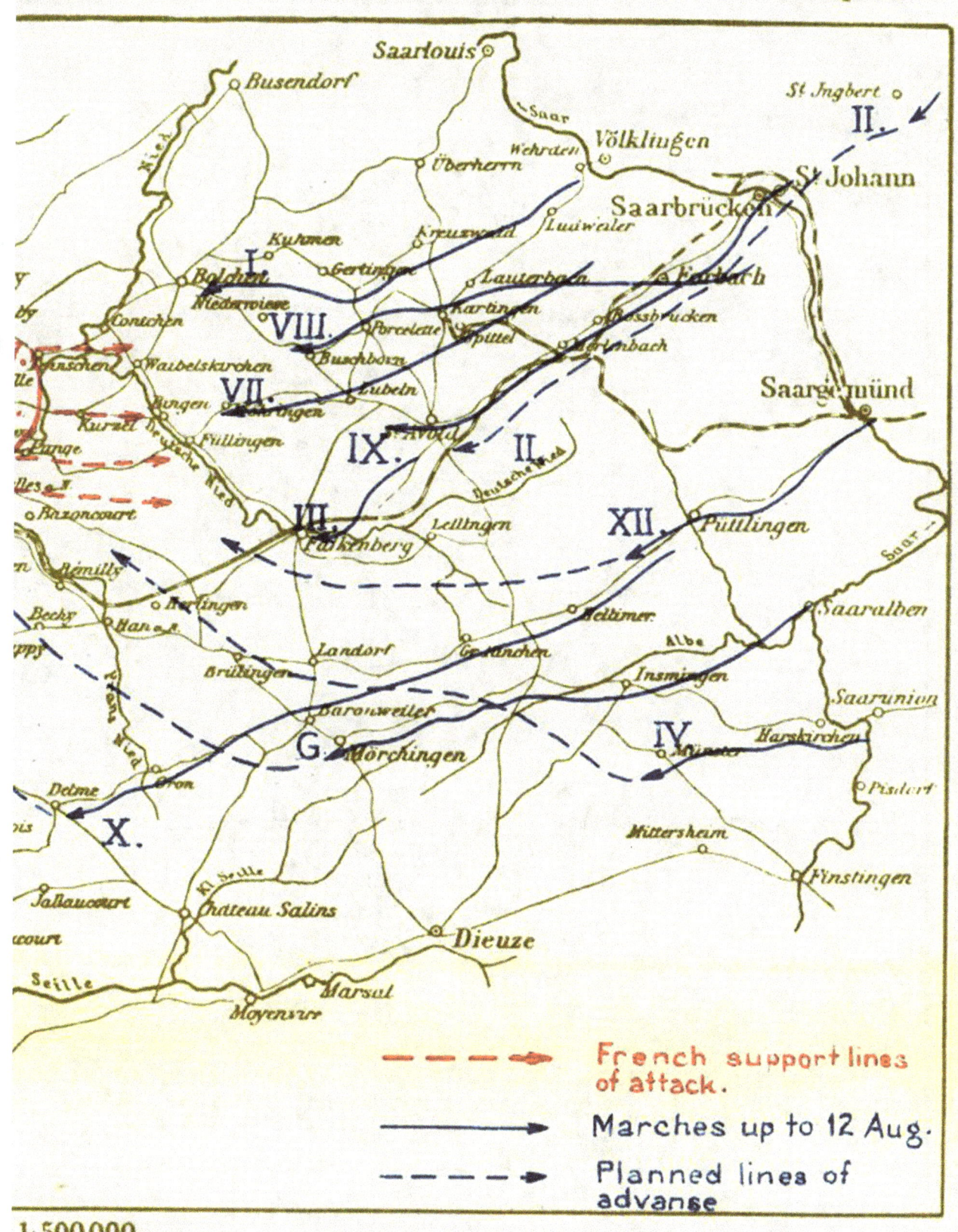

SITUATION ON THE EV

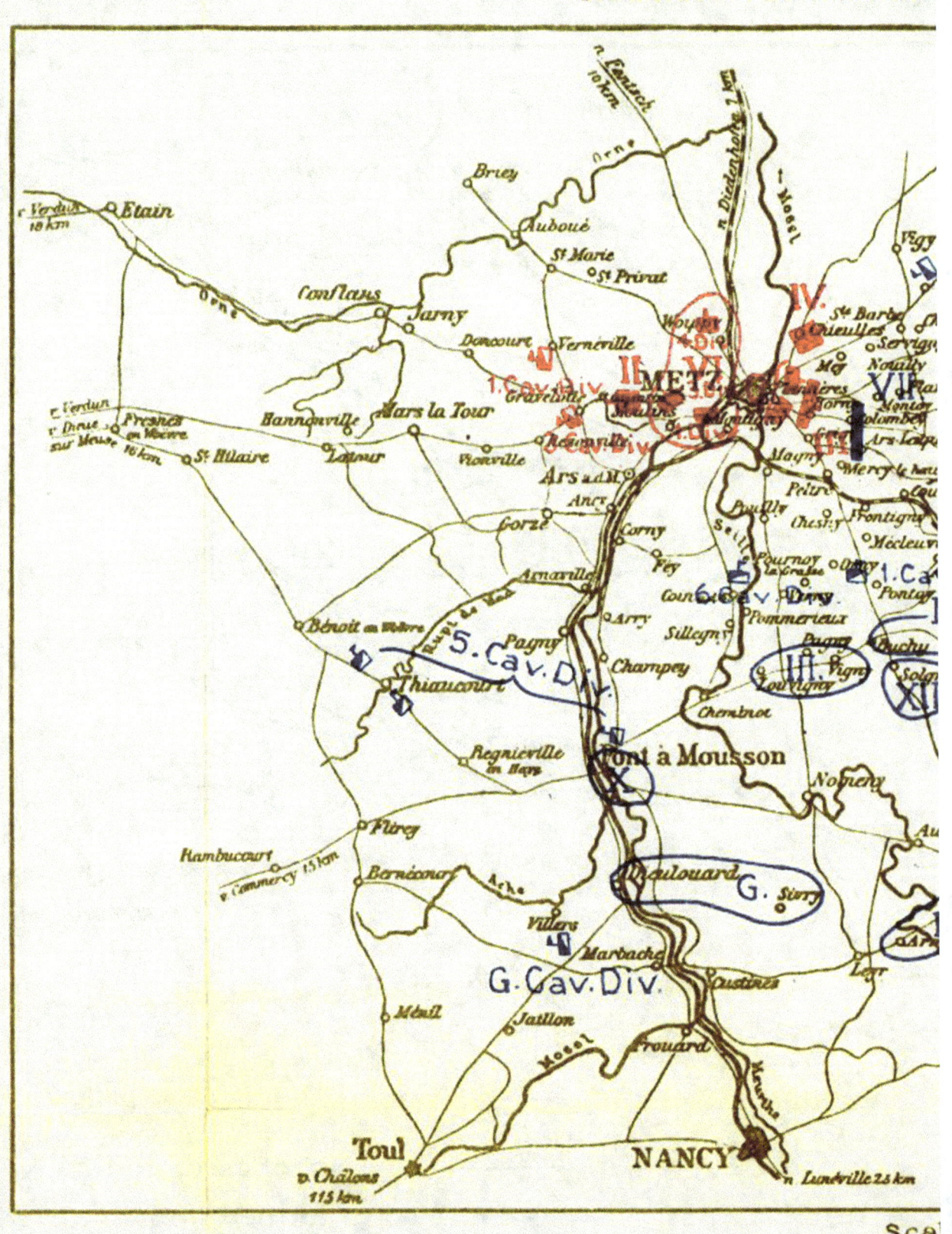

ENING OF 14 AUGUST. Map 75.

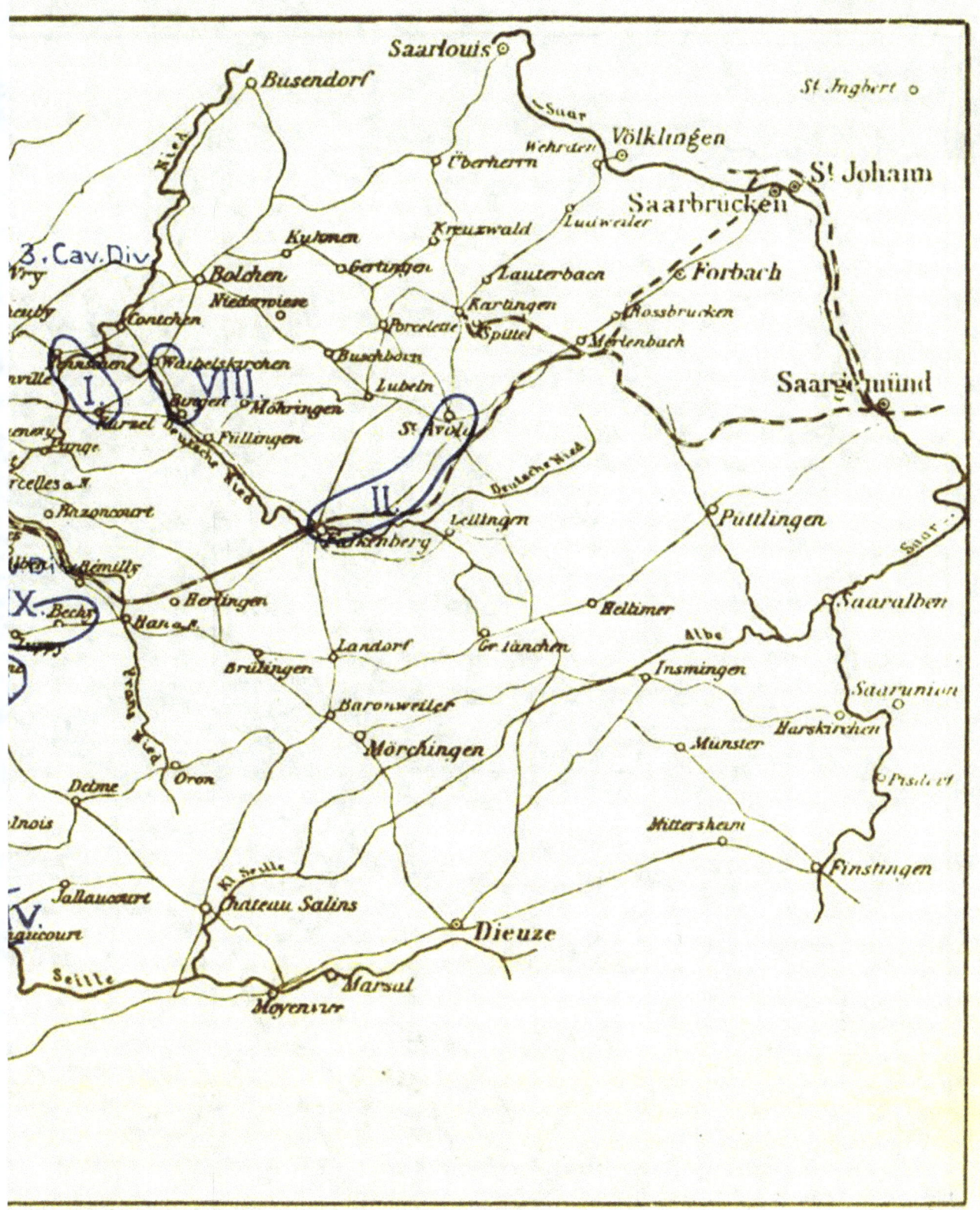

SITUATION ON THE EVEN[ING]
FOR THE FURTHER ADV[ANCE]

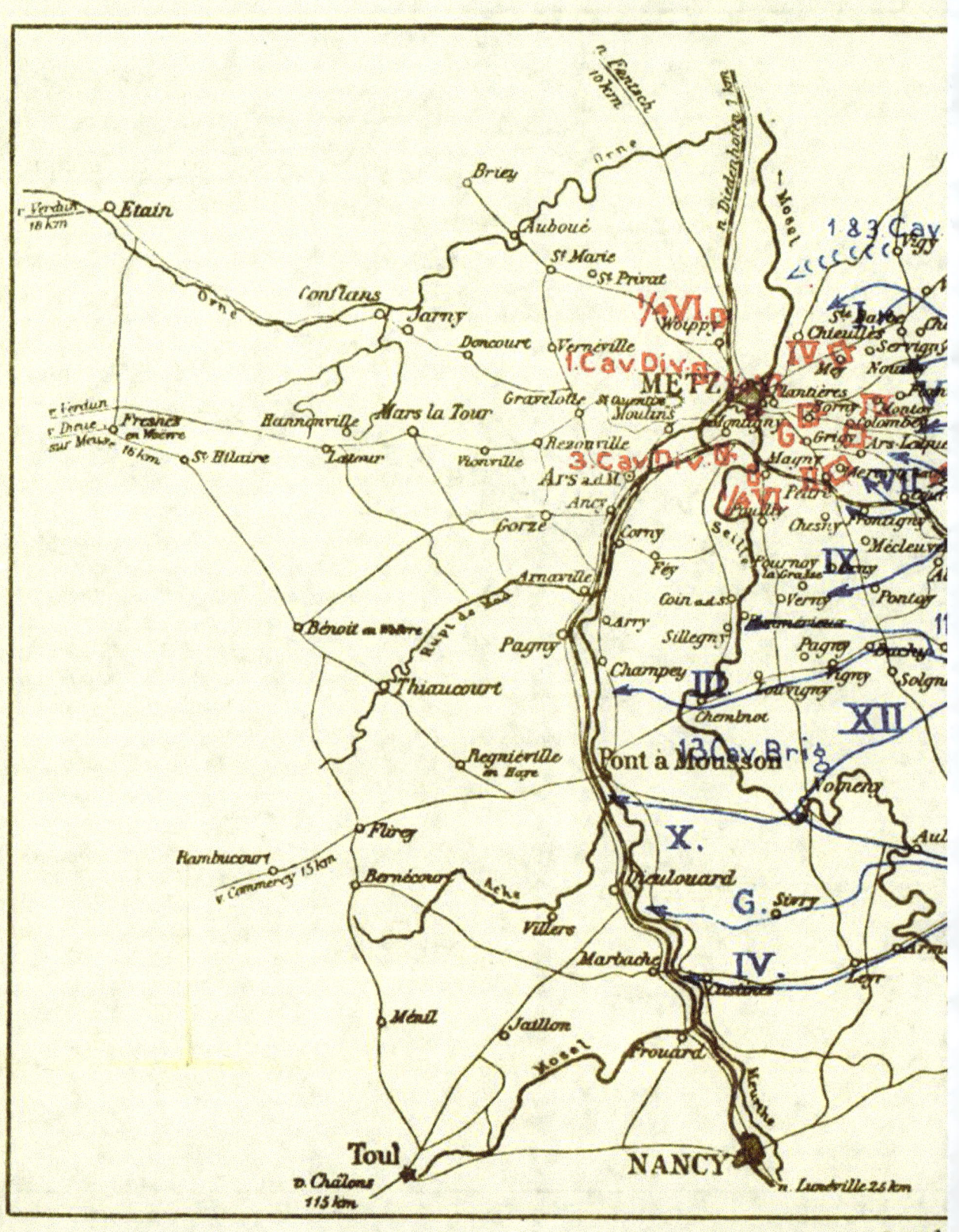

NG OF 12 AUGUST. PLAN ANCE TO THE MOSELLE

Map 76.

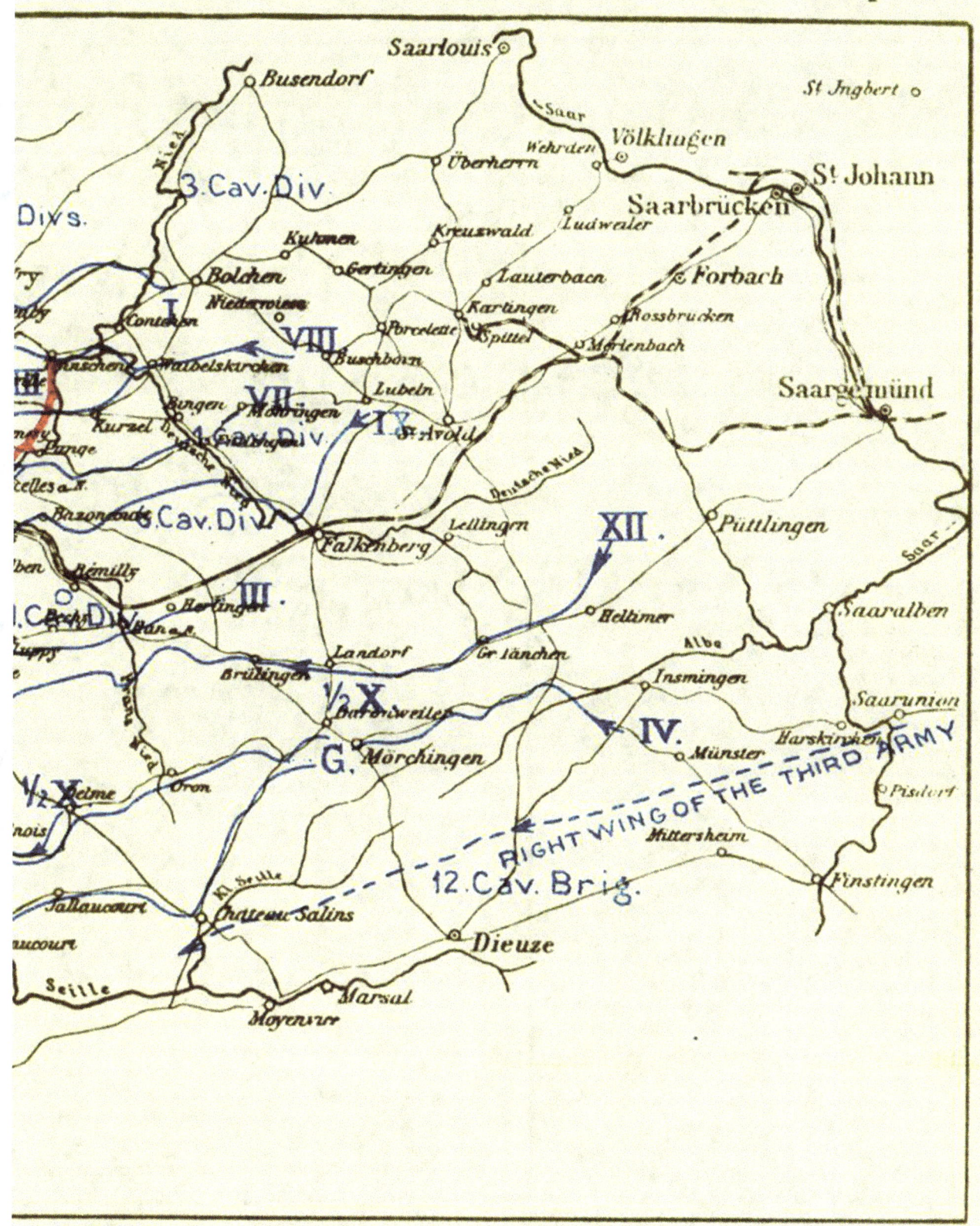

BATTLE

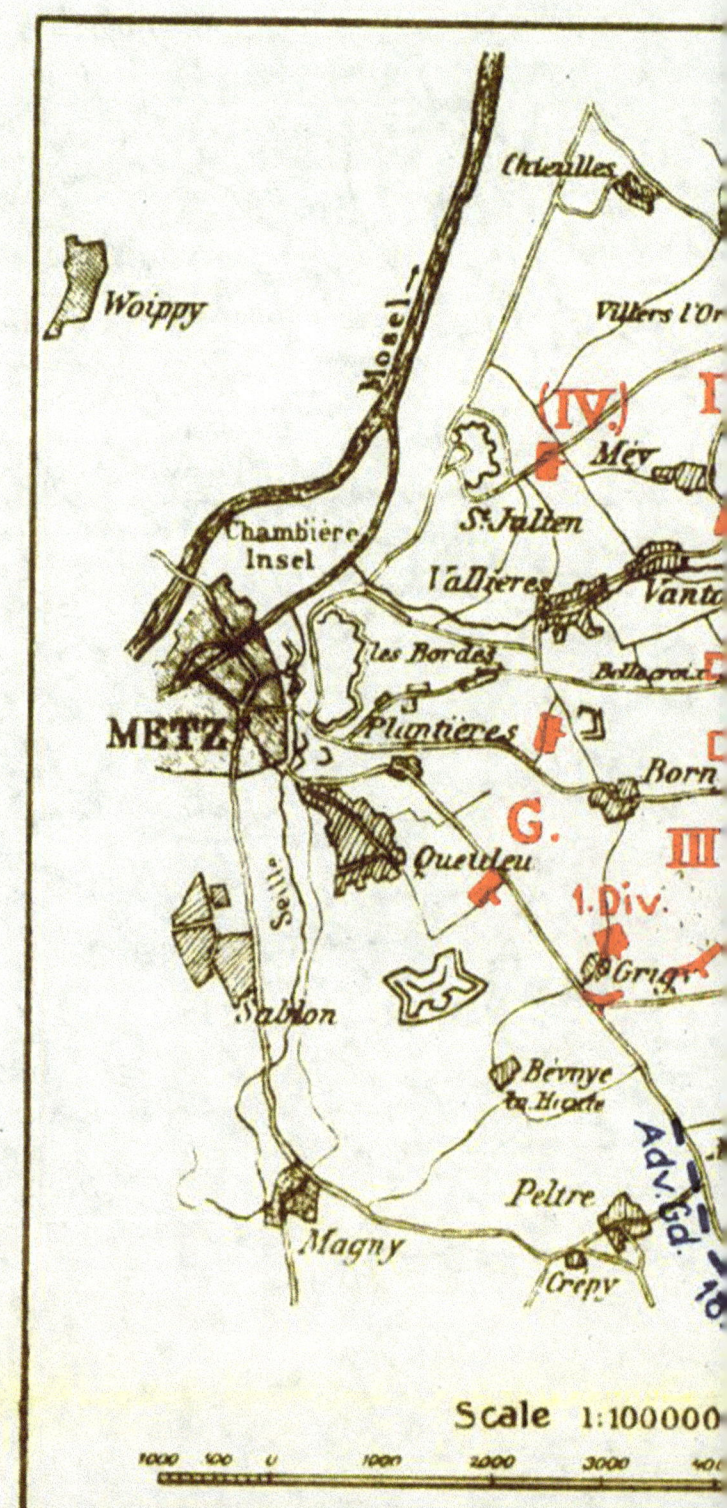

OMBEY-NOUILLY.
ust, 1870.

Map 77.

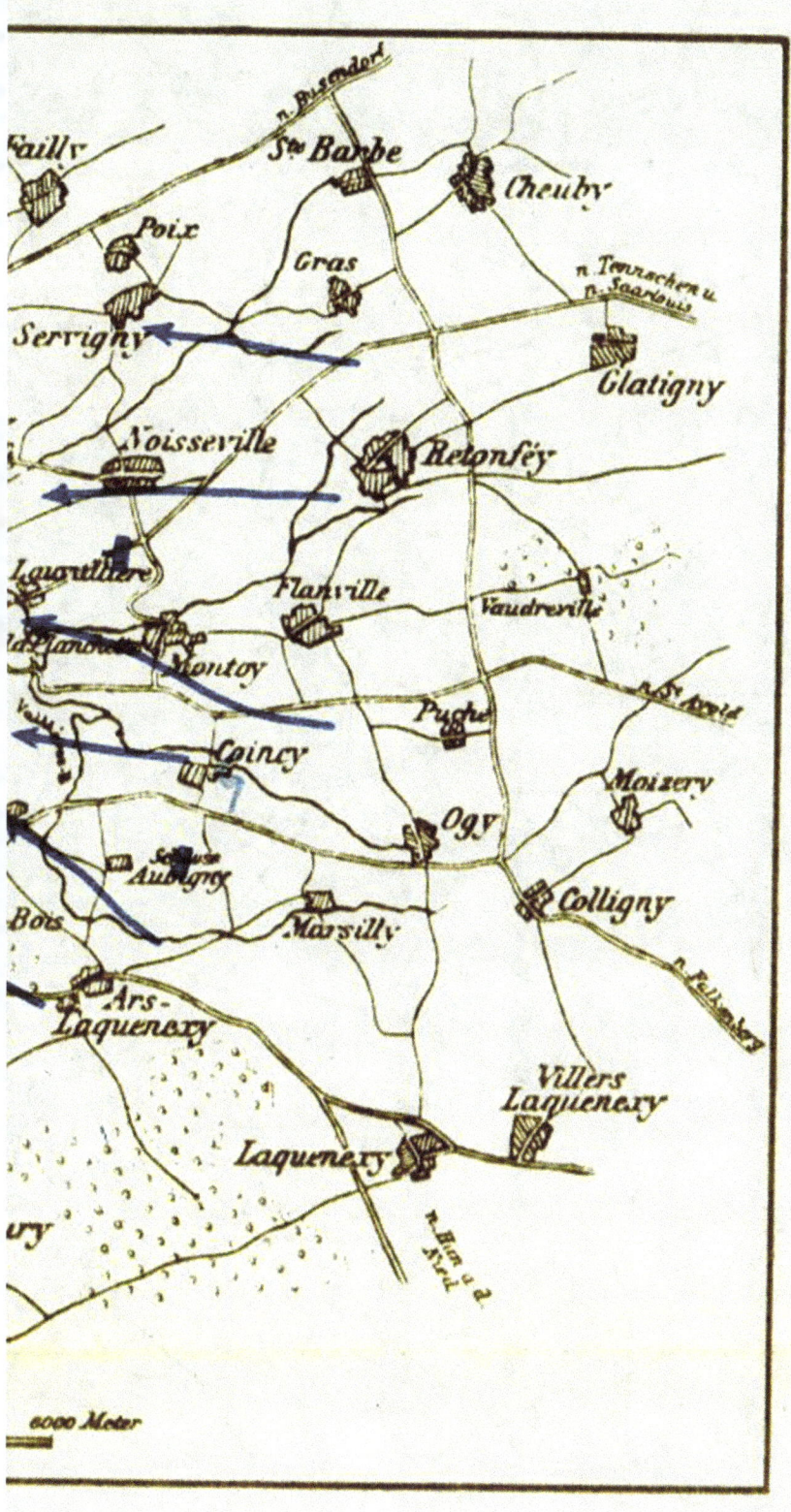

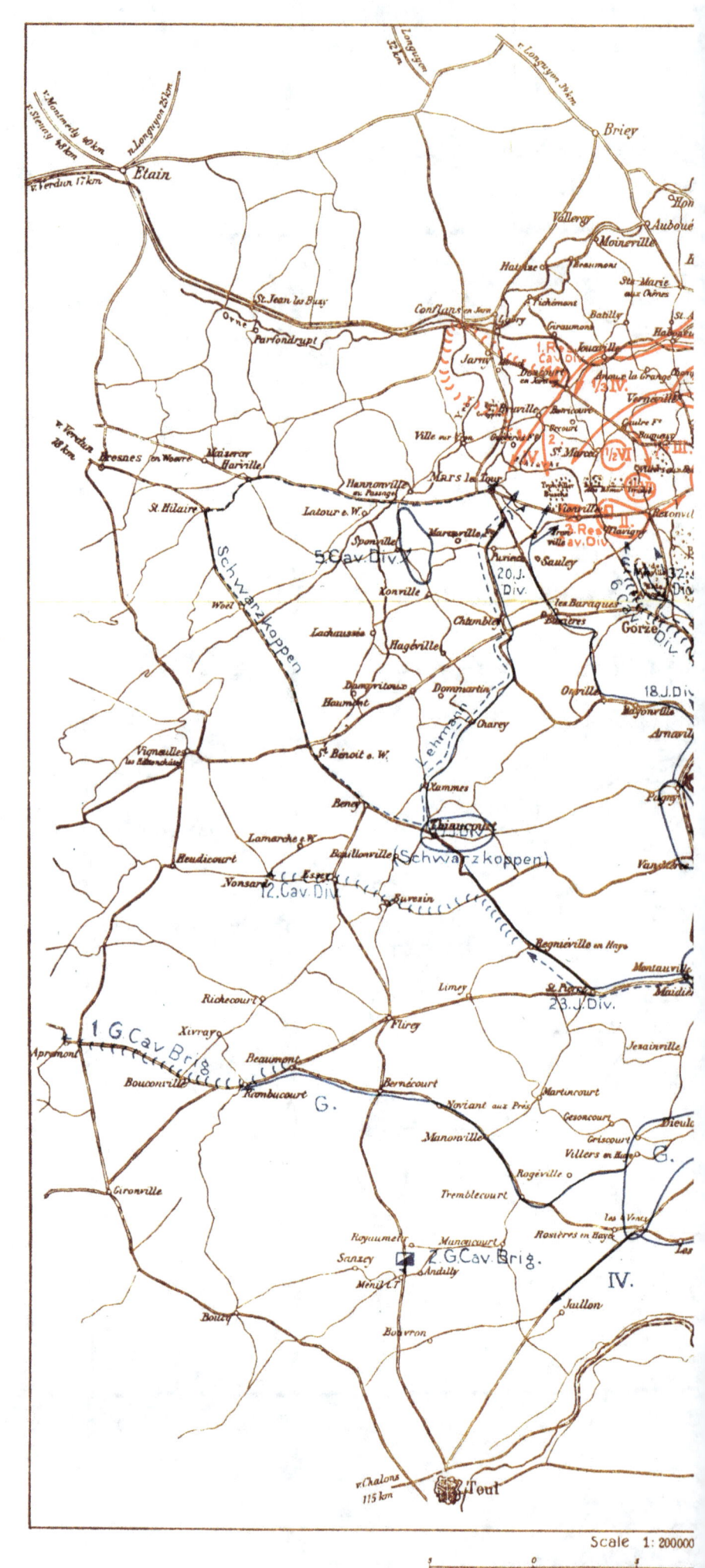

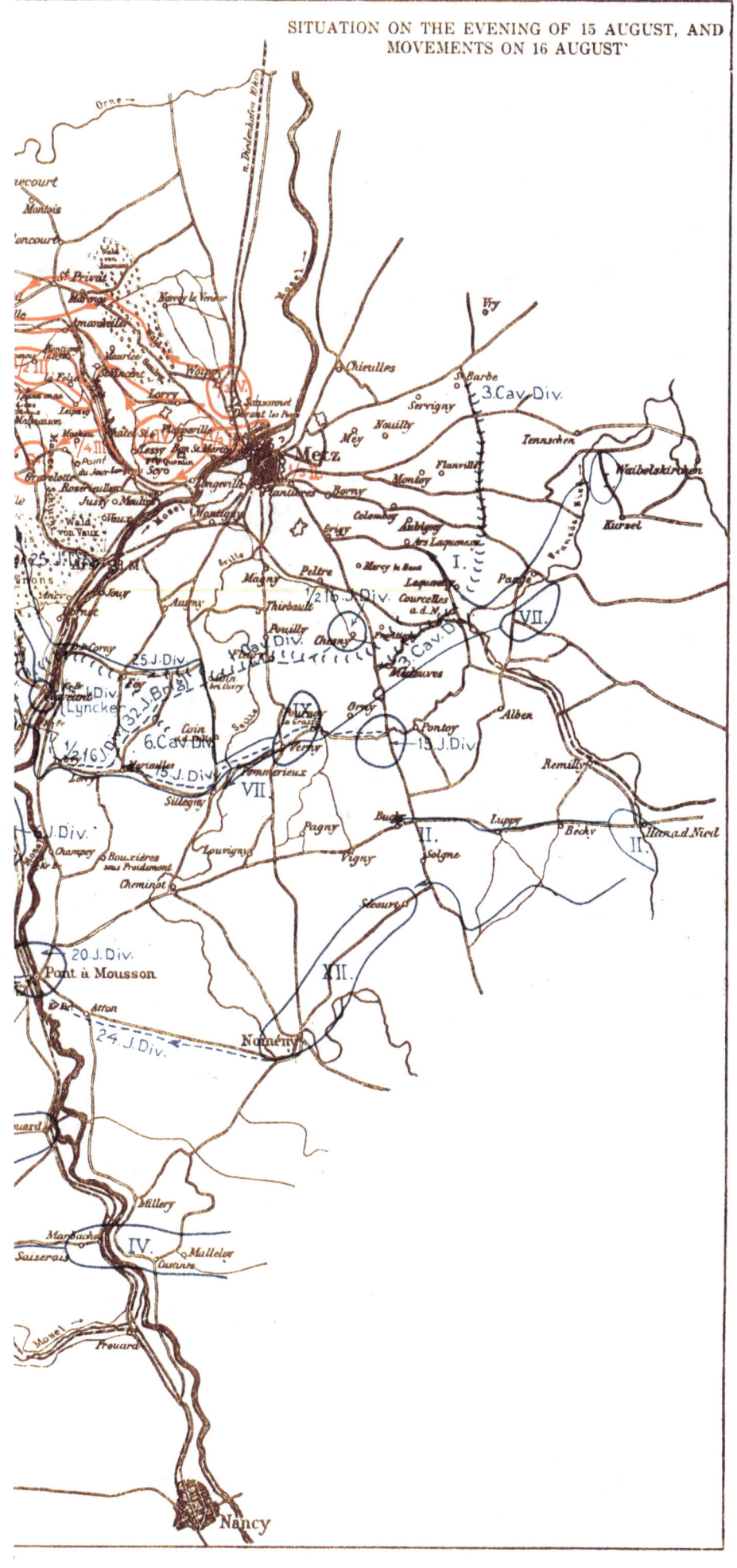

Map 78.

SITUATION ON THE EVENING OF 15 AUGUST, AND MOVEMENTS ON 16 AUGUST

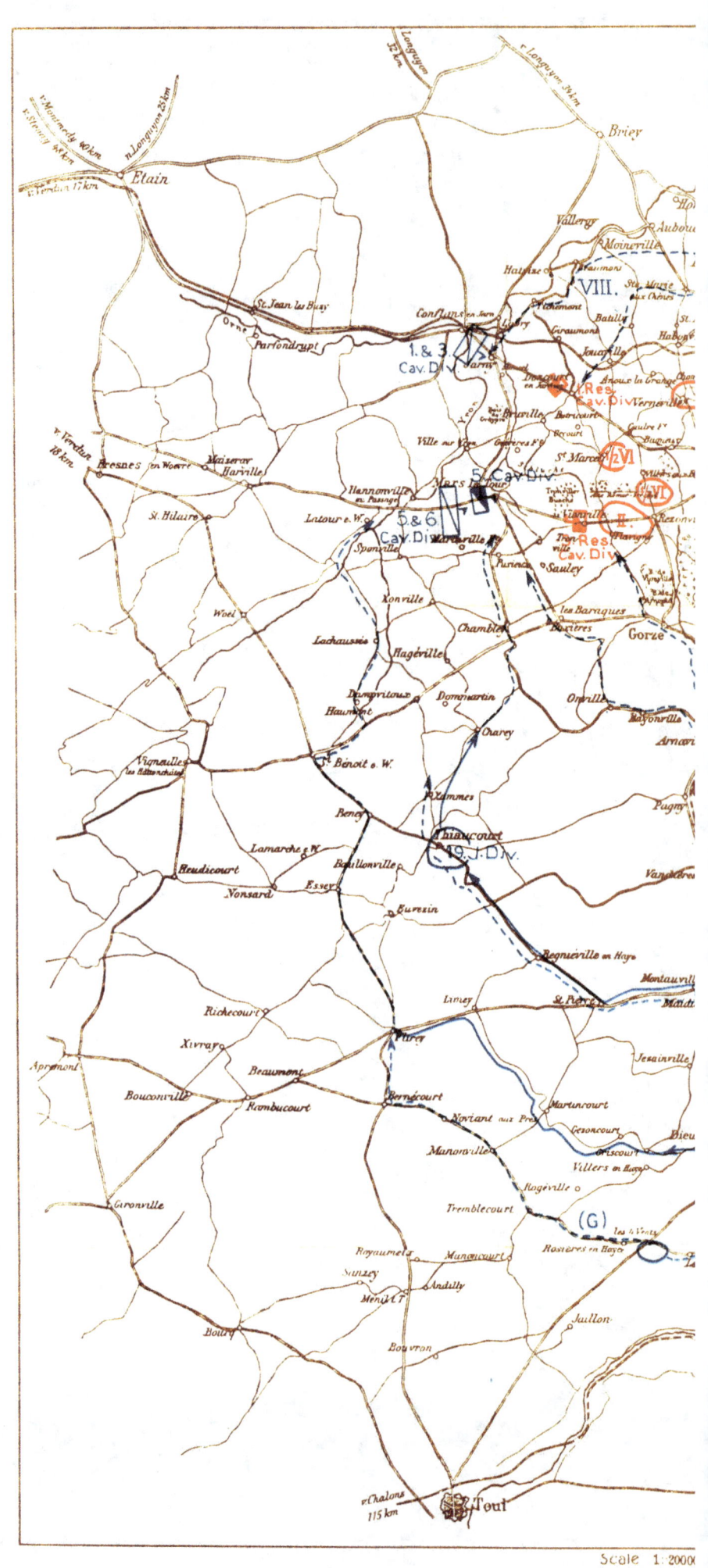

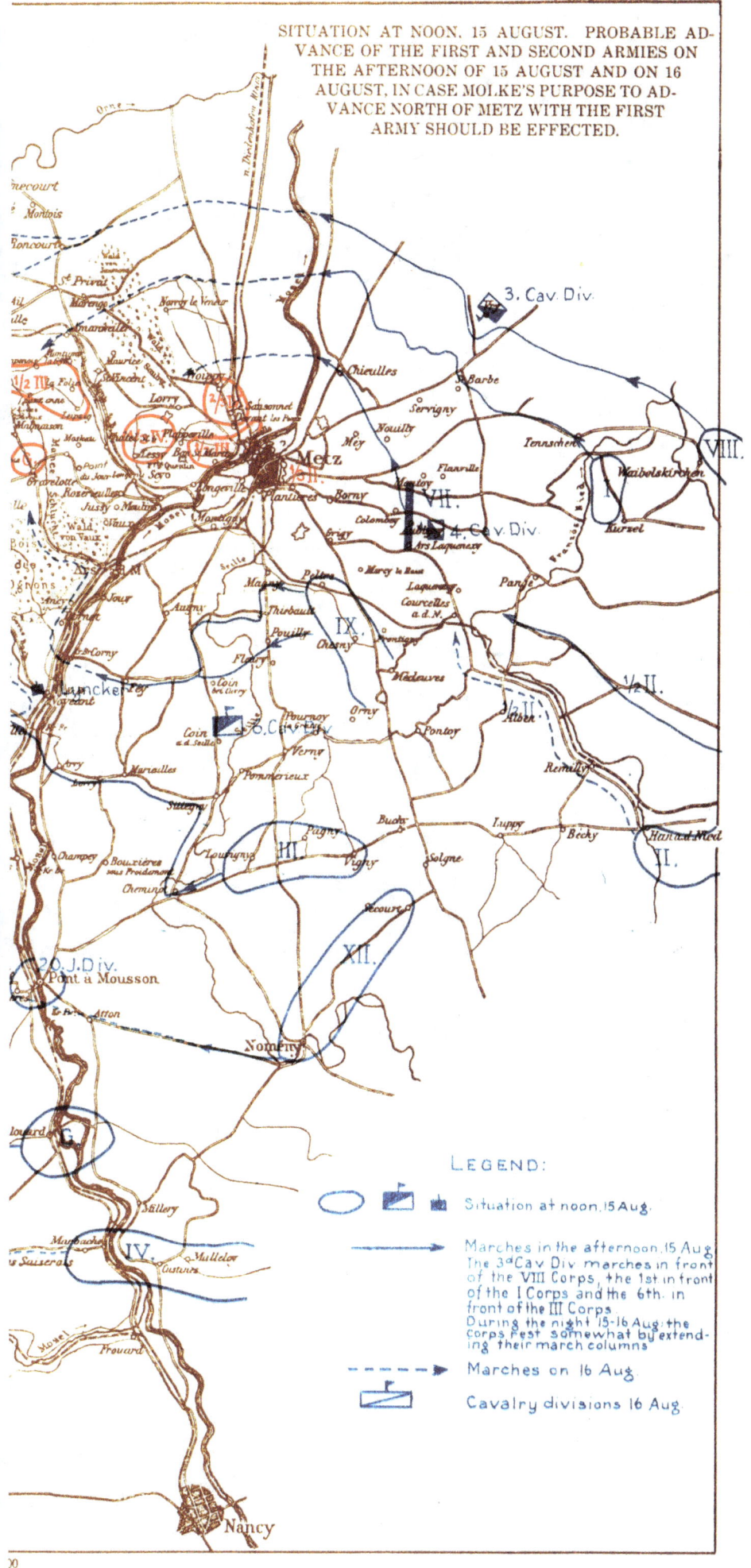

MARS LA TOUR 16 August, 1870

LEGEND:
GERMAN / FRENCH
Movements up to 2:00 P.M.
Situation 2:00 P.M.
Movements in the afternoon.

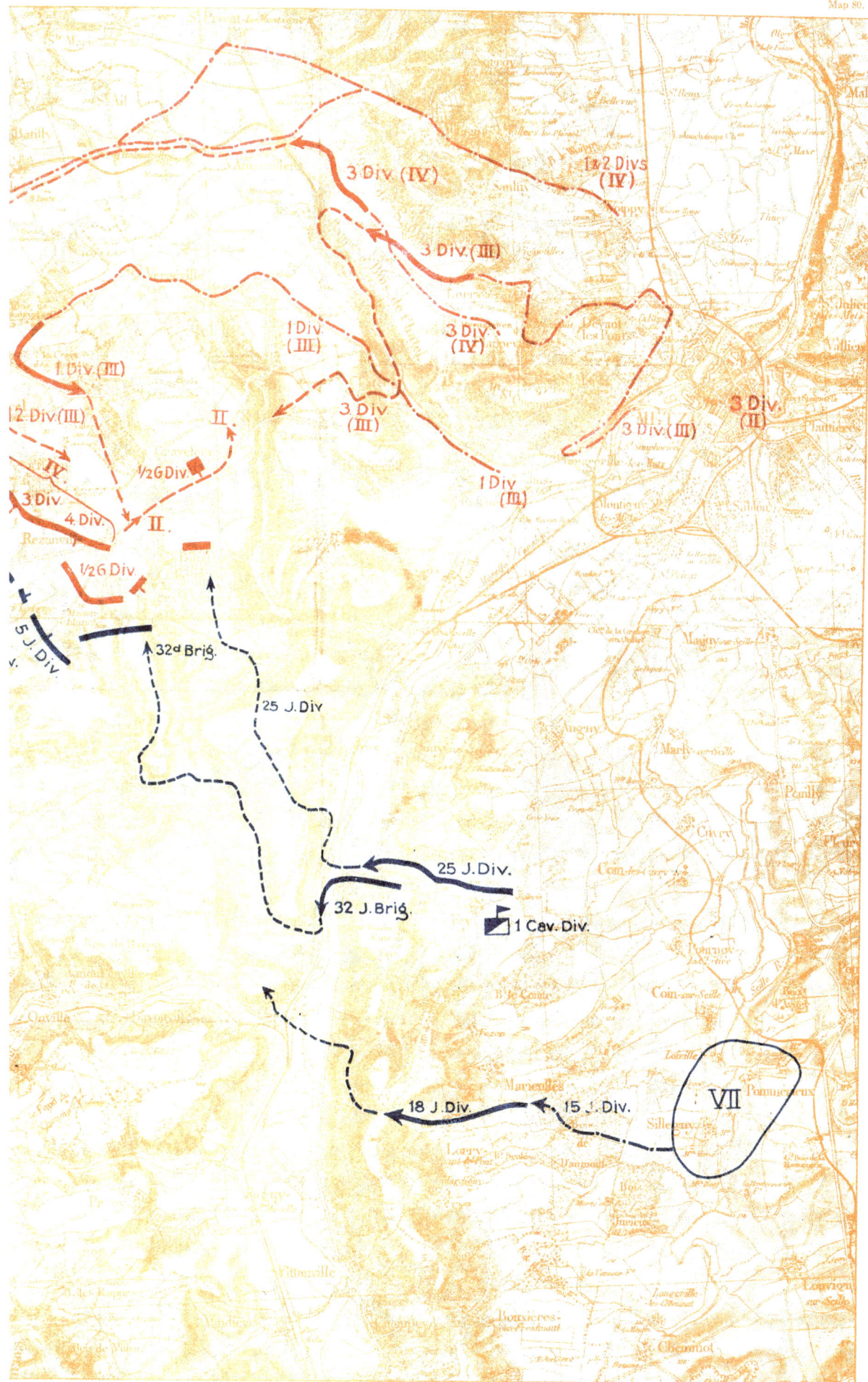

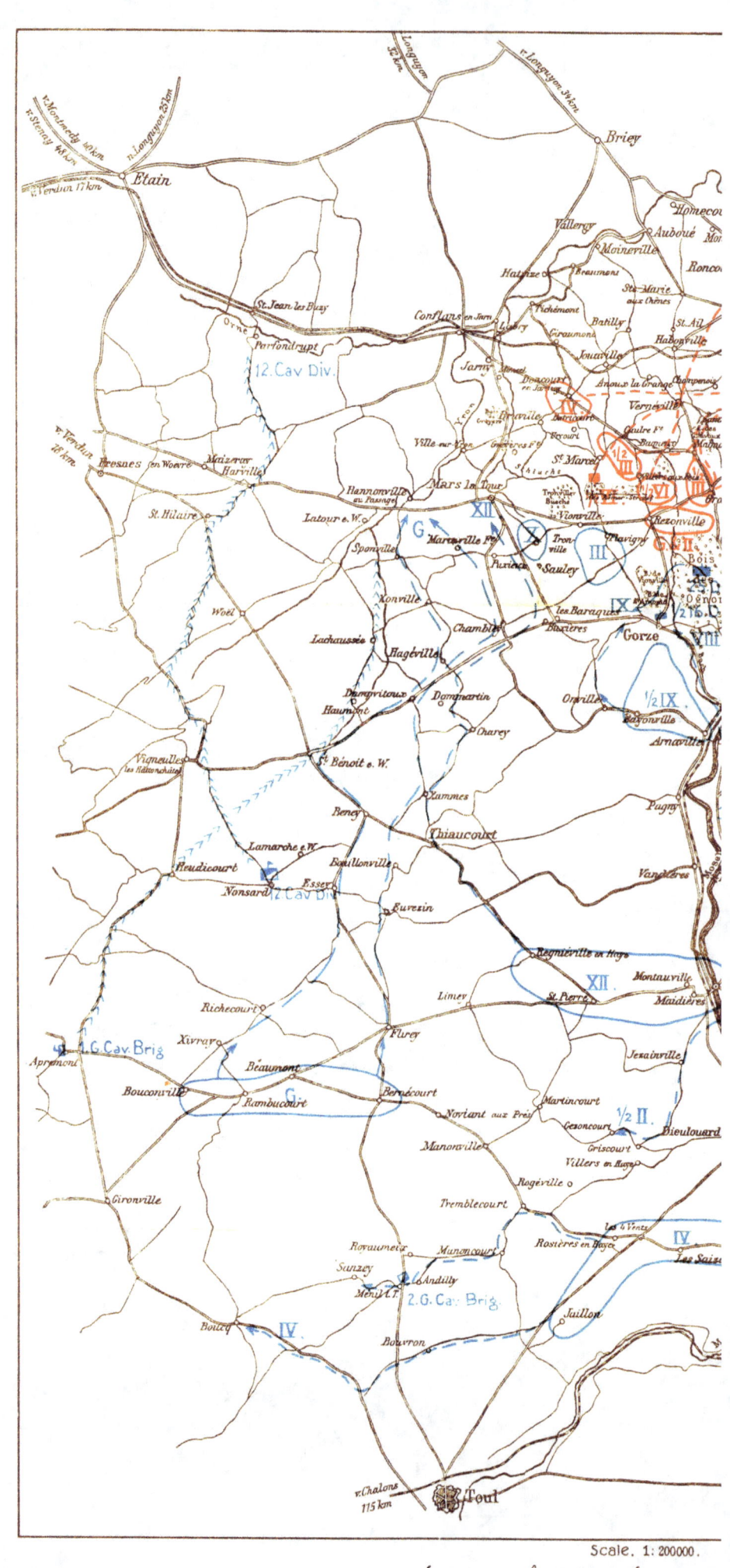

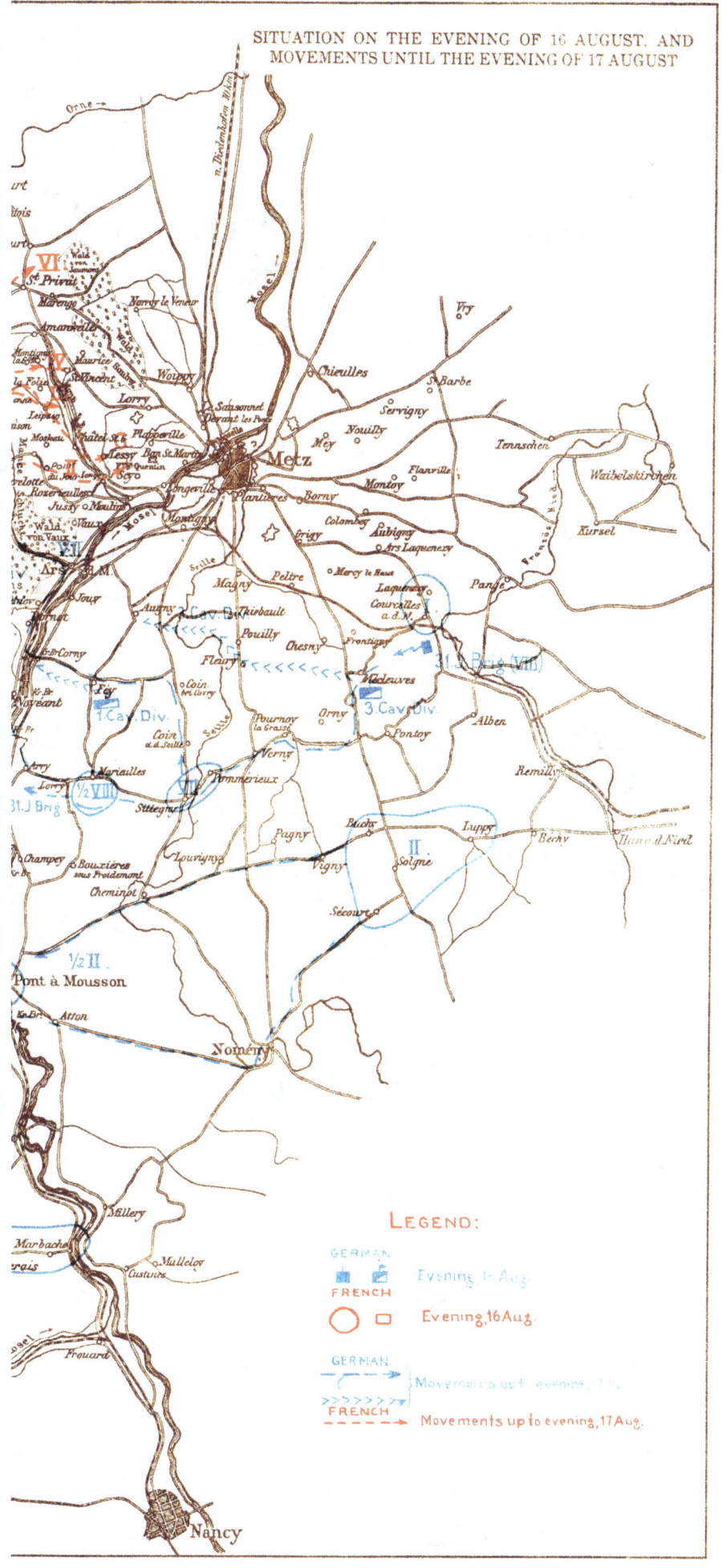

...NT OF THE GERMANS ON
... 17 AUGUST, AND FOR
... ON 18 AUGUST

Map 82.

Map 83.

SITUATION ON THE MORNING OF 18 AUGUST, AND
ADVANCE OF THE GERMANS

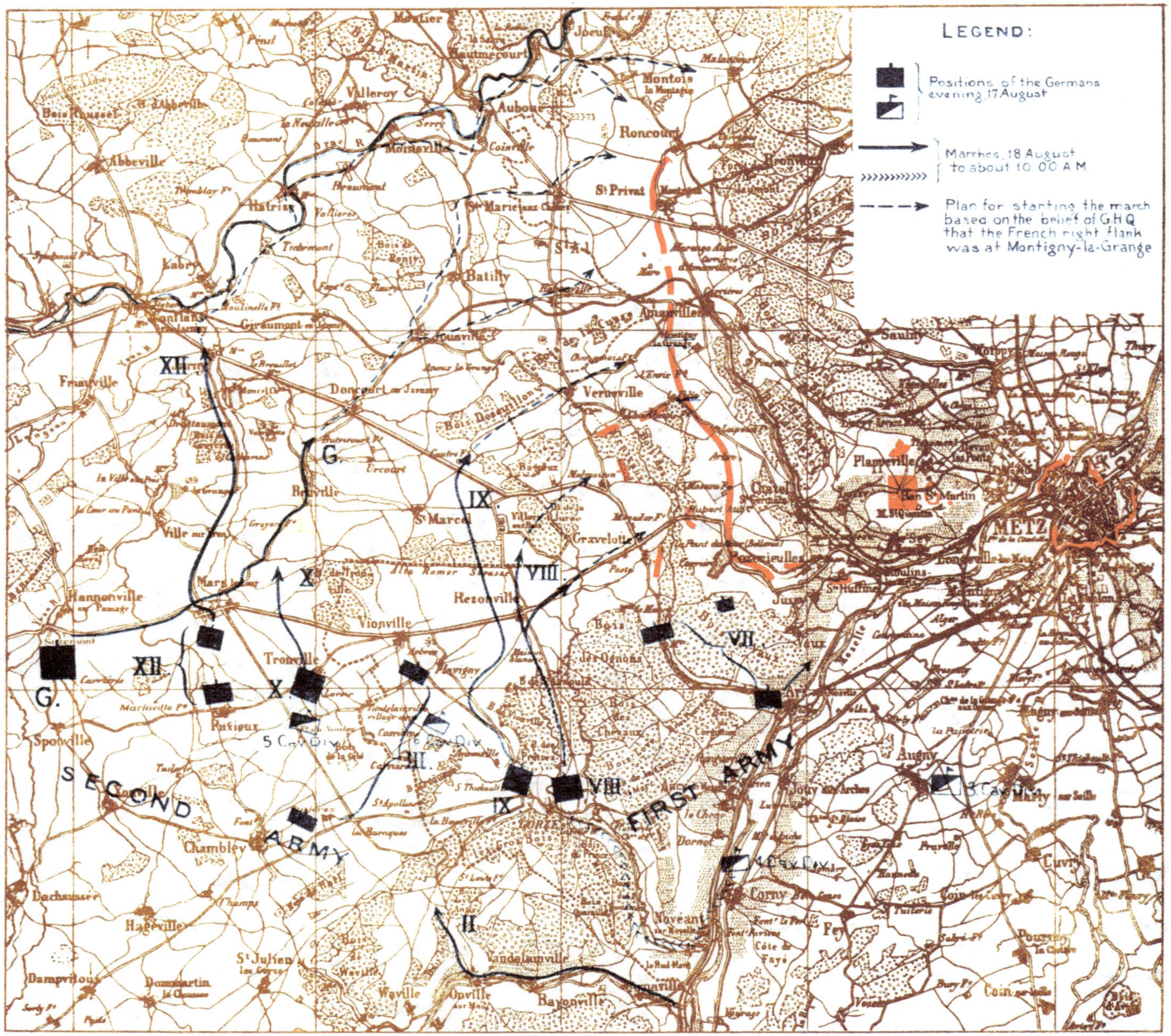

LEGEND:
Positions of the Germans evening 17 August
Marches 18 August to about 10:00 A.M.
Plan for starting the march based on the belief of GHQ that the French right flank was at Montigny-la-Grange

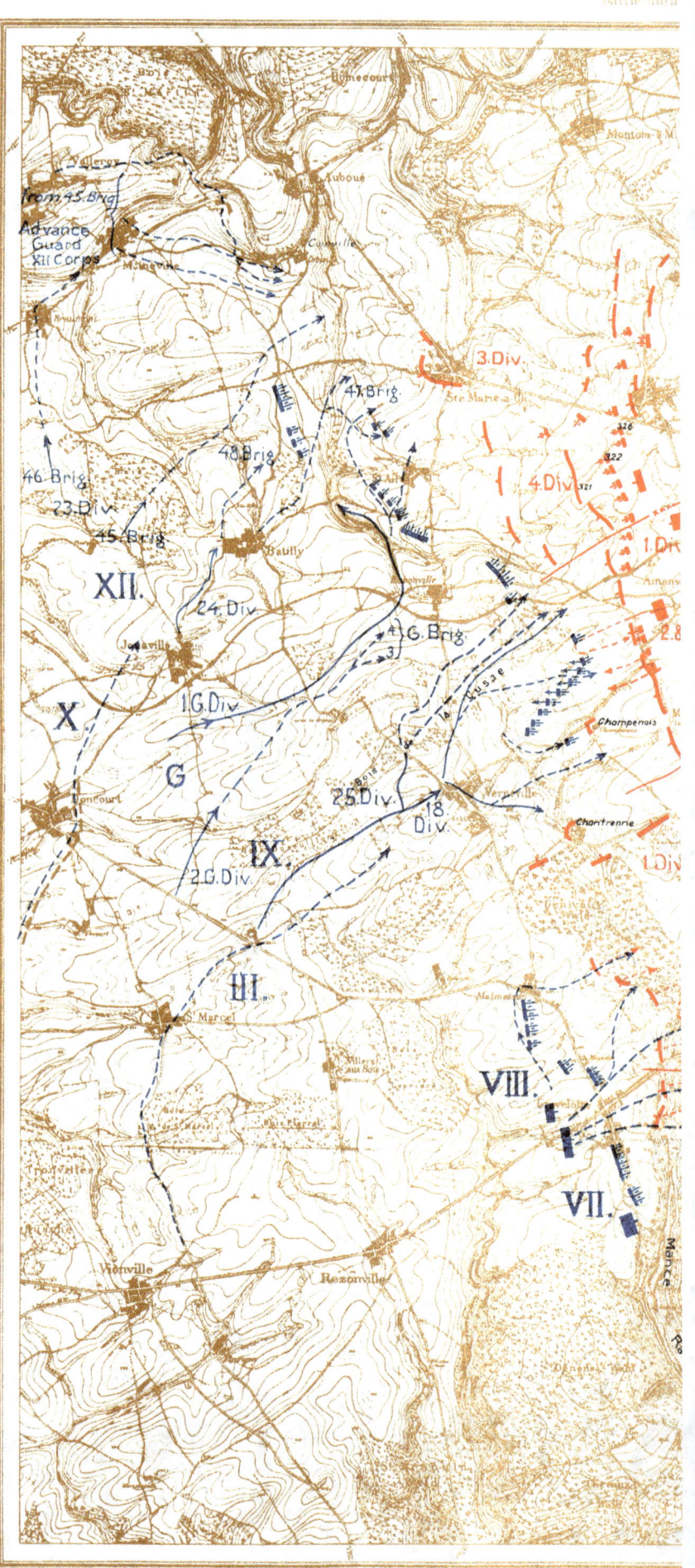

VELOTTE-ST. PRIVAT

Map 84.

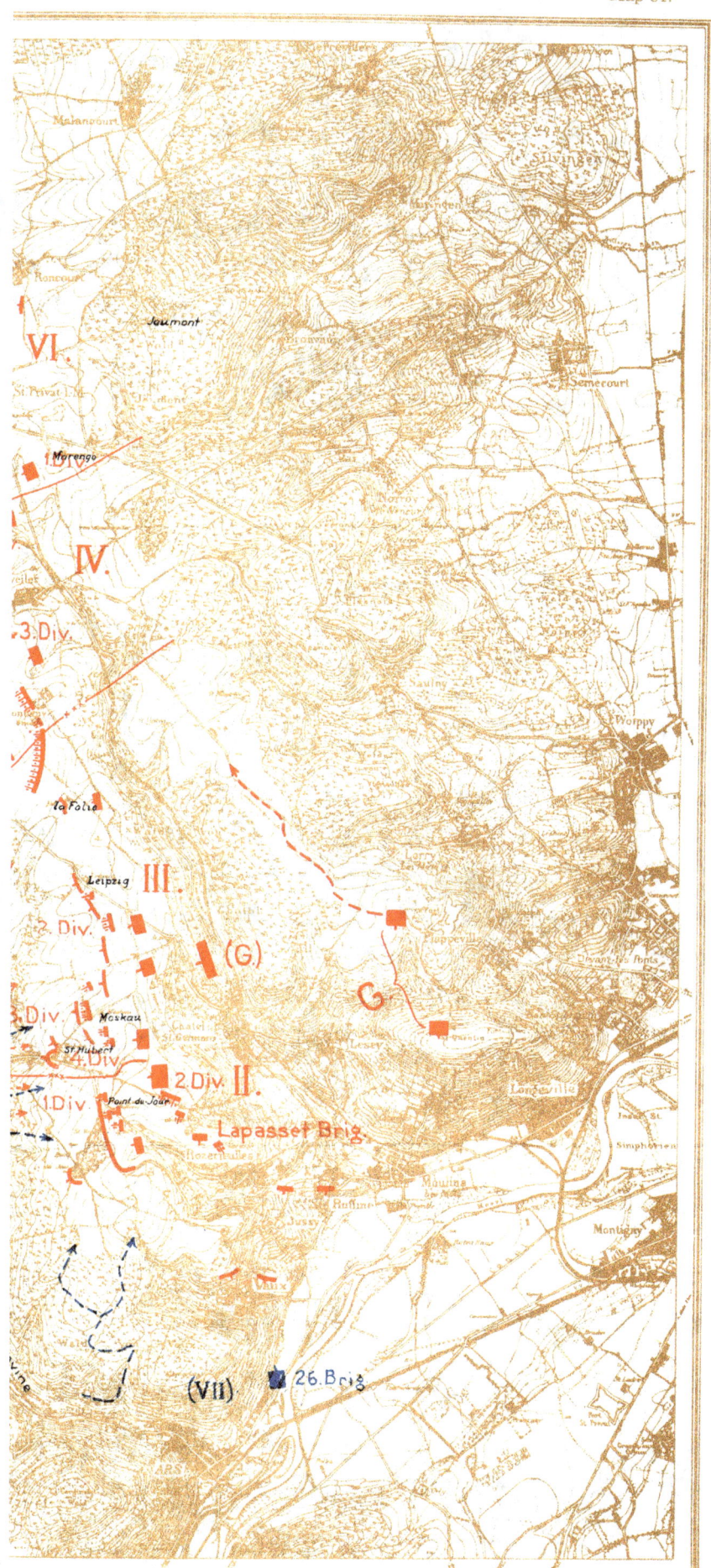

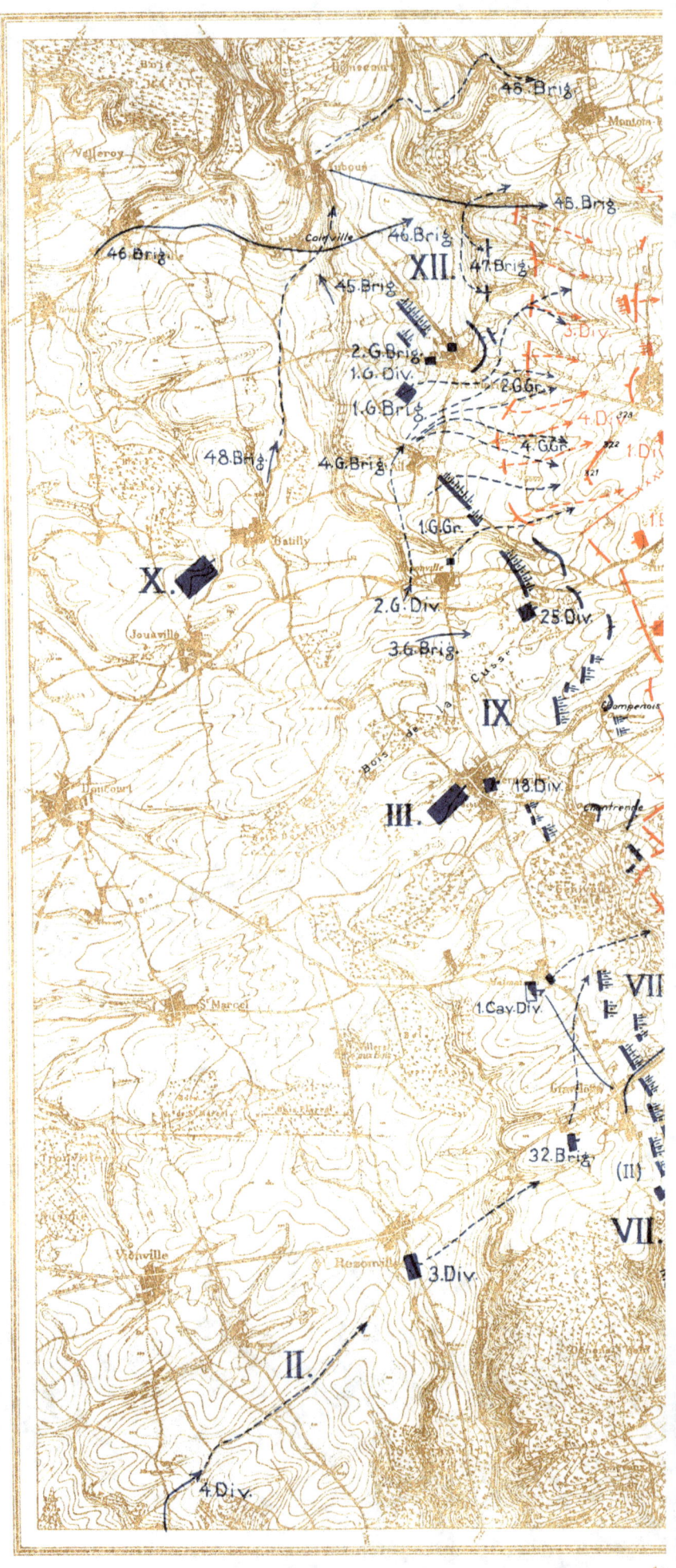

VELOTTE-ST. PRIVAT
m 3:00 P.M. until about 6:00 P.M.

Map 85.

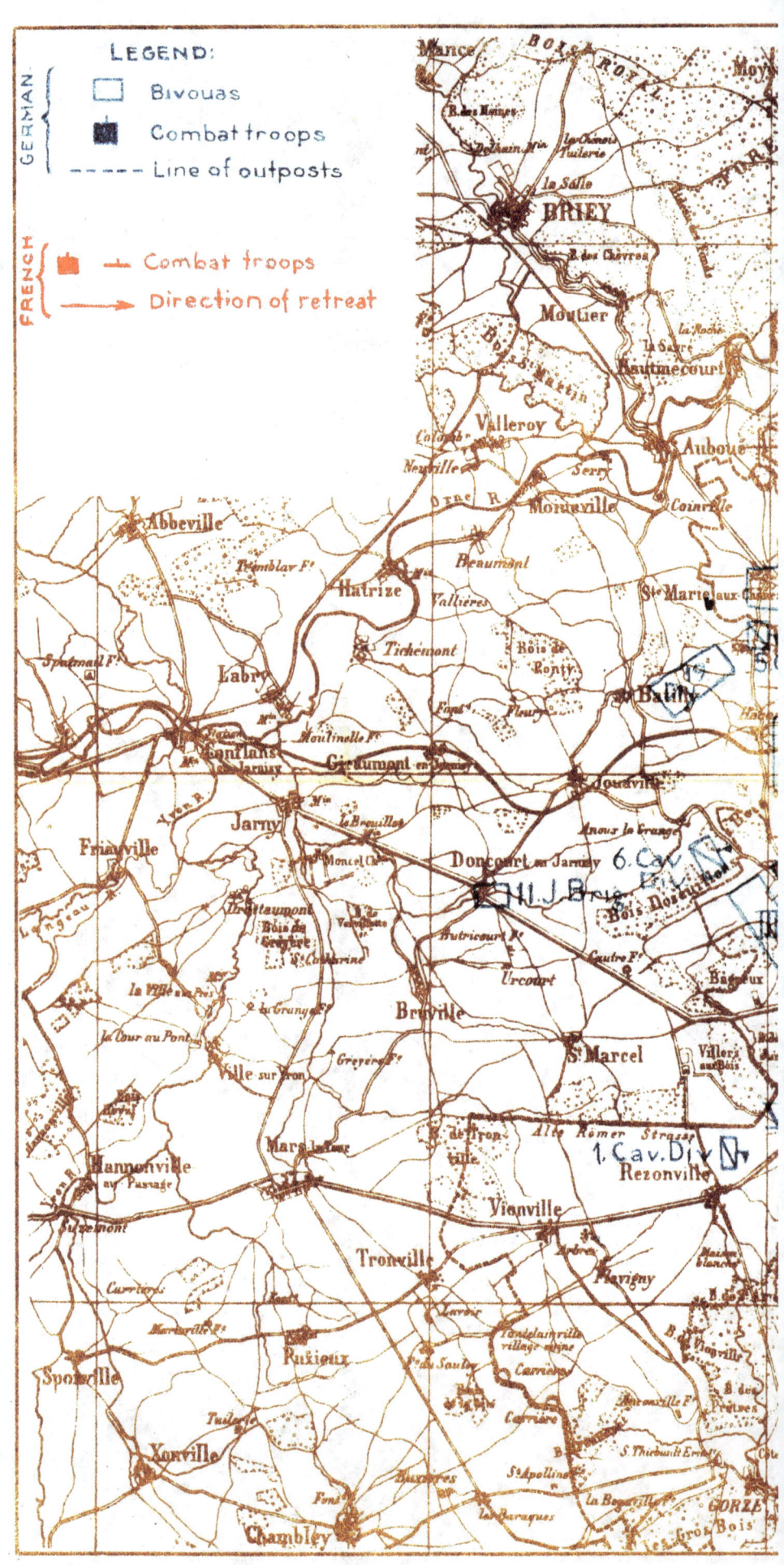

HT 18-19 AUGUST, AND RE-
THE FRENCH

Map 88.

:100 000.

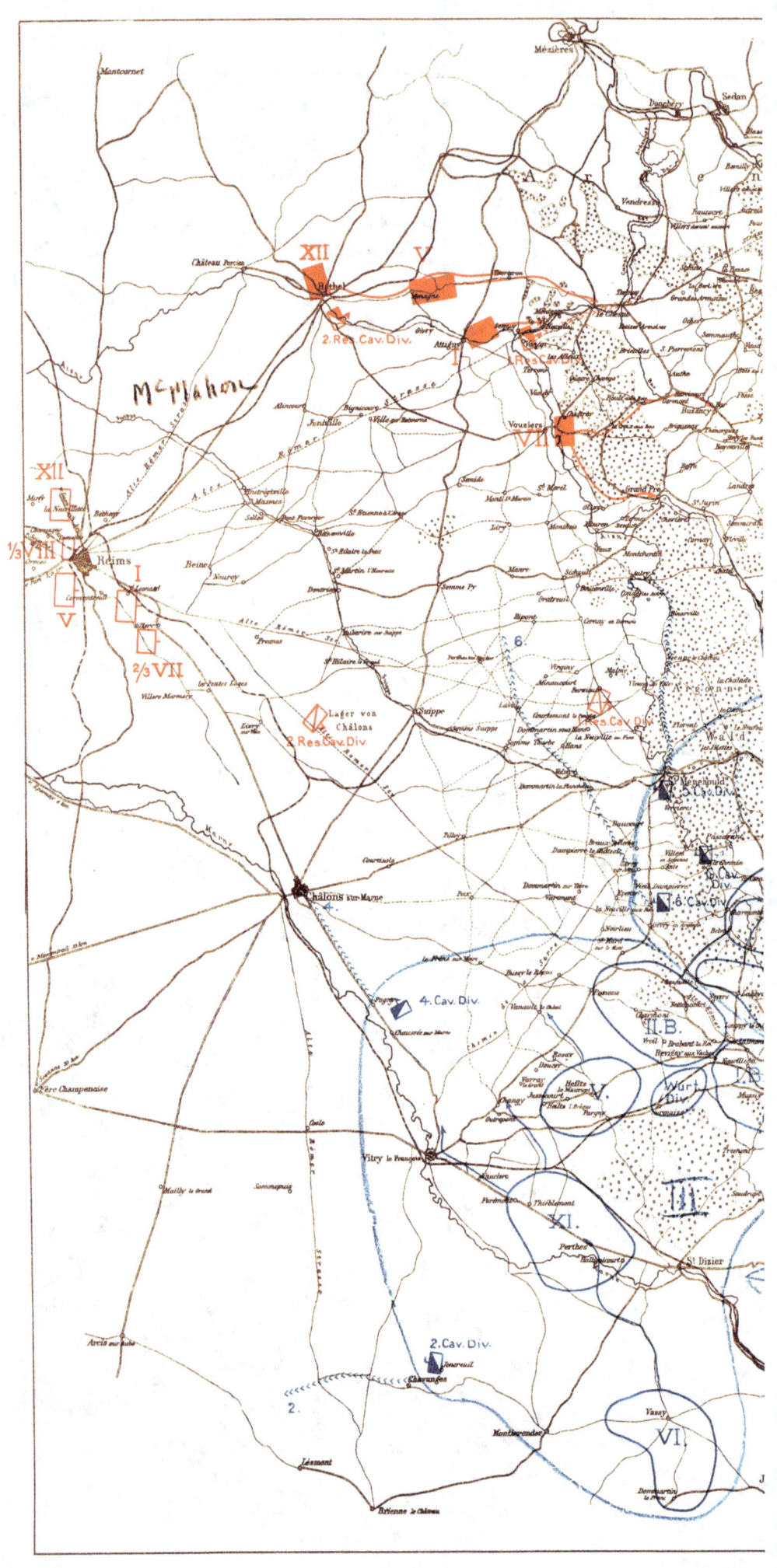

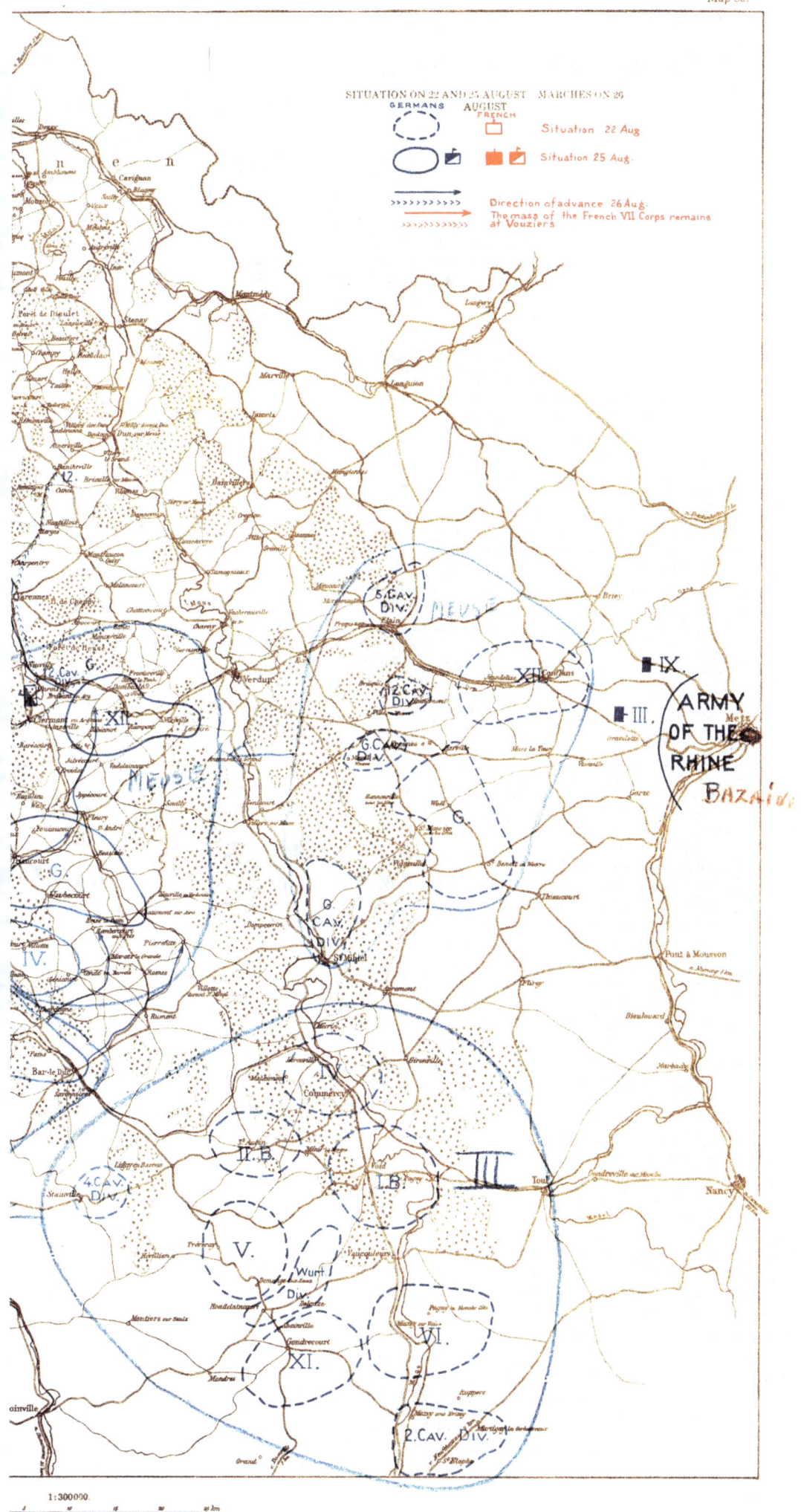

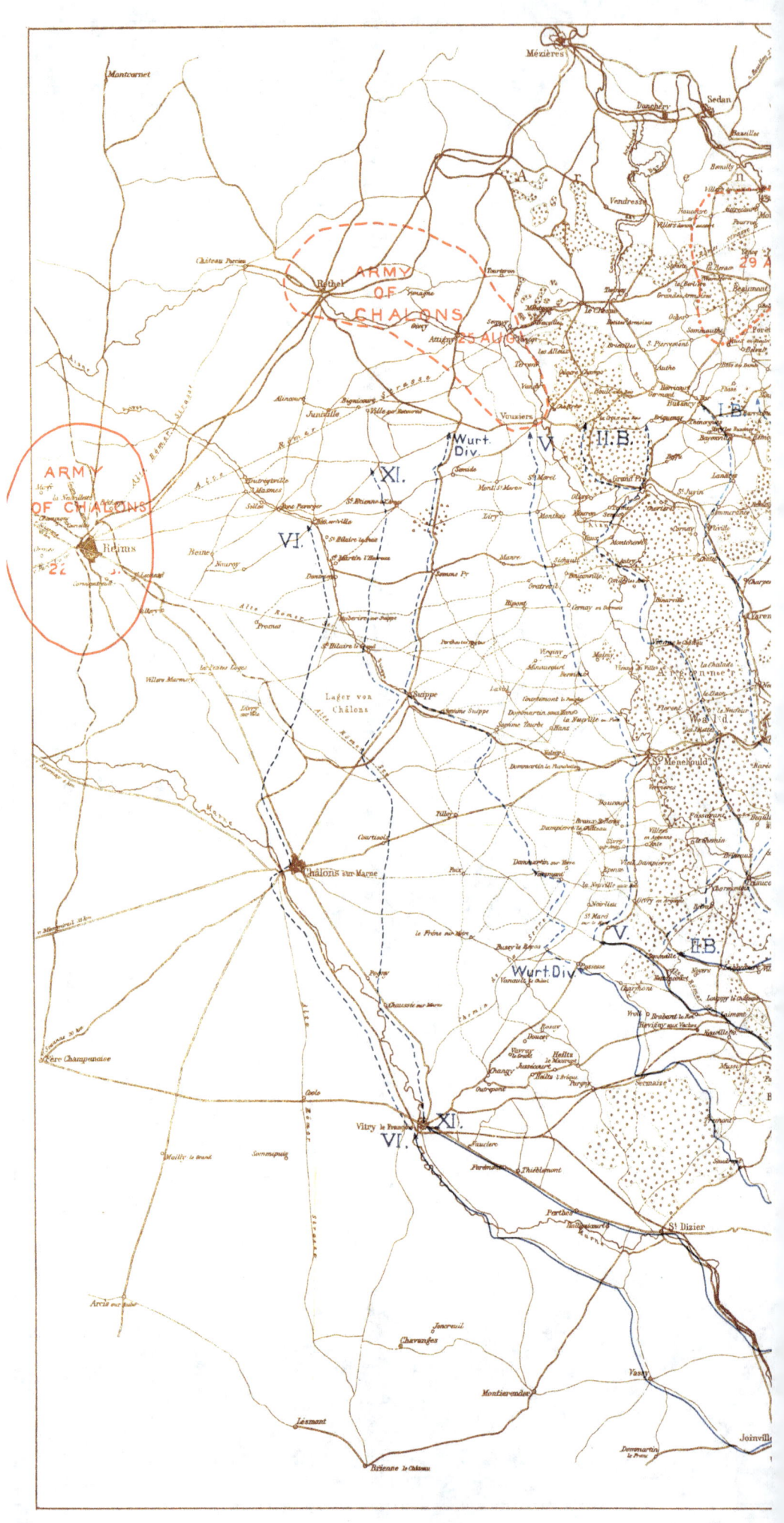

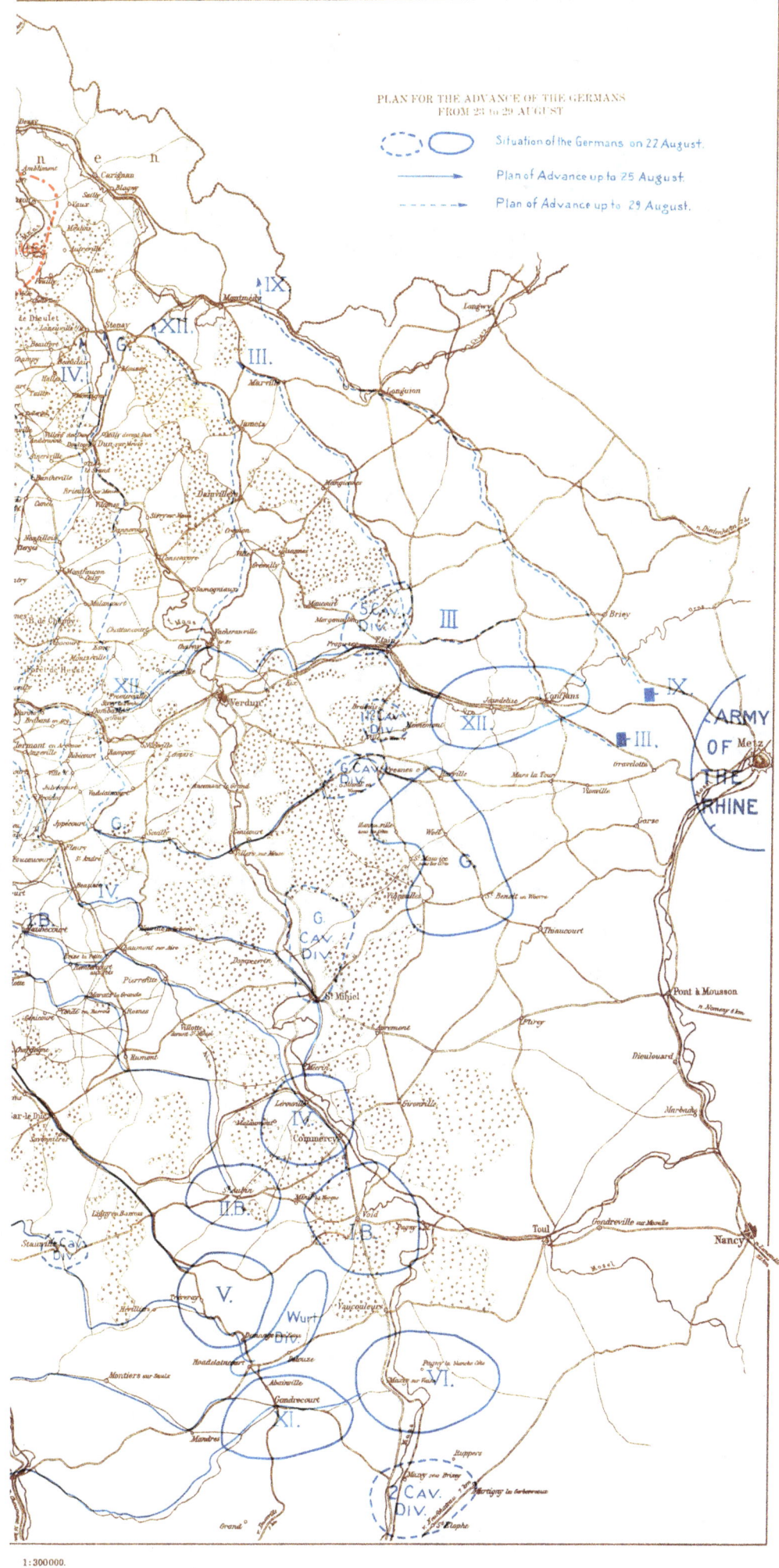

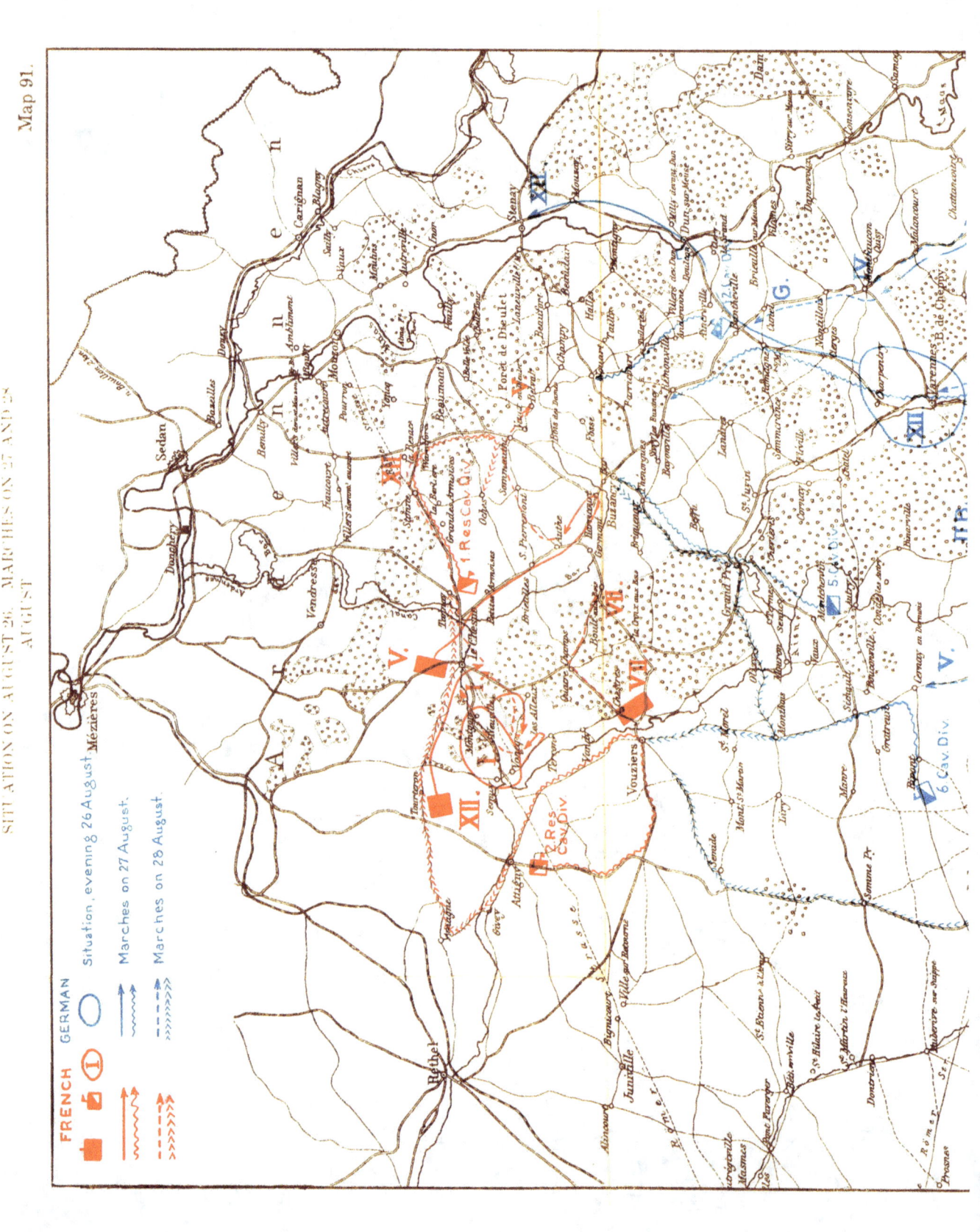

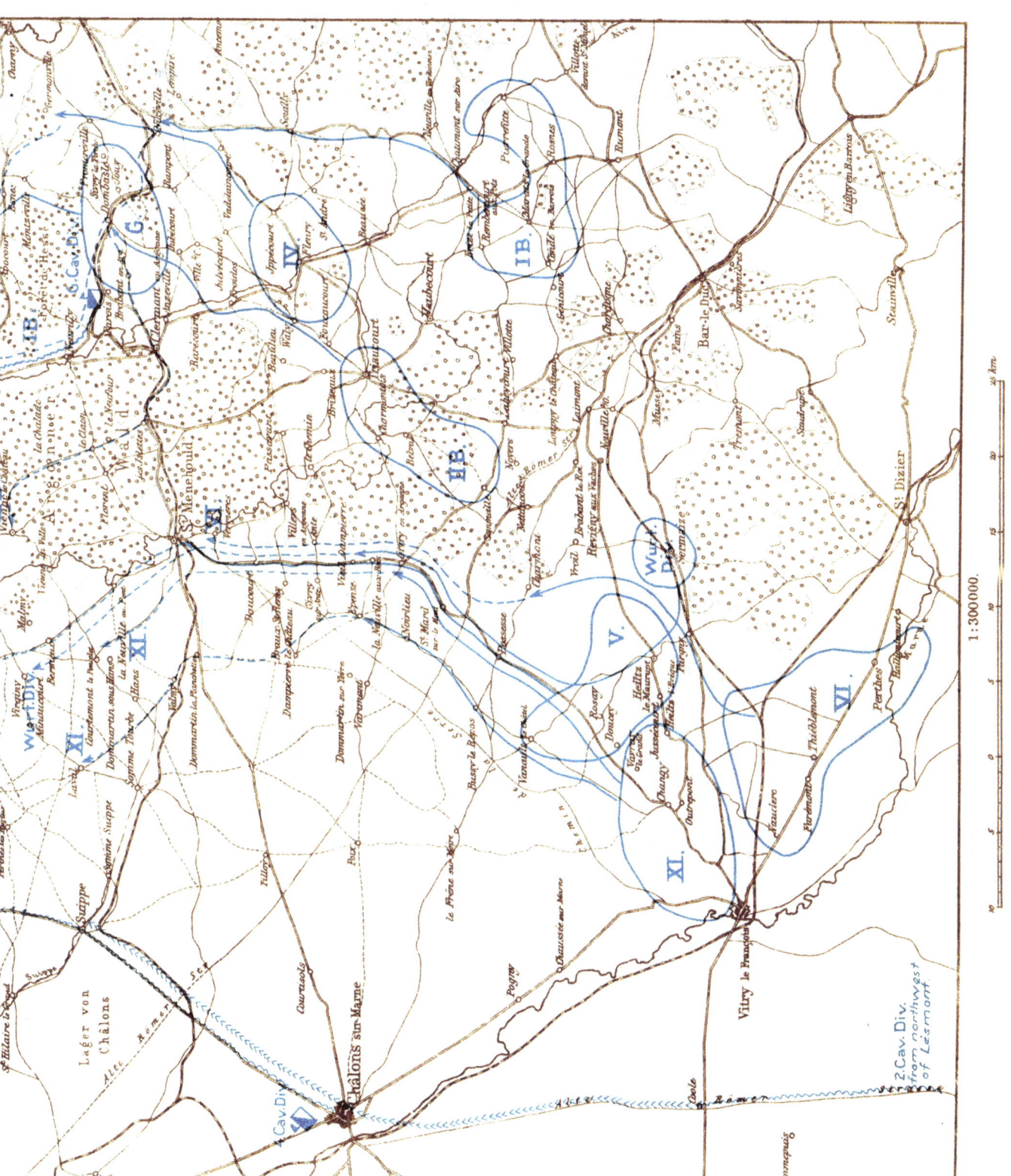

Map 92.

SITUATION ON THE EVENING OF 25 AUGUST. MOVEMENTS ON 25 AUGUST.

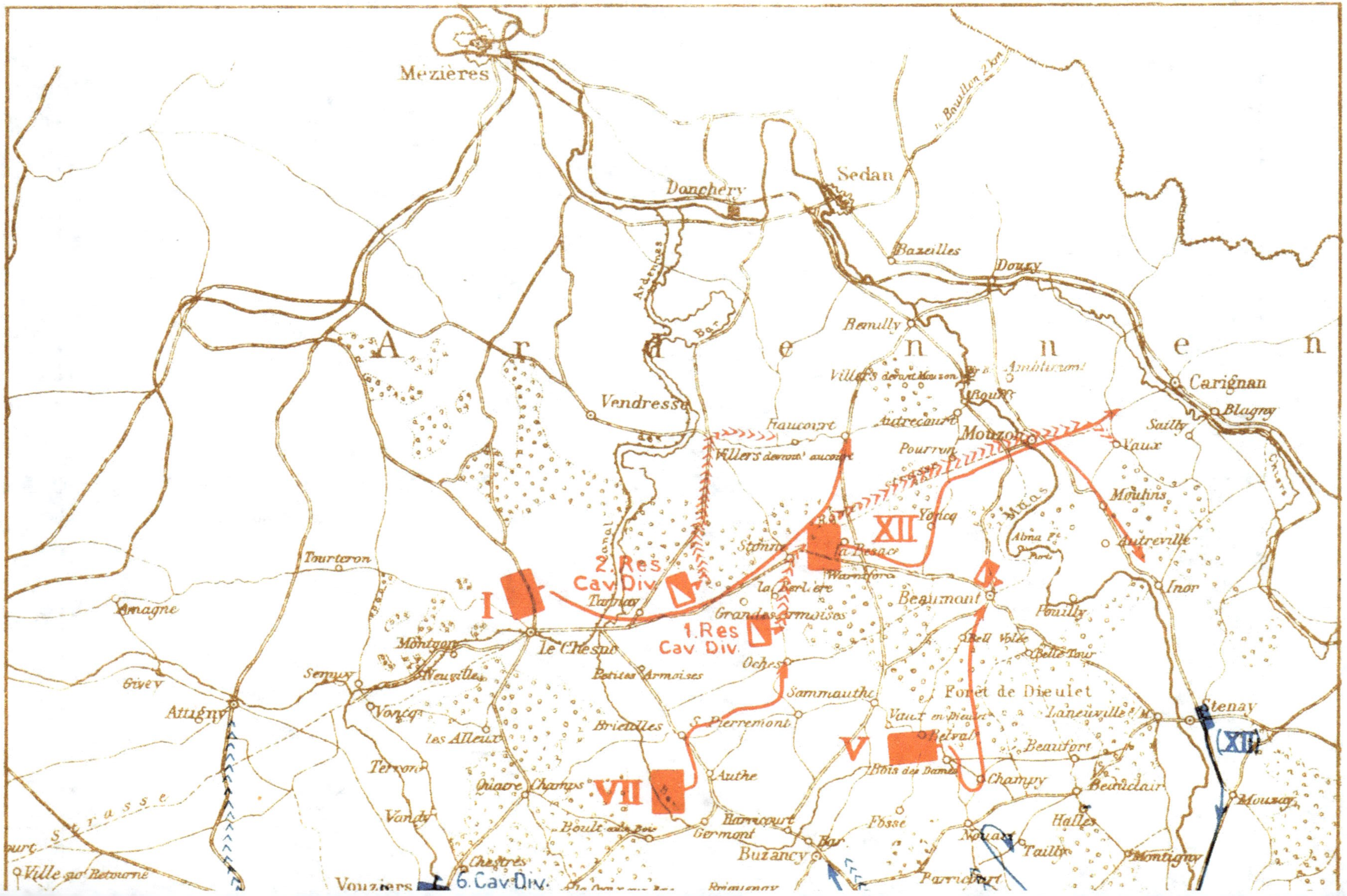

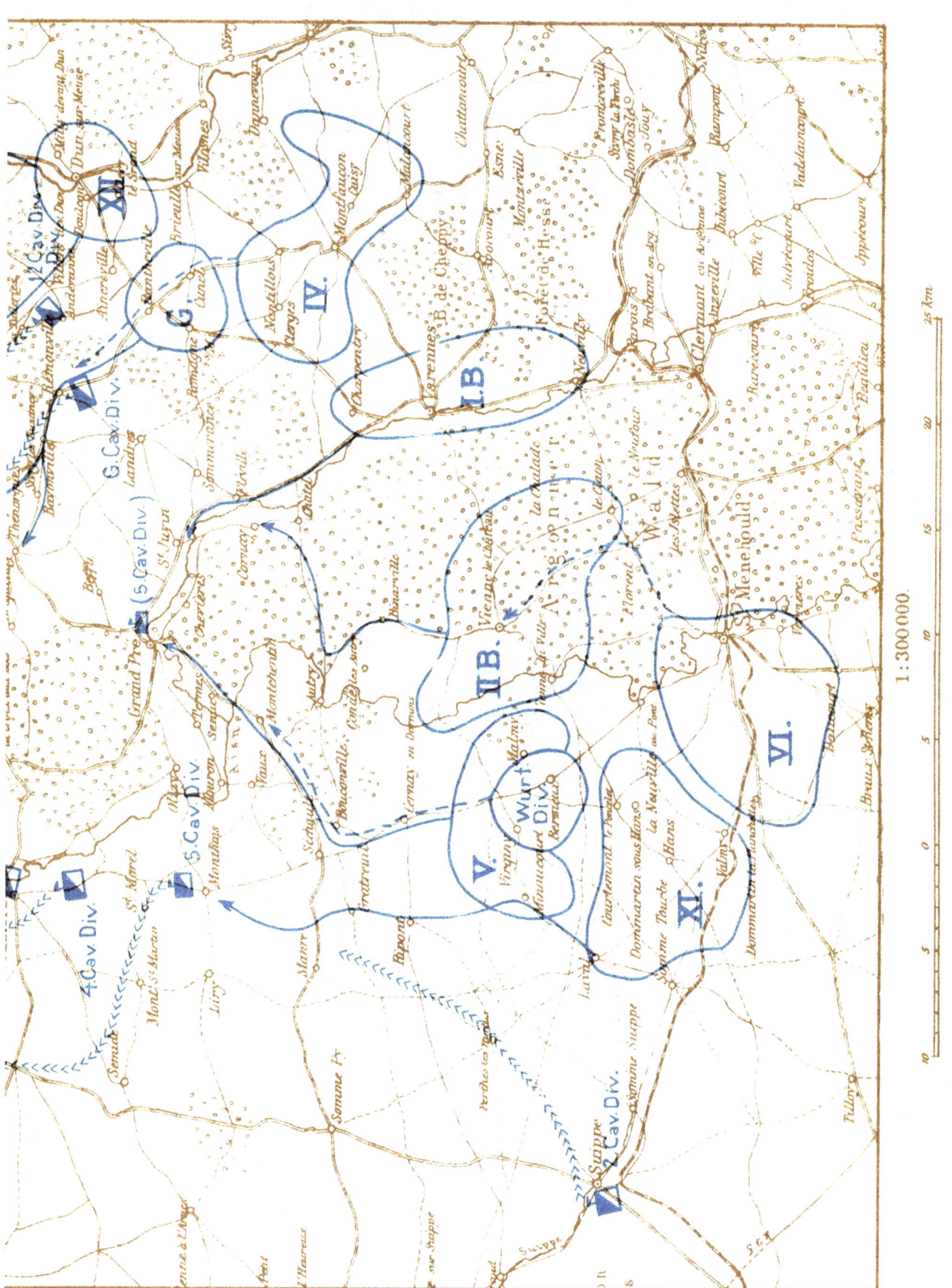

Map 93.

SITUATION OF THE GERMANS ON THE EVENING OF 29 AUGUST. MOVEMENTS OF THE GERMANS AFTER 30 AUGUST, ACCORDING TO MOLKE'S PLAN

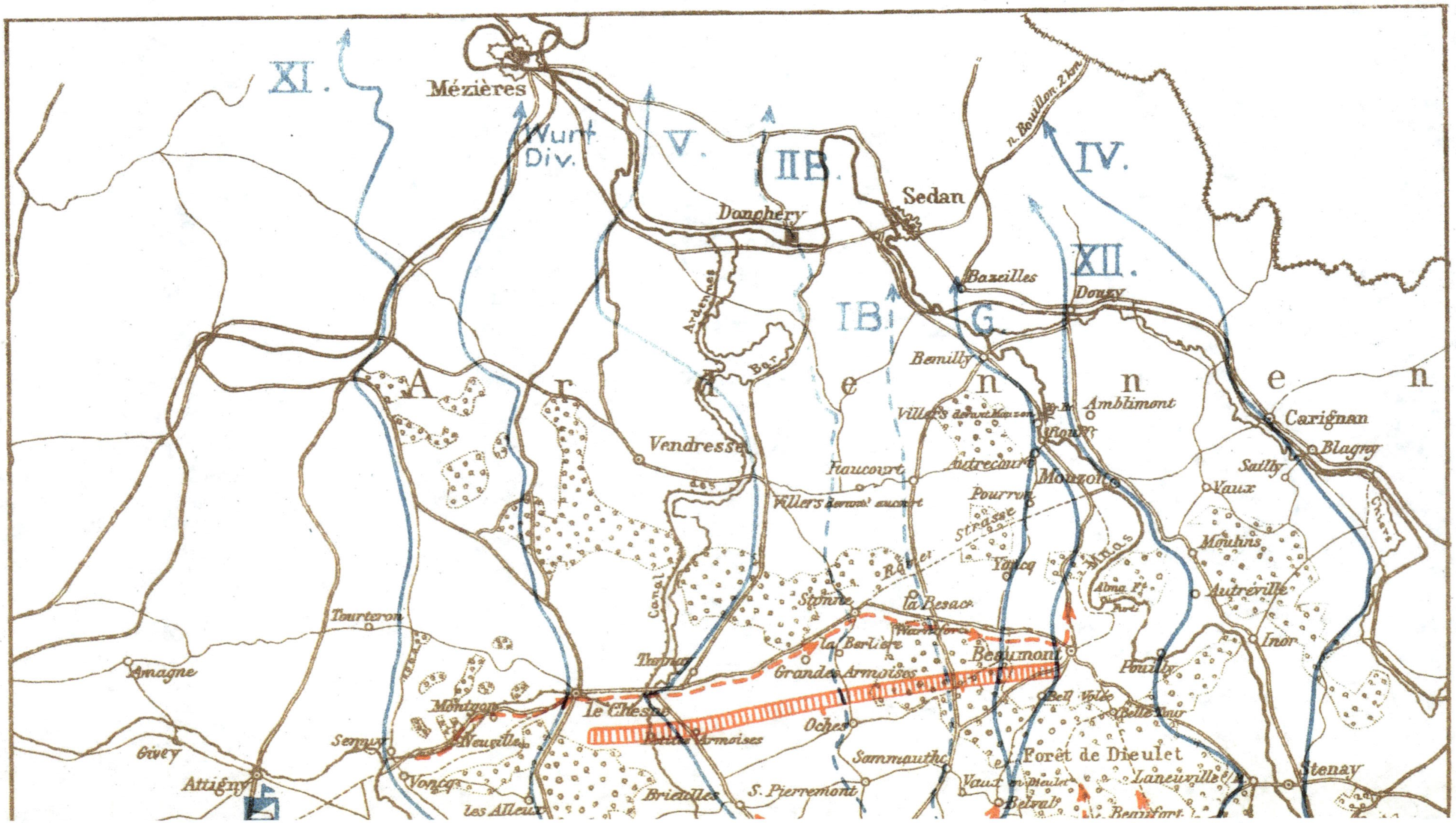

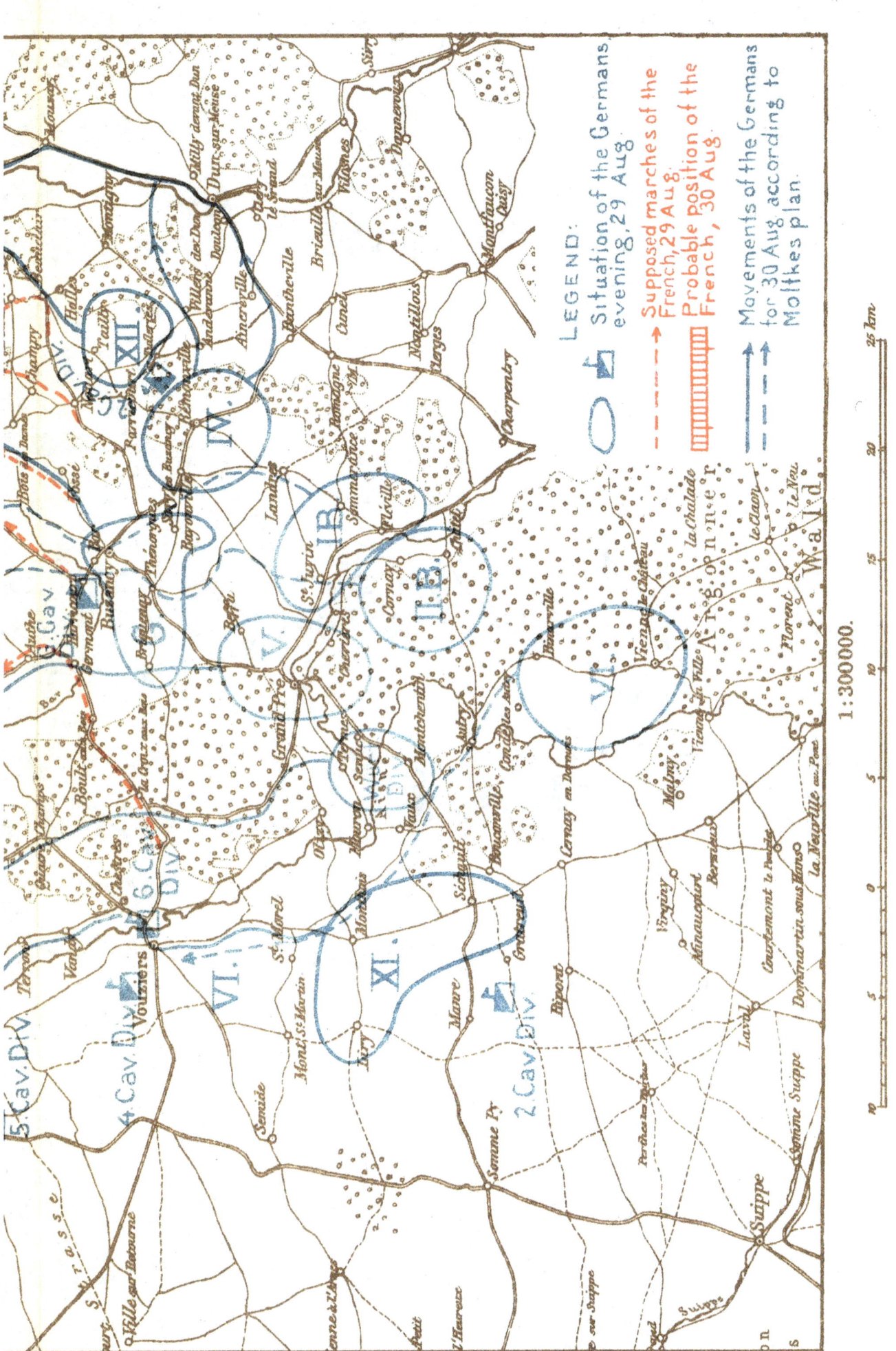

Map 94.

SITUATION ON THE EVENING OF 29 AUGUST. MOVEMENTS ON 30 AUGUST

LEGEND:
⇢ Marches ordered for the German Army Corps on 30 Aug.
⇢ Marches made by the French about 30 Aug.

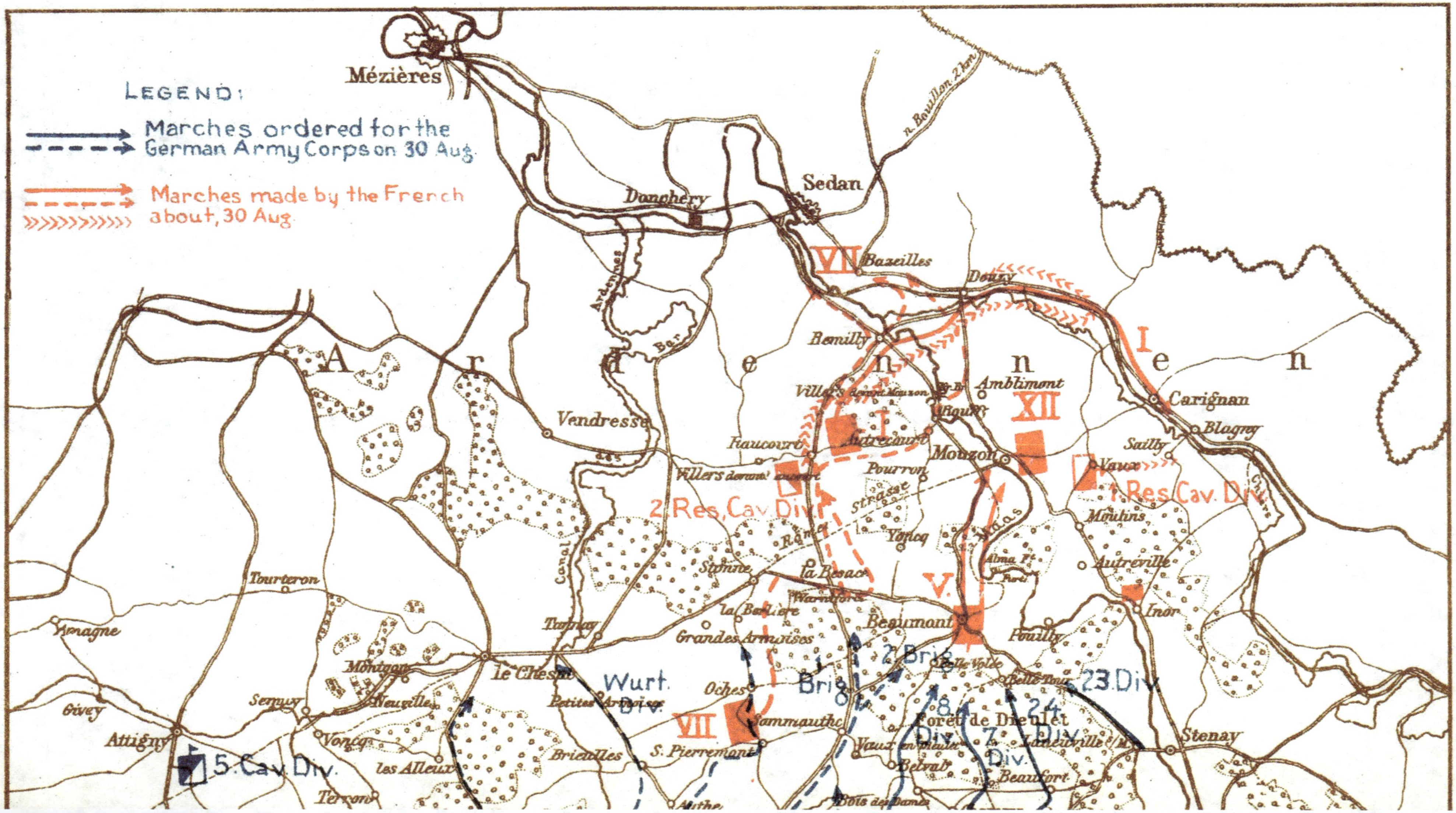

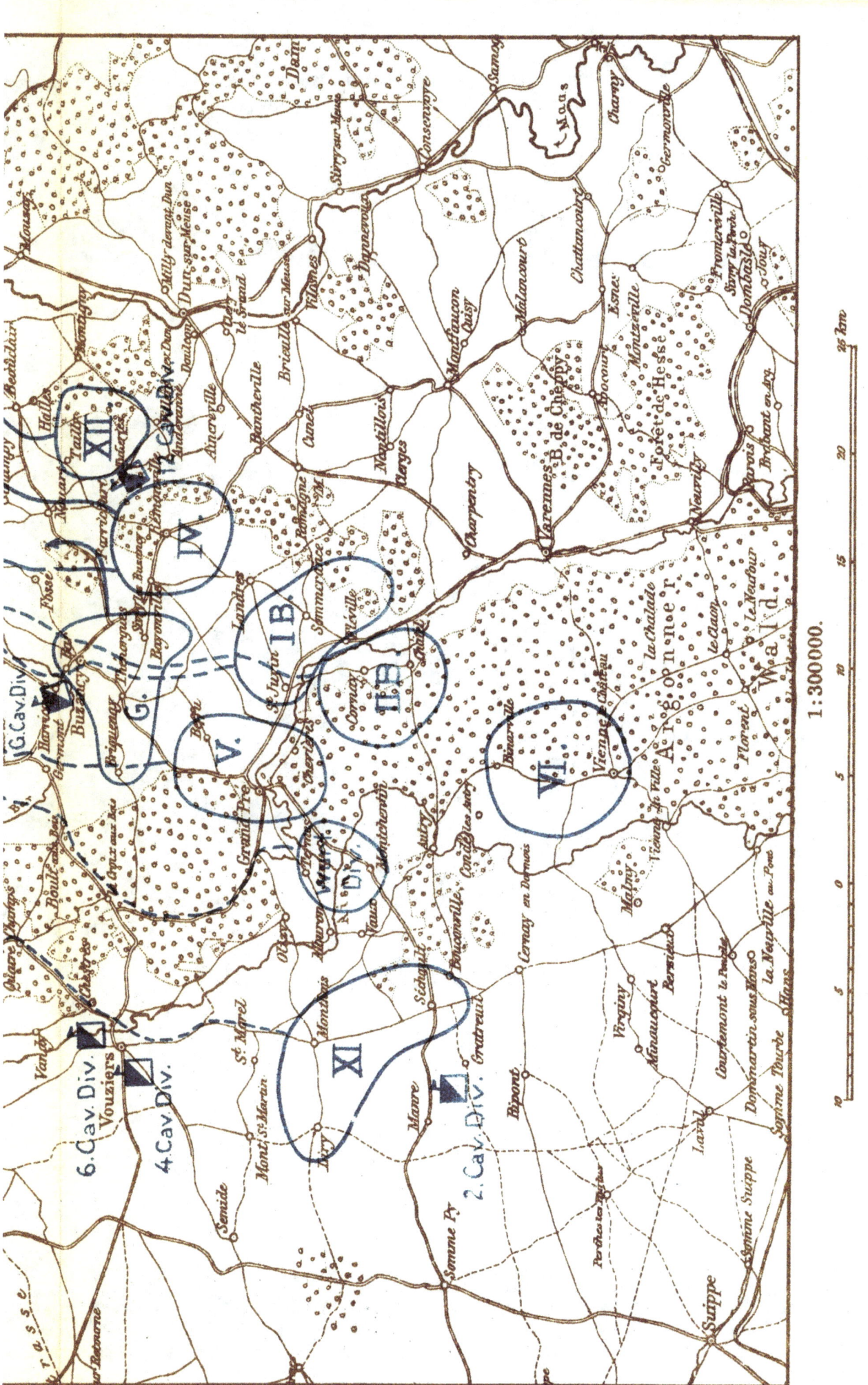

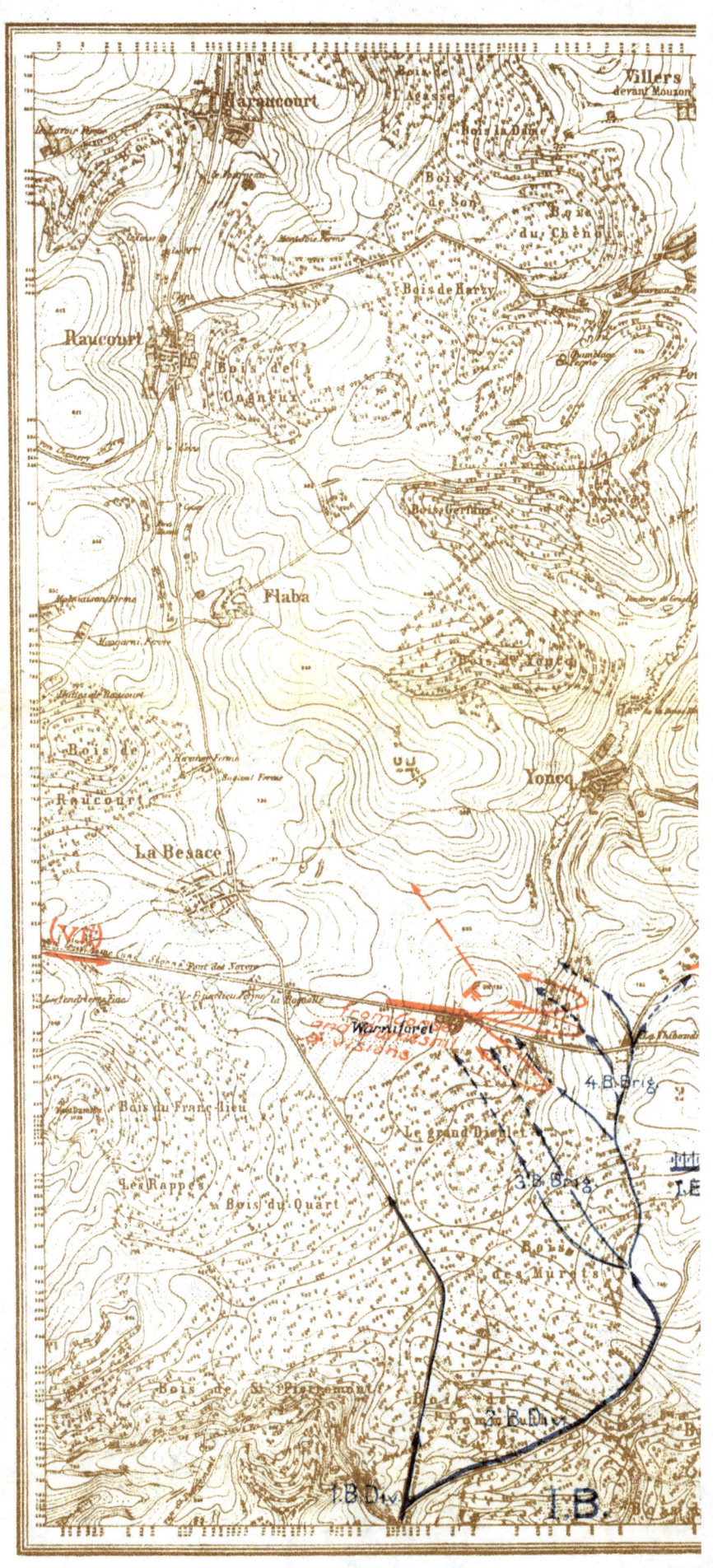

BEAUMONT
1870
until about 3:00 PM.

Map 95.

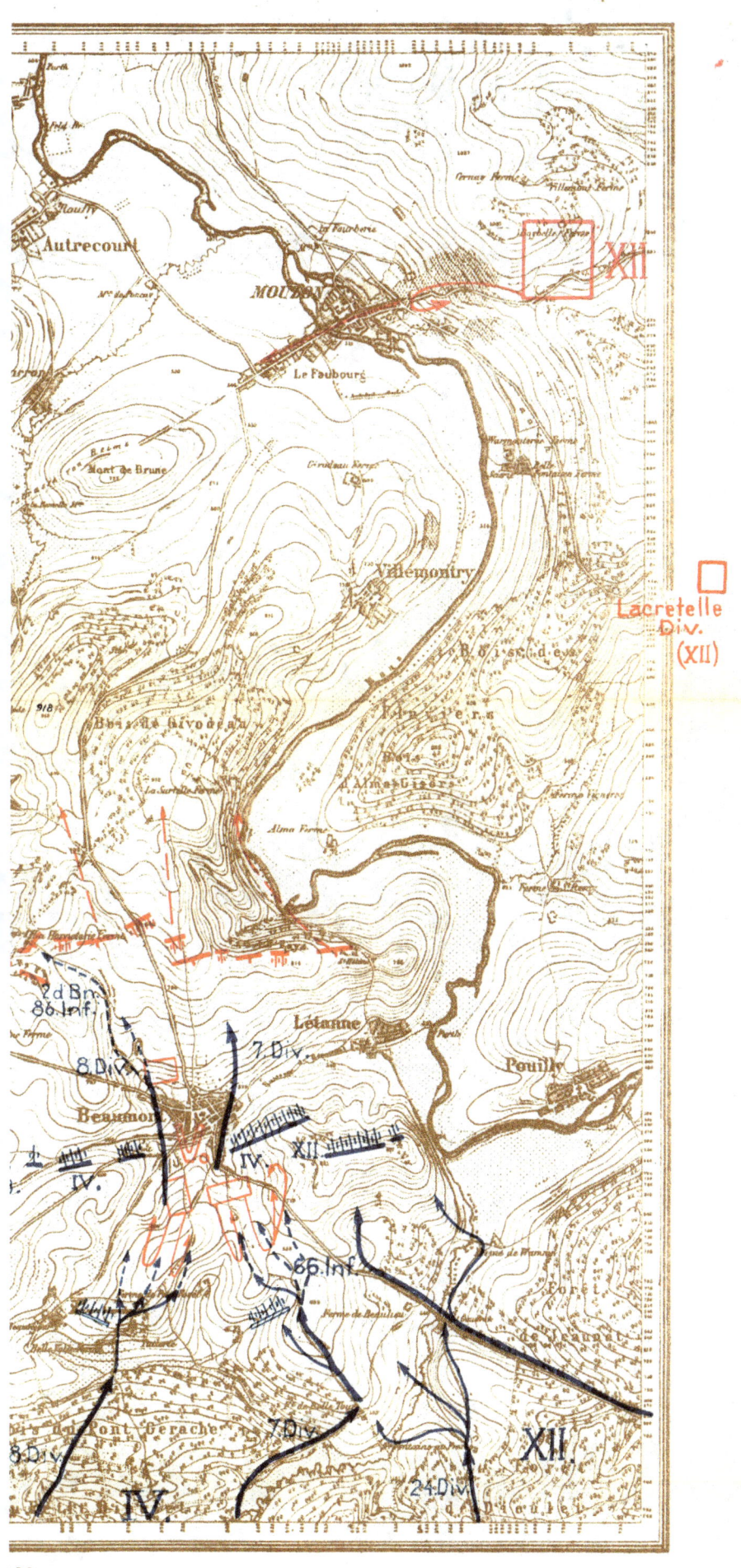

2 km

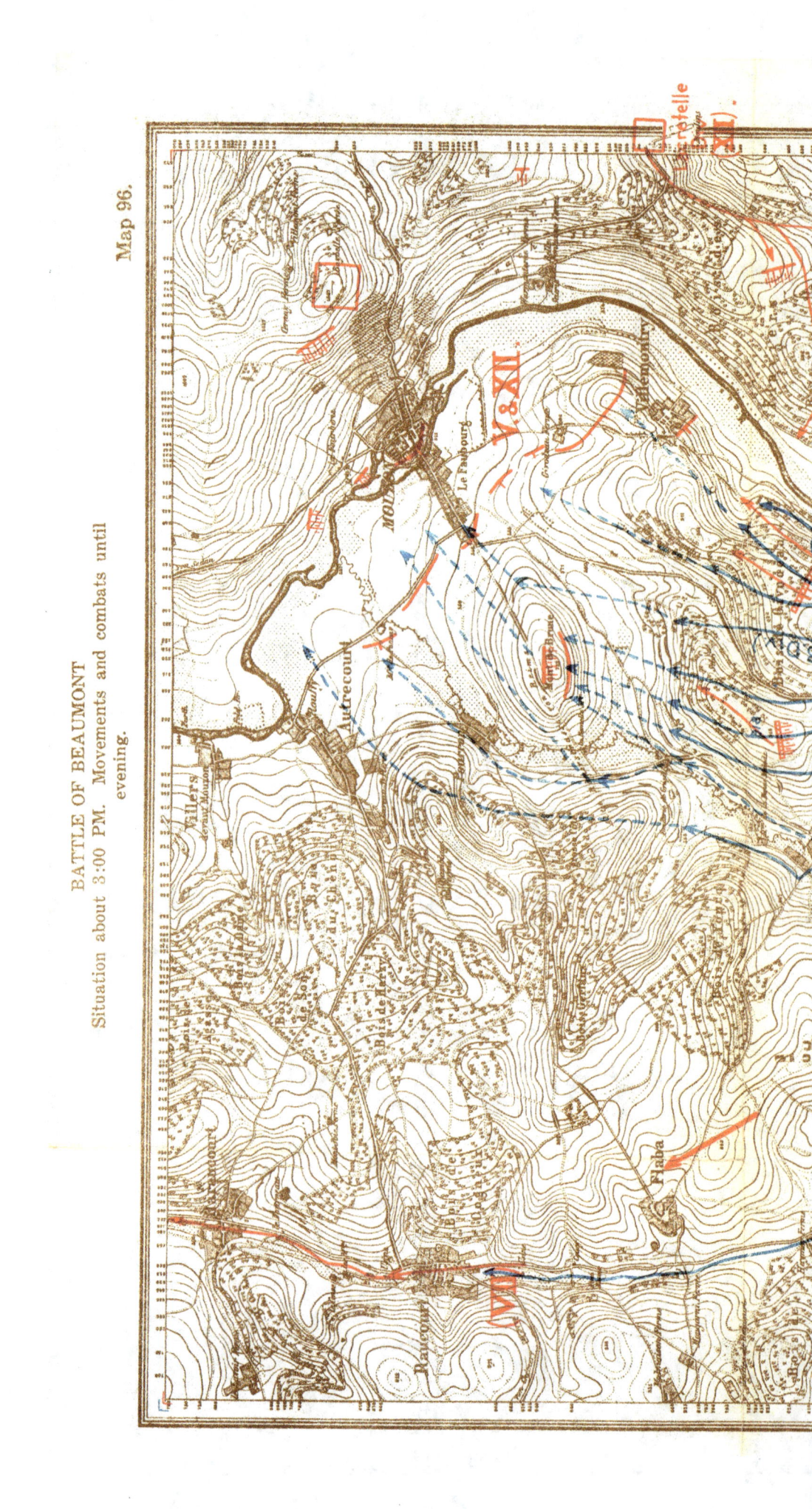

Map 96.

BATTLE OF BEAUMONT
Situation about 3:00 PM. Movements and combats until evening.

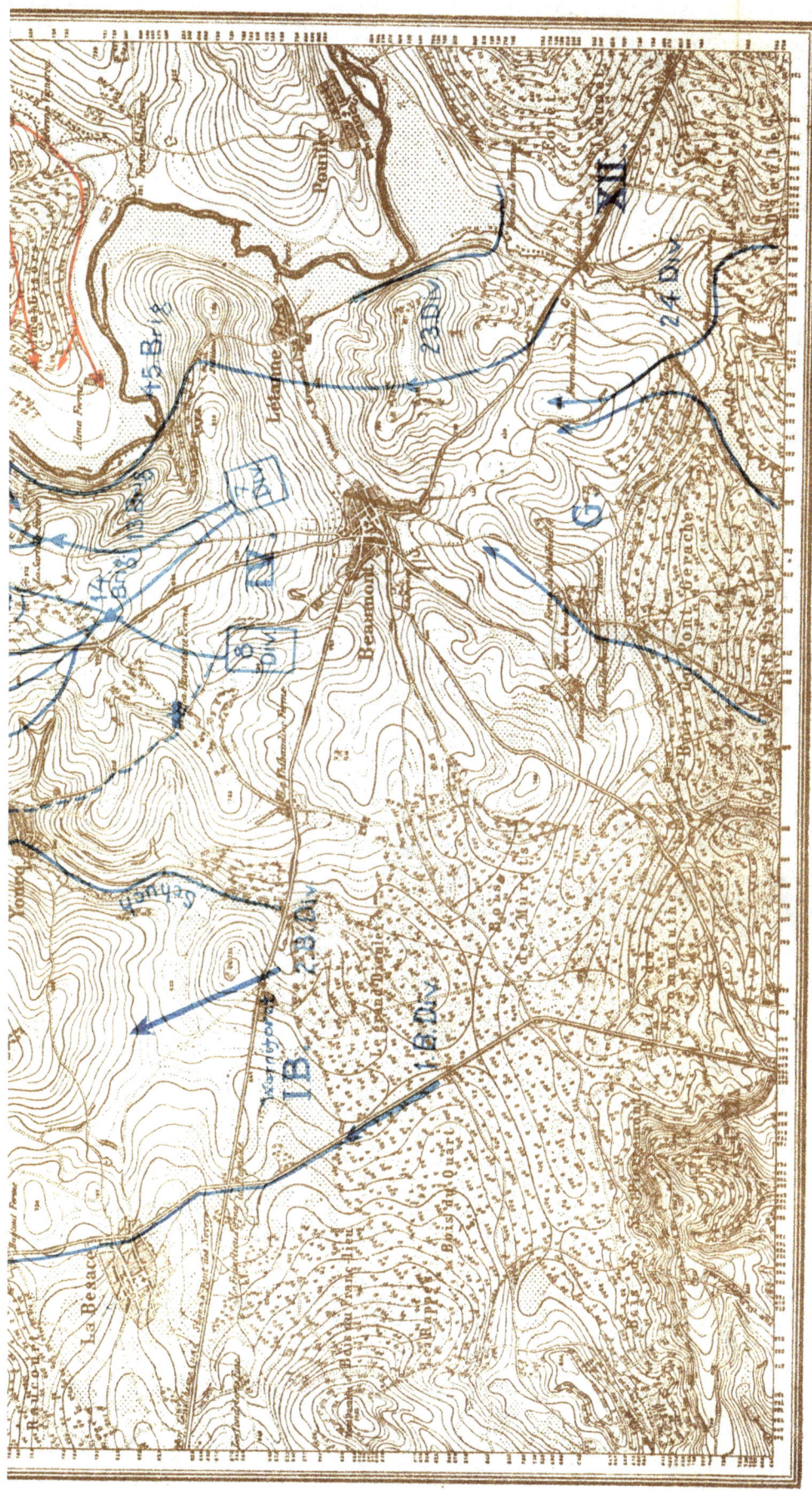

SITUATION ON THE NIGHT, 30-31 AUGUST.
MARCHES ON 31 AUGUST

Map 97.

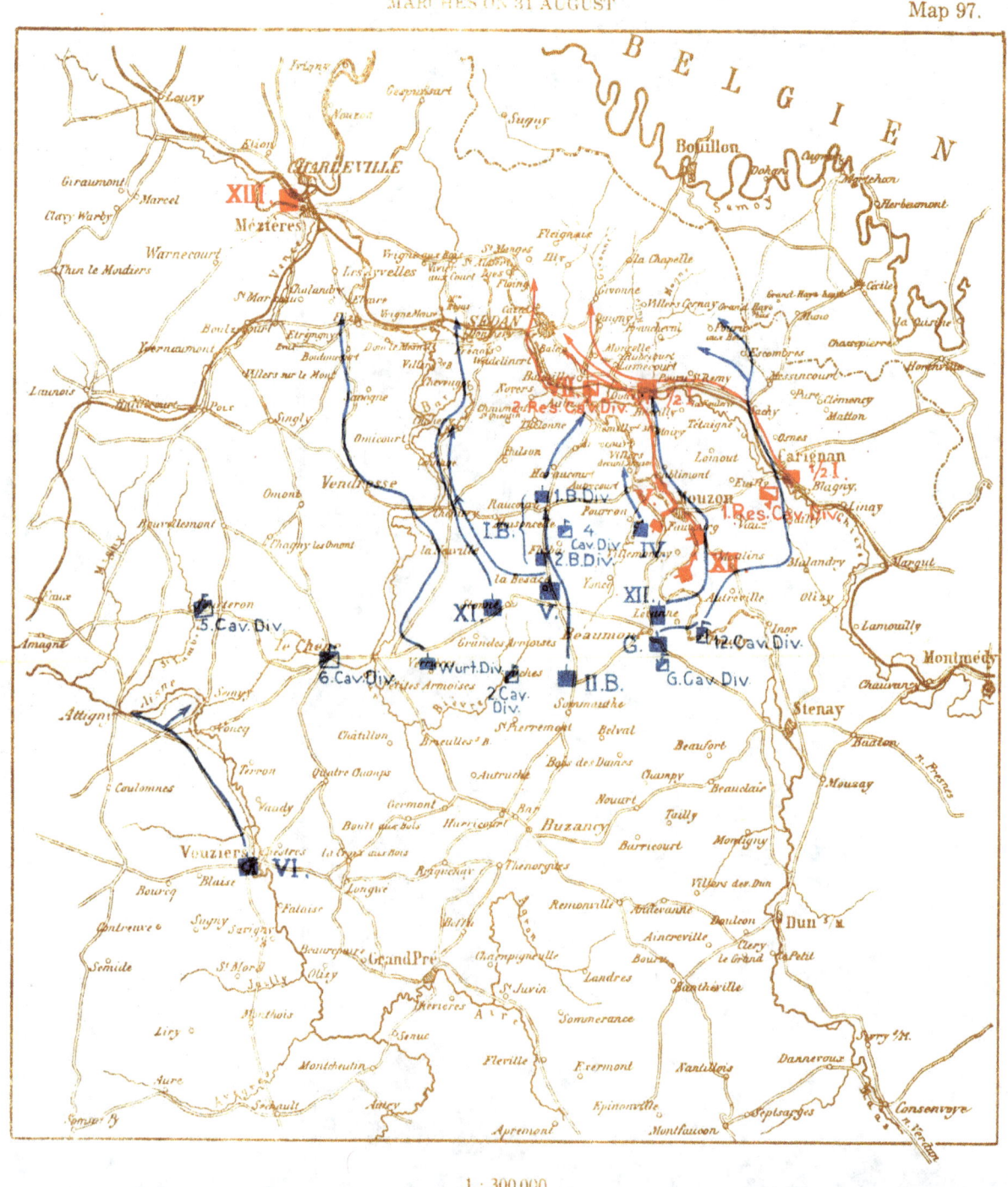

1 : 300 000

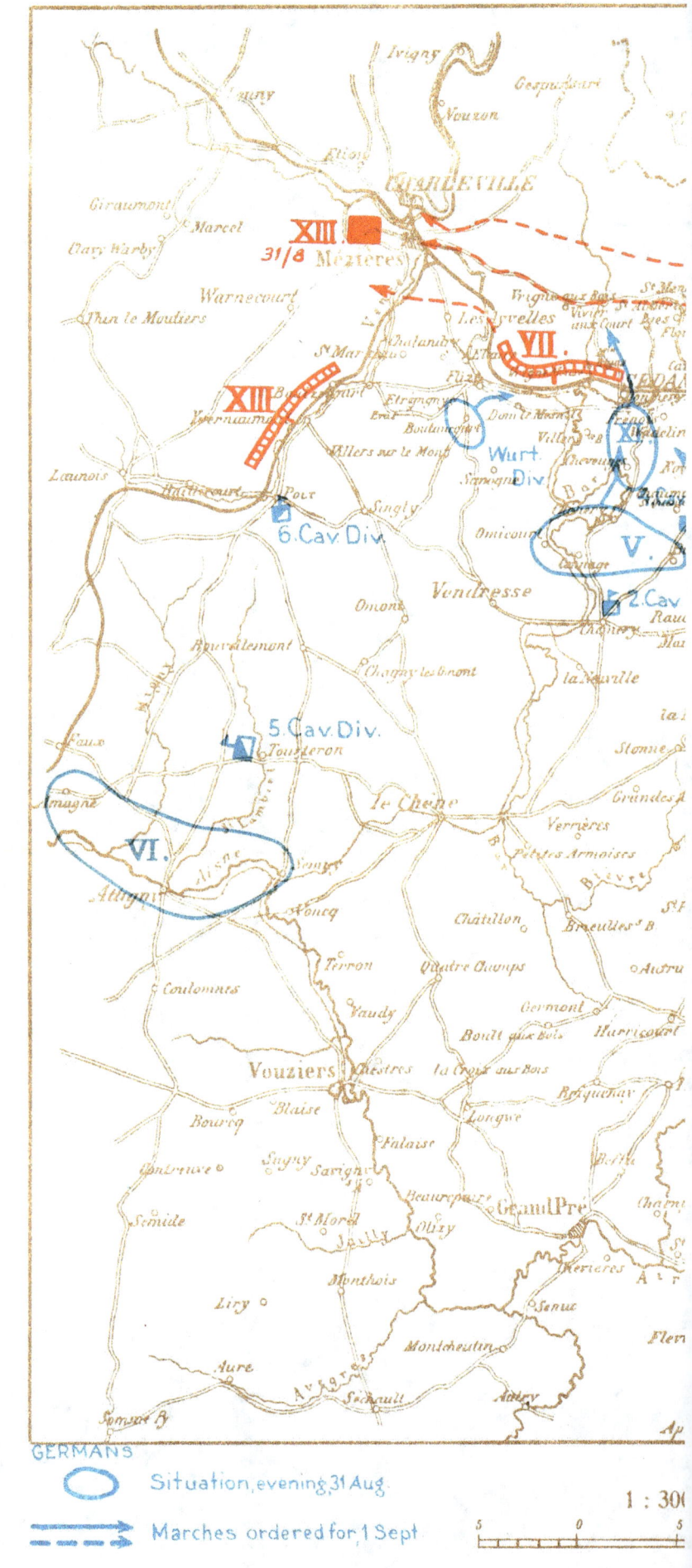

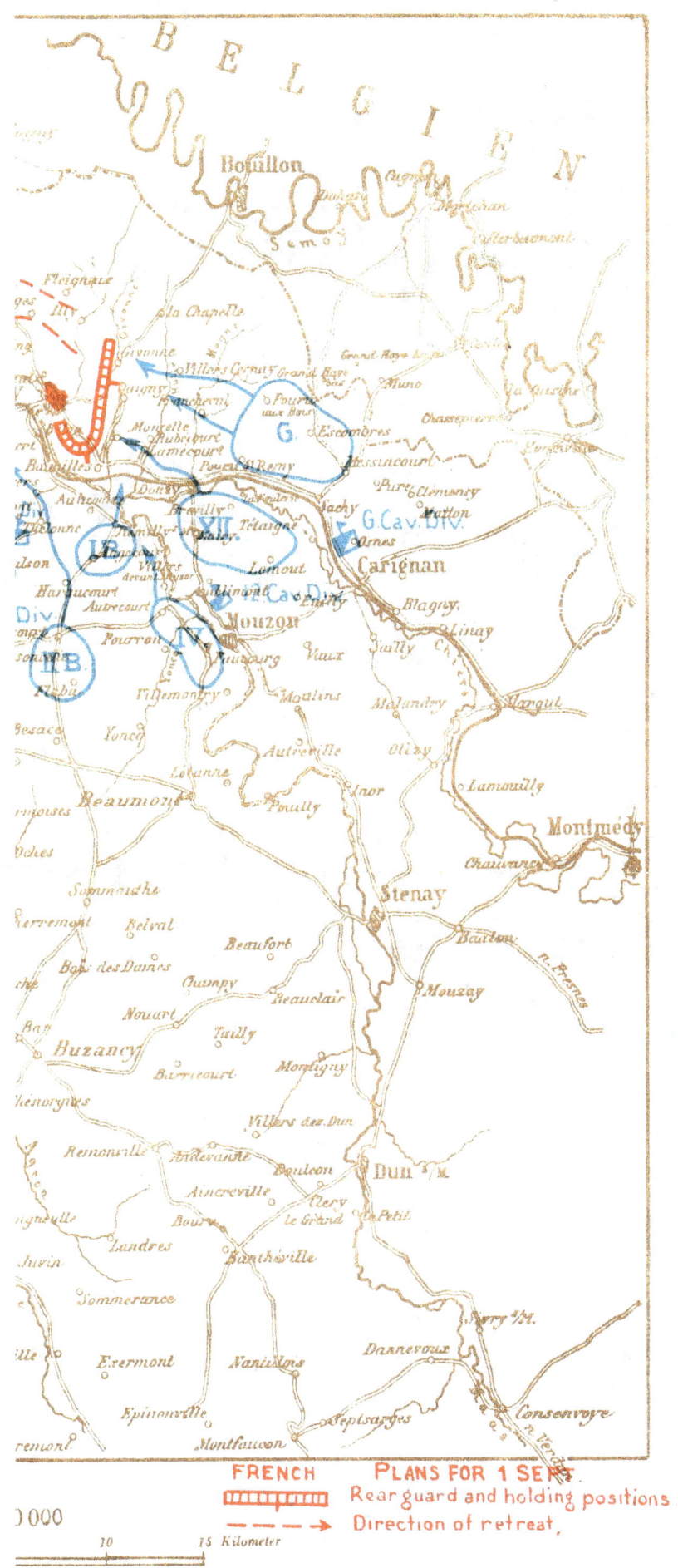

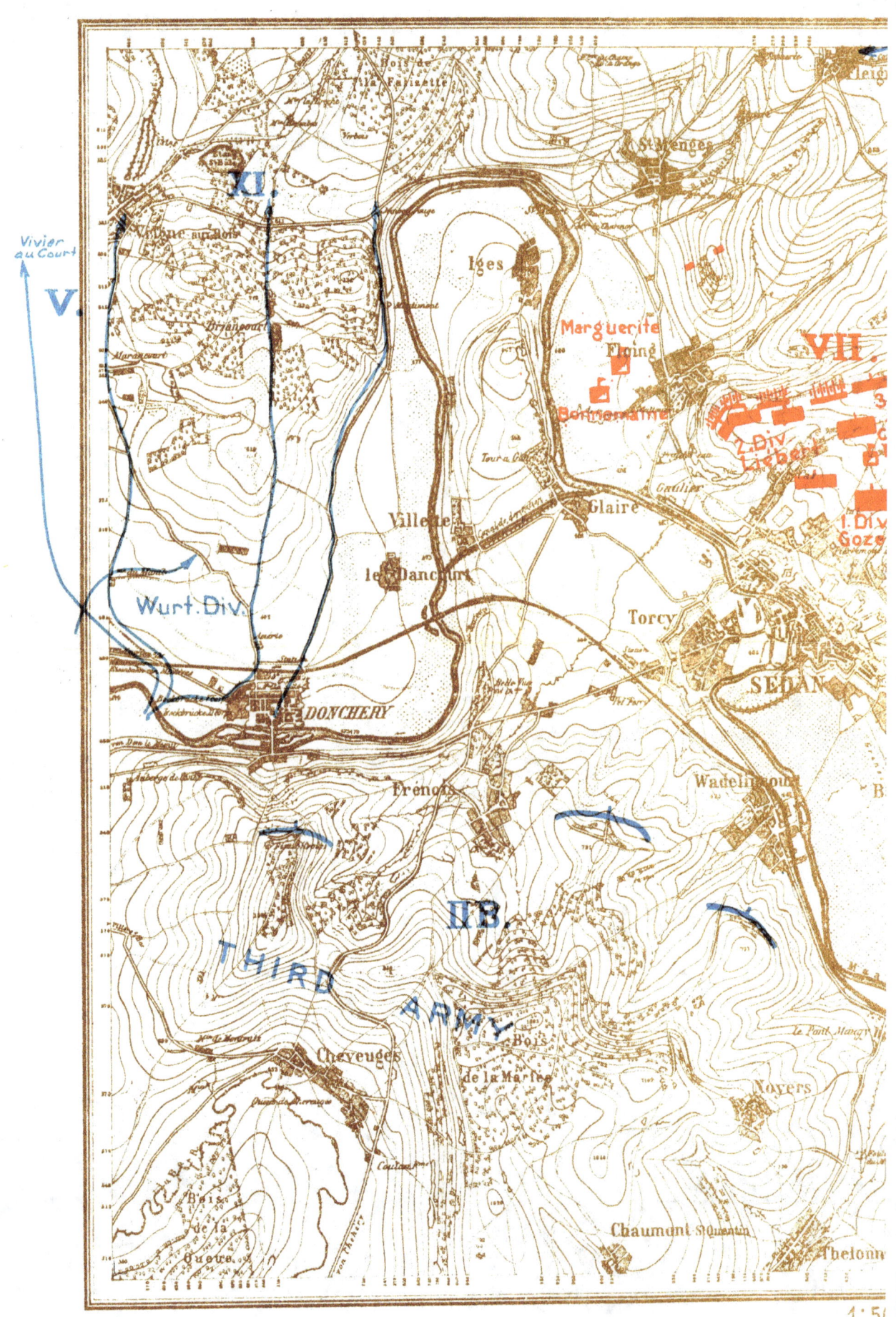

OF SEDAN
ber, 1870
September. Advance of the
order from general head-
plan for the advance
use Army.

Map 99.

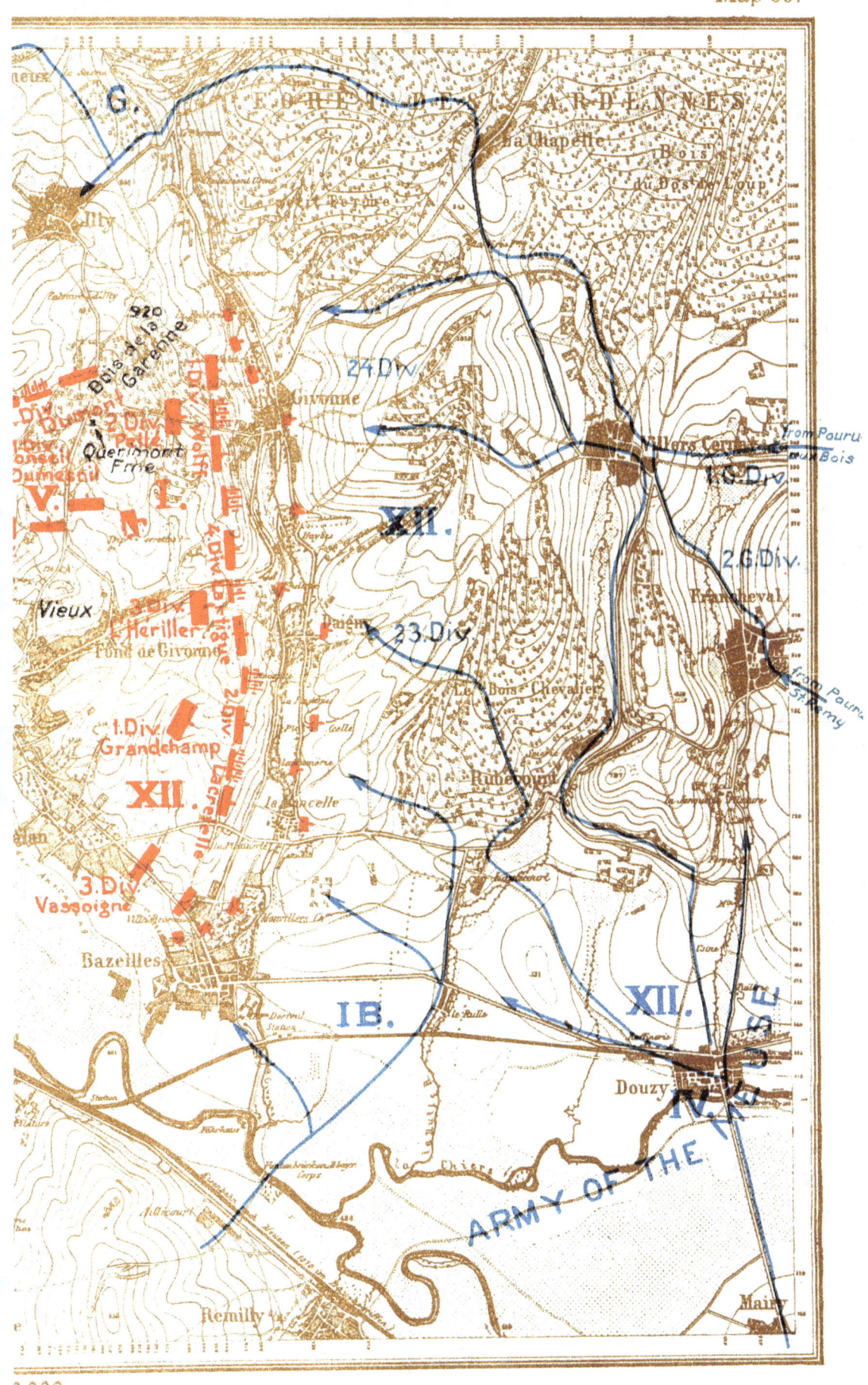

E OF SEDAN
ngagements up to noon.

Map 100.

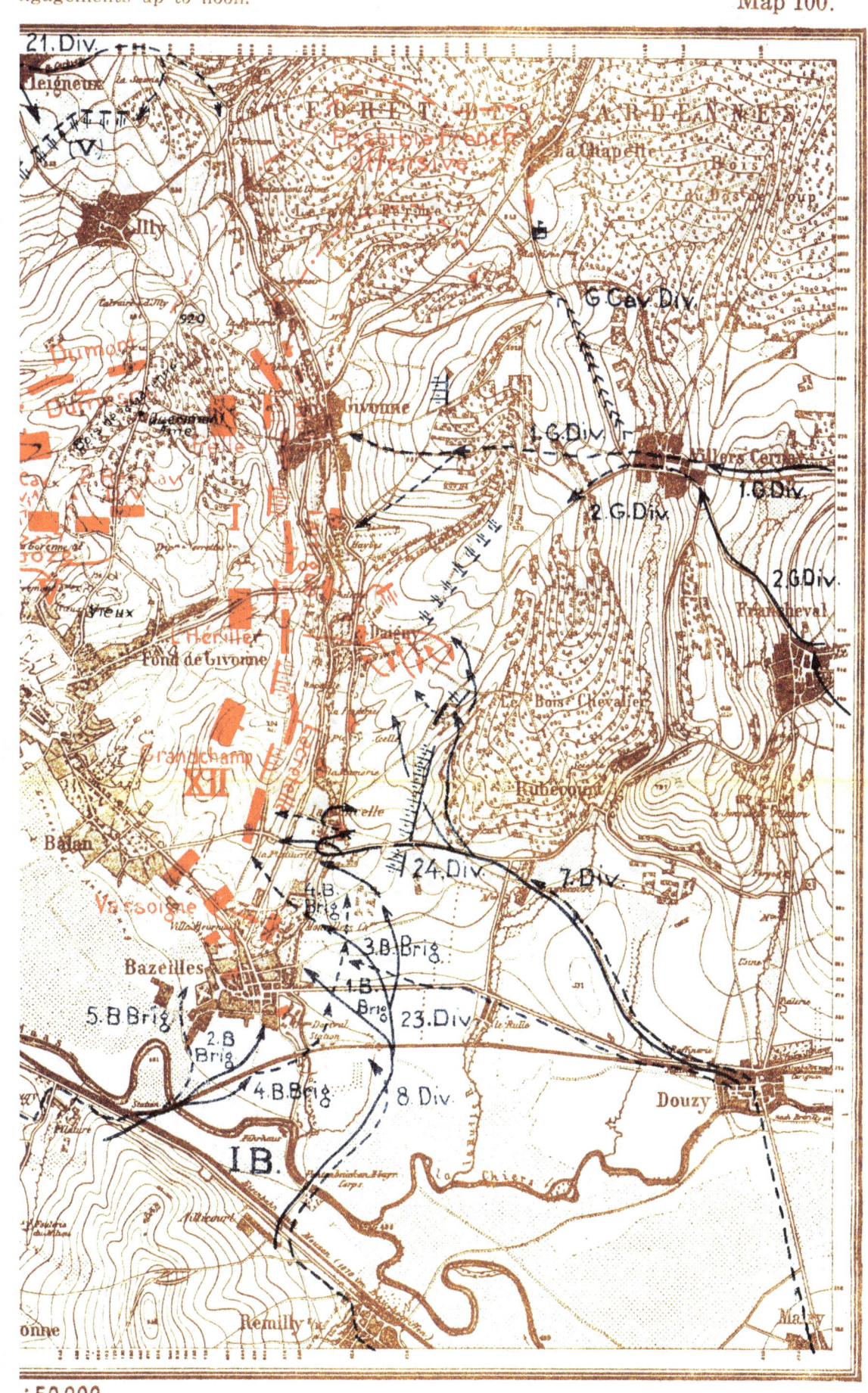

1:50 000.

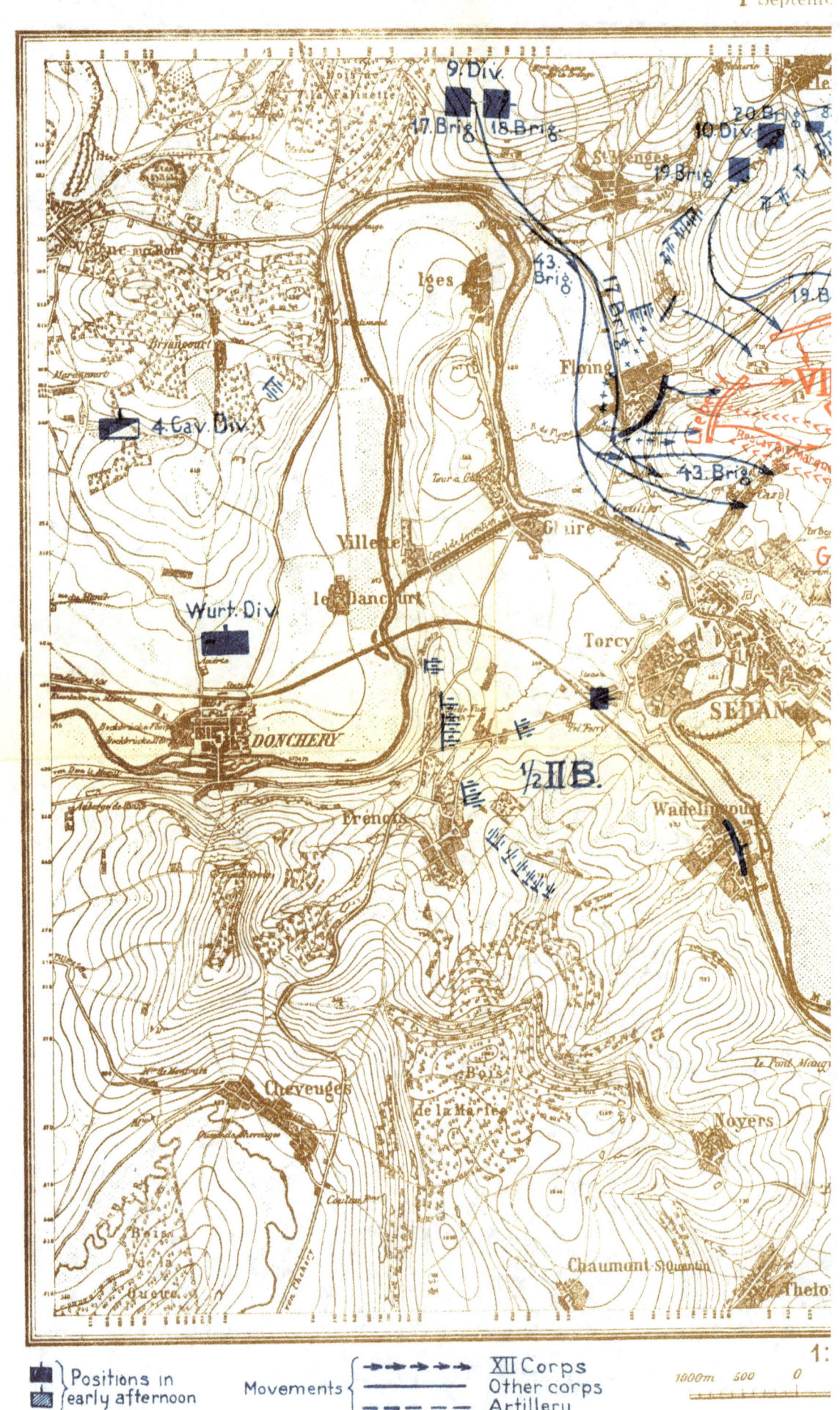

SEDAN
on the afternoon of
er.

Map 101.

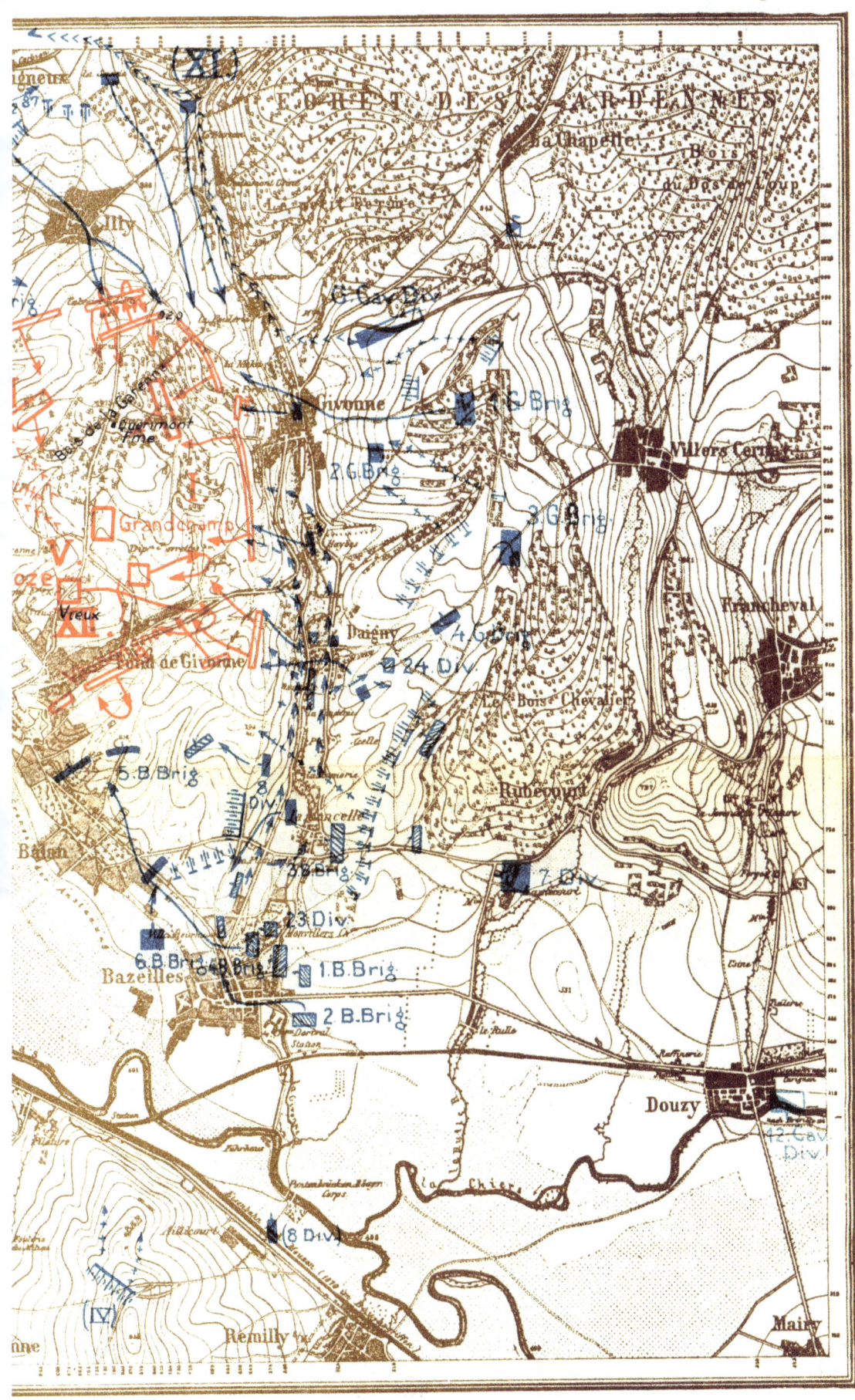

50 000.
1 2km